"This book is fuel for igniting curiosity and creativity. Wesley Phillipson has a knack for encouraging original thinking and writing, and his essay prompts are a gift to teachers, students, and everyone who believes in the power of the pen."
    Adam Grant, *#1 New York Times bestselling author of THINK AGAIN and HIDDEN POTENTIAL, and host of the podcast Re:Thinking*

"I've taught writing on the college and high school level for 30 years and this is the book I needed. Grab it. Your students' lives and, dare I say, yours will be changed."
    Victoria Redel, *Guggenheim Fellow and Sarah Lawrence College Writing Professor*

"In *Teaching the Anti-Essay*, Wesley Phillipson authoritatively deconstructs the standard format essay (5 paragraphs, anyone?) of the past and paves a delightfully liberating path to teach the essay of the future."
    Avis Cardella, *author of* Spent: Memoirs of a Shopping Addict, *published by Little, Brown and Company*

"As a high school student, Wes Phillipson was the first teacher who inspired in me a love of writing and helped me understand that I had a voice which could be expressed in print."
    Jimmy Vielkind, *Reporter at The Wall Street Journal and WNYC Radio*

"When most teachers are trying to figure out a way to work with or work around AI, Wes Phillipson has figured out a way for all of his students to become skillful and original writers, and something more, and something lasting: they learn to be themselves. This is an invaluable gift to the profession."
    Jeff Berger-White, *Bard College's Institute for Writing and Thinking*

"Mr. Phillipson has given us all a unique and illuminating deep dive into the mysterious world of creative writing. The many paths to fulfillment he guides us to discover in this challenging universe are a true testament to his professorial genius. I highly recommend *The Anti Essay* book to those involved in all ends of the creative writing spectrum."
    Richard Rudolph, *Writer and Producer of the #1 Hit Song "Lovin' You" – CEO Rudolph Productions | Chief Visionary at Vault/Headshell Books*

"Wes Phillipson will lead you to the thing all great writers find – clarity and truth. He will teach you to leap right into the fray with both feet, and go from there."
Jeff Goodby and Rich Silverstein *of Goodby, Silverstein & Partners, Creators of the "GOT MILK?" Advertising Campaign*

"*The Anti-Essay* is a deep, personal, immersive experience that explores the habits of life and mind that create an excellent writer and, in turn, an excellent essay."
Beth Raymer, *Author of* Fireworks Every Night: A Novel, *and* Lay the Favorite: A Memoir

"Wes Phillipson redefines the student-teacher dynamic with *The Anti-Essay*, turning rote assignments into meaningful self-explorations. By modeling vulnerability and authenticity, Wes inspires students to find their voices and craft work that resonates beyond the classroom. His thoughtful approach to teaching the art of writing is not just innovative—it's transformative."
Brandi Dugal, *CEO and Founder of The Fidget Game/ Fastest Growing Shark Tank Educational Product*

"Wesley Phillipson's out-of-the-box teaching style and support shaped me not only as a writer, but also as a thinker. He encouraged me to submit my writing for a National Council of Teachers of English (NCTE) Achievement Award in Writing and my entry pushed me to articulate what I found fascinating about early American history. It was these same interests that have propelled me to my graduate work. His book provides an exceptional opportunity to reflect on diversifying teaching in ways that students, myself included, will take with them far beyond their high school classrooms."
Emily Yankowitz, *Yale University/PhD candidate in History*

"At a moment when the disorienting acceleration of Artificial Intelligence is leading all of us in education to reassess every aspect of the high school writing experience, Wes Phillipson's 'Teaching the Anti-Essay' serves as an exceptionally timely and immensely thoughtful contribution to that critically important, ongoing conversation."
Adam Weisler, *US & AP US History Teacher since 1998*

"Mr. Phillipson is one of the teachers who I can confidently say changed the course of my life. He got me to understand how writing is a skill that can never be devalued. As an educator, he is fully engaged with the evolving needs of students, and his insights into essay writing will hold true in any context."

Oscar Tirabassi, *Wesleyan University '24, English Major*

"For the first time, I experienced the freedom to write what was in me without the constraints typically imposed by formal education. What a relief! Pure joy of true expression which I carry with me to this day."

Tess Brandwein, *University of Wisconsin-Madison, 2008, Political Science and Legal Studies UC Law San Francisco, 2014*

"Through Phillipson's guidance carried over to college applications, assignments while in college, and will continue to make me a writer whose perspectives are worth reading."

Ethan Hersch, *Cornell University '25, Honors Computer Science & Mathematics*

"As an educator in Harlem, I teach the same writing strategies that I learned in Mr. Phillipson's class eight years ago. I stress ideas, not formulas. I prioritize thinking, not replication."

Jack Waxman, *Teach for America/Social Studies Department, Harlem HS, New York/Cornell '23/Founder and Executive Director of Students Against Nicotine*

"Wes cared about the embodiment of our racing thoughts. He'll have you throwing out your word counts, cited source requirements, and rubrics. If you want your students to create something new and meaningful, let them write how they think."

Charlie Hirschhorn, *The University of Pennsylvania/Economics and Cinema Studies/Founder and CEO of The Friendly Fridge*

"Mr. Phillipson unlocked something in me by dismantling the rigid frameworks that often stifle artistic expression in high school writing courses. He invited me into a creative realm where my voice could resonate freely and authentically."

Sasha Forman, *University of South Carolina '26/Media Arts Major*

"I was lucky enough to have Wes as my HS English teacher. This was a difficult period in my life and Mr. Phillipson encouraged me to express myself through my writing. I flourished in his class and eventually went on to major in creative writing in college. I don't think I'd be where I am today without his influence."

Courtney Ires-Cohen, *SUNY Purchase, '06, Liberal Studies & Creative Writing*

"My first essay in Wesley Phillipson's classroom demonstrated a belligerent disregard for the semiotic substructure of a text. Rather than grade it, Wesley had me write a new version, excluding everything that wasn't "absolutely necessary." The following attempt was met with the same response: less. Several drafts came and went, and my essay gradually morphed to resemble a mathematical equation. The system of signs it both represented and itself was—straddling the diaphanous border between the essay and the text it was describing—now stood as a monolith before me. And I understood."

Axel Ahdritz, *Claremont McKenna College '22/ Double Major in Literature & Data Science*

"I discovered literature's hidden beauty, now seeing it as the art of communication rather than a struggle. And while I have what should be debilitating dyslexia, Wes brought me deeper into a world of words, unlocking a passion I never knew existed."

Masashi Kawabata, *University of Rochester '21/ Business & Finance/Bloomberg Tokyo*

"So much of what made Wes Phillipson's class special was his immovable trust in us, the students. He always pushed for our honest thoughts and opinions to shine while creating a lyrical framework to better articulate them."

Miwa Sakulrat, *School of Visuals Arts '17/Film Editing*

"His class helped me vocalize my complicated memories and thoughts, recalibrating my ability to read, write, and consume literature. Wes Phillipson empowers students in ways no other teacher or professor compares."

Peyton Lusk, *Connecticut College '26/History & Government*

"Taking a class taught by Mr. Phillipson gave me hope for the future of English education. I learned to surpass boring essay tropes and have fun with writing."
      Adam Otsuka, *Union College '27/Electrical Engineering & Computer Science*

"These essays were my first real chances to figure out who I was and what moved me."
      Daheun Oh, *Yale University '25/B.A. in Computing and the Arts*

"My years as his student learning about "form vs. content" helped prepare me for my career in advertising, where I've written high-visibility ads including a Super Bowl spot and a TV campaign parodied by SNL. I trace my success back to my years with Phillipson and his constant challenge to the class: "Tell me something I don't already know!""
      Jonathan Goldstein, *Graduate of Washington University in St. Louis*

"Wes Phillipson was my eleventh-grade English teacher. Immersed in deep, thoughtful explorations of postmodernism, signifying, and the complexities of modern rap music, he taught me how to think and how to write. It was hard and confusing. But it was also inspiring, empowering, and exciting. Now, as a medical student and future medical educator, I carry with me lessons from his course and his teaching in my academic career."
      Beatrix Thompson, *Medical Student, Harvard Medical School*

"I had never found writing to be as fun and creative as I had in Wes Phillipson's class. I can still remember my sophomore year when I learned that no matter the topic, writing an essay can be personal, argumentative, artistic, and interesting all at once. In every writing assignment I tackle today, I make sure to find those distinctions, forms, and stories that bring my essays to life."
      Jake Feuerstein, *Lehigh University '26/Biomolecular Engineering & Global Studies*

"I wrote essays I wanted my peers to read."
      Oryna Bludova, *NYU Tisch Drama '28 (Production & Design), BFA in Drama*

"Wes was unlike any teacher I have ever had. He taught me how to write. He showed me how to use form, syntax, and tone to enhance my writing. Every driven student in this world should have the opportunity to take a Wes Phillipson English class because they will be enlightened."

Kyle Kahan, *University of Michigan '27/ Wealth & Asset Management*

"It's been over fifteen years, and I still talk about Mr. Phillipson's class with my colleagues and students. I can trace the spark for my love of writing back to his classroom, where on any given day, we would jump from Biggie's rap lyrics to Sylvia Plath's poetry to F. Scott Fitzgerald's prose. Thanks to *Anti-Essay*, everyone can now pull up a seat and learn how to think and create differently."

Marissa Shandell, *PhD Candidate at The Wharton School*

TEACHING THE ANTI-ESSAY

Teaching the Anti-Essay helps secondary school English Language Arts (ELA) teachers introduce literary nonfiction and creative nonfiction essay writing to their students, demonstrating how writing is a fun and engaging activity where students can see tremendous value in "thinking on paper." Meaningful essays are also, by default, analytical.

This book offers English teachers and their students 18 different essay prompts that challenge student writers to take calculated risks on paper, leading to essays that students *can write and want to write*, allowing them to add something new to the conversation in the process. Each chapter explores a unique essay prompt, along with rationale, the targeted skills, teacher models, student models, and reflections. The book is intended to be a tool for change in the English classroom at large by motivating students through tried and tested prompts, demonstrating that anyone can write like a journalist, a professional blogger, a creative nonfiction essayist, becoming an author with one's own voice and style.

This is a great resource for in-service middle school and high school ELA teachers, and beyond.

Wesley Phillipson has taught writing for 30 years – most of that time at Scarsdale High School, on the same campus where Kohlberg conducted much of his field research on community-based education.

Also Available from Routledge Eye On Education
(www.routledge.com/eyeoneducation)

Teaching Reading and Literature with Classroom Talk: Dialogical Approaches and Practical Strategies in the Secondary ELA Classroom
Dawan Coombs

Pop Culture Literacies: Teaching Interpretation, Response, and Composition in a Digital World
Mia Hood

Teaching Poetry in a Digital World: Inspiring Poetry Writing through Technology in Grades 6-12
Stefani Boutelier & Sarah J. Donovan

Teach This Poem, Volume I: The Natural World
Madeleine Fuchs Holzer and The Academy of American Poets

Grammar Inquiries, Grades 6–12: An Inquiry- and Asset-Based Approach to Grammar Instruction
Sean Ruday

The Antiracist English Language Arts Classroom
Keisha Rembert

The Literacy Coaching Handbook: Working With Teachers to Increase Student Achievement, 2nd edition
Diana Sisson and Betsy Sisson

TEACHING THE ANTI-ESSAY

18 Creative Nonfiction Essay Prompts for the English Classroom

Wesley Phillipson

NEW YORK AND LONDON

Designed cover image: Louis Basso

First published 2026
by Routledge
605 Third Avenue, New York, NY 10158

and by Routledge
4 Park Square, Milton Park, Abingdon, Oxon, OX14 4RN

Routledge is an imprint of the Taylor & Francis Group, an informa business

© 2026 Wesley Phillipson

The right of Wesley Phillipson to be identified as author of this work has been asserted in accordance with sections 77 and 78 of the Copyright, Designs and Patents Act 1988.

Angela Chiang has provided all of the illustrations for this work.

All rights reserved. No part of this book may be reprinted or reproduced or utilised in any form or by any electronic, mechanical, or other means, now known or hereafter invented, including photocopying and recording, or in any information storage or retrieval system, without permission in writing from the publishers.

Trademark notice: Product or corporate names may be trademarks or registered trademarks, and are used only for identification and explanation without intent to infringe.

ISBN: 978-1-032-98785-9 (hbk)
ISBN: 978-1-032-98784-2 (pbk)
ISBN: 978-1-003-60056-5 (ebk)

DOI: 10.4324/9781003600565

Typeset in Optima
by KnowledgeWorks Global Ltd.

Access the Support Material: www.routledge.com/9781032987842

This book is for my students who have inspired me to get up and teach writing every day for thirty years, and to discover more of myself in the process. I owe you all more than just words.

And to my wife Stephanie and sons Brady and Riley: I write so that you may understand a deeper part of me that I don't get to show at home nearly enough.

SUPPORT MATERIAL

This book contains additional materials and a glossary that are available on our website as free downloads, so you can easily print or reproduce them for classroom use. You can access them by visiting the book product page: www.routledge.com/9781032987842 (or search for the book title on www.routledge.com). Click on the tab that says "Support Material" and select the files. They will begin downloading to your computer.

CONTENTS

Meet the Author — xv
Author's Note: Teaching the Anti-Essay — xvi
Preface by Toby Rosewater, Managing Sports Editor,
 The Amherst Student — xxii
Acknowledgments and Shout-Outs — xxvi
Introduction by James Treadway, CEO of GrowthWise
 Tutoring — xxviii

1 The Wax Pack: Breaking Wax — 3

2 The Philosophy of You: Your Students Are Deeper
   Than You Think — 11

3 Consider the Lobster — 17

4 When the Hitmakers Knock, You Answer — 33

5 The Unicorn College Essay — 45

6 Emily's Way and How to Wrangle a Guest Speaker — 57

7 My Lipogram: The no "E" paper — 67

8 The Usual Suspects: A Dialogue Essay from England
with Love   67

9 *The Living Artists* Literary Research Paper   91

10 Nice to Meet You and Goodbye: 7 Intros and 7 Outros   109

11 Ranting and Raving: Why Complaining Is Good for
Your Students   131

12 Dave's Way: The Humor Essay a la Dave Barry   141

13 The Poetry Forgery Unit: How Imitation Breeds Greatness   153

14 The Feature Article: Journalism Your Classroom Needs   163

15 The Autopsy of You: When Students Metacognate
Good Things Happen   179

16 Ebert's Way: Lessons from a Late-Great Film Critic   191

17 The Video Essay Is Not Just for YouTubers   201

18 The Interrogative Mood: Questions Only, No Answers   209

19 Grading Essays Means Never Having to Be Alone Again   215

MEET THE AUTHOR

Wesley Phillipson is a writing, literature, and media studies teacher at Scarsdale High School in New York. He holds a B.A. in English, and a Masters in English and Education. Wesley has taught grades 9–12 for the past 30 years in New York *with an emphasis on creative nonfiction writing*.

In 2006, he presented a master class on advertising and copywriting at the NCTE Convention in Nashville entitled From Ithaca to Madison Avenue: 2000 Years of Rhetoric. That year the theme was "The Compleat (sic) Teacher."

During his academic career, Wesley has collaborated on classroom lessons with Oscar winning writer Christopher McQuarrie (The Usual Suspects), Pulitzer Prize winning nonfiction writers Hua Hsu (Stay True), Dave Barry, and Emily Nussbaum, number one songwriters Richard Rudolph, Mario Winans, and Sam Hollander, NYT number one bestselling author John Gray (Men Are From Mars), and – among others – National Book Award and PEN/Faulkner Award-winning novelist Don DeLillo.

Phillipson is the son of noted English teacher Brainerd F. Phillipson (of Newton North High School), and the great-grandson of Thomas Boyd. Boyd was close friends with F. Scott Fitzgerald, who edited (along with Maxwell Perkins) his first war novel Through the Wheat. Boyd was a member of The Lost Generation along with Hemingway, Dos Passos, and Stein.

Wesley's grandfather, Karl Nash, built the newspaper conglomerate Hersam Acorn (begun in 1937 as The Acorn Press), which independently published 19 weeklies across Connecticut before being purchased by Hearst Communications.

Please connect with Wesley at wphillipson@scarsdaleschools.org or @wesphillipson on Instagram.

AUTHOR'S NOTE: TEACHING THE ANTI-ESSAY

Today is Monday, October 7, 2024 and I started seeing "patients" at 7:35 AM and taught four 50-minute English classes in-between my one-on-one writing and grading conferences. By day's end, I'll have sat down with a total of 13 students separately, each one for 15-minute sessions, before heading home to Armonk at 4 PM.

When I attended a Tony Robbins seminar in 1997 called The Competitive Edge, I remember hearing that "salesmen who spend most of their time in front of the client are more successful than those who don't." That idea stuck with me. I started "grading with students" about ten years ago, and I've massively expanded the practice since.

When I first meet students in September of each academic year, I immediately try to teach them two things:

1 Overwrite.
2 Embrace the mess.

At present, I teach sophomores through seniors, but there's a common denominator across grade levels – nearly all students underwrite, their voice is more flattened affect than engaging conversation, and their essays are heavy on formula, structure, and confirmation bias.

The reason I've written this book in my 30th year of teaching HS English is because I spent the first decade of my career not knowing what I was doing, nor how to do it, nor why. I attended Holliston High School in the late 1980s – it's an upper-middle-class town near Wellesley – but I have no recollection of anyone "teaching me how to write." I had two undergraduate and two graduate professors who actually took the time to impart **an idea (or two)** that has stuck with me.

And I don't think that my educational experience with writing is unusual. **But I want it to be.**

I want first-year English and Composition teachers to have access to proven writing prompts, and to know what I know. I want veteran teachers who have "seen it all" to get a fresh take on approaches to crafting intros and conclusions. I want the parents of middle and high school students to read this book and see what is possible – creatively on paper – for their child. I want English Department chairs to understand my unique philosophy about teaching and assessing writing so they'll give their own charges more running room to innovate and risk-take.

More than anything, I want this book to be an extension of my English classroom – Room 207 – a space constructed in 1917 with leaded-glass bookcases and millwork featuring gothic arches that match and mirror the facade of Scarsdale High School itself. It's where I've taught for 22 years straight, surrounded by my personal library of used and rare books (20th-century novels), elegantly framed vintage movie posters (everything from Butch Cassidy to Dog Day Afternoon), and a view of the organic garden that colleague and good friend Amanda Filley transformed from a small plot of land to a campus institution just years ago.

Yes, I have it good. I also didn't start out teaching in Scarsdale. This is high school number four for me. And you could get here too, or somewhere like this place, should you choose to pursue a career in teaching – or stay in the game long term. Some of you have started at a school with a national reputation. Yet others of you will dedicate yourself to working with populations who are challenged, and challenging.

Regardless, this book takes you through 18 of my most successful writing assignments, my thinking behind each one, and the larger context for how they came to exist. You'll read my "version" of each assignment (my teacher model = finished essay), accompanied by successful student samples for each prompt (students' finished essays). Also included in each chapter are teacher and student reflections: What was it like to write a "No E Paper," or work directly with the author of your research paper's novel? How did I navigate the pushback or the anxiety that comes with assigning non-traditional essays?

As I've alluded to, we don't do "enough" writing with our students, and we do even less "skill-building" than we've done in decades. But with the onslaught of Artificial Intelligence platforms and add-ons, there's a need for this book today, now, more than ever before, because we're not just teaching writing we're modeling for students how to think (not what to think), and how to conduct meaningful inquiry (not confirm existing biases that we pass down to them).

And it never mattered *where I taught* high school English. I wasn't always in Scarsdale.

Writing is the most important work that we do with students whether it's a Blue Ribbon or magnet school, or a place with low graduation rates and gang problems.

My first paid teaching job (post college) earned me $27,000 a year in a remote Western Massachusetts town near Amherst. The year was 1995, and the median income in America was $34,000.

So no, we don't do this work for the money.

That high school had a gun club – like actually, a gun (Bang! Bang!) club. Students would bring their rifle and pistol cases into the building each morning and place them in their lockers. On the opening day of hunting season, many of my students would be absent to pursue (instead of the written word), the blood of rabbit and deer. In the 1980s, Orange, MA had been a thriving factory town: tool and die, paper, sewing machines, and automobiles. By the time I got there, it had become part of the Massachusetts rust-belt, a distressed area that spilled over into its near neighbor, New Hampshire.

Many of the parents there were educated but blue-collar, often attending trade-schools to gain practical skills for the factories that had, as of 1995, shuttered.

From the beginning in Orange, MA, I was pretty stubborn about my writing standards, despite not really knowing what constituted a strong paper from a young teen. I didn't know what I didn't know – a classic case of unconscious incompetence. *But I was dogged about diction*. I left most essays covered in red ink and pink-or-yellow highlighter. It's been 30 years since, but I vividly recall a freshman (Phoebe) asking another student in the class: "What does Mr. Phillipson expect from us? We're just 13. Take it easy."

After three years there I moved on to a large high school in (way) upstate New York, just a short trot from Saratoga Springs. A good chunk of the parents were government workers (it's right by Albany), as well as doctors, lawyers, and other professional types.

But I taught a skills-level course at Shenendehowa HS. The students had extensive Individualized Education Plans (IEPs), longer than most career criminals' rap sheets. I also instructed an honors class called "World Culture & World Literature" and worked with regular level sophomores who were – on paper – unremarkable. Two of my students died around that time – Christy Massa and Victoria Nesbitt. Christy was a straight "A" student who'd ask me clarifying questions about comments I'd left on her essays; Victoria was someone who ran with the party crowd, and I had the sense that before my class she'd never really taken an interest in literature.

(It's strange – the things we remember from our classrooms. It's been 25 years and I can still, verbatim, recall an exchange I had with Christy who asked,

"When you write 'clarify' here, do you mean that it's clear, or I need to make it clearer?" I can also remember being in the Shen HS parking lot and Megan Breedlove (a classmate of Vic's) asking me, "Are you going to Vic's service?" Sadly, that same English class Vic was a part of had another death years later. Matt Gorka, a young man who didn't want to buy into my program at all – who wouldn't even give me a hello when I'd drop off work for him at detention – came to be the liveliest contributor in the room. He died at 31. I believe that one other student from that group of 19 or 20 has since passed away, too].

Shen was also where I met 14-year-old Louise Gava who was quiet (at times), but always thinking. She was in that "unremarkable" tenth grade class that I came to find was anything but. Shen – as an HS – is broken up into East and West campuses, with a behemoth footprint. Louise was part of my final year there at the smaller West building, and she couldn't understand why some of her classmates didn't immediately respond to my thoughtful prompts or discussion questions. I appreciated her enthusiasm for what I was trying to do, but I can't blame the students: I was still working things out.

Next, I landed 150 miles south in West Nyack, NY at Clarkstown South – a big suburban school with just one tiny, narrow road on or off campus. The Clarkstown Police Department once shot a deer on that same road after it ran into the side of a school bus. With students looking on from the relative comfort of their green Naugahyde seats, one cop pulled out a shotgun and delivered a fatal blow to the badly injured doe. It reminded me of my time in Orange, MA, where I lived on White Pond and would sometimes wake up to the sound of gunshots from deep in the woods just beyond my cabin (or – occasionally – students driving their muscle cars on the ice in late January).

Clarkstown South had an AP course, but I didn't stick around to teach it. I spent three years there as well – just enough time to earn tenure and move on to the next big thing. It was a pattern that I'd hoped to break when I got to Scarsdale or Chappaqua (the only two places I was considering "leaving for").

Long before Bill Cosby was canceled (as a performer and a human being), he had a short-lived show called just "Cosby" that ran from 1996 to 2000. One episode, "Superstar," revolves around actor Doug E. Doug's character Griffin who dreams that educators are suddenly as culturally significant (and well-paid) as NBA players. The episode references Westchester County, New York (by name) as the equivalent of the major leagues. The dream sequence has sports commentators asking Griffin if he'll sign with a Westchester school district, as he's the number one draft pick. After seeing that show on NBC, I remember resolving to move to New York to teach in a place like Bronxville, Armonk, Rye, Harrison, Briarcliff Manor, or – naturally – Scarsdale.

All I can tell you is the show profoundly distorts the value placed on teachers in Westchester County per se. There's tremendous variety to this area. There's upper and lower. There are impoverished parts and uber-wealthy ones. The

Greenburgh Eleven Union Free School had an anemic 17% graduation rate in 2022. Scarsdale HS has a graduation rate of 100%, and a college placement rate of 99% (that's a blend of four- and two-year programs; the 1% differential can be accounted for by students who take gap years).

But Clarkstown South was an odd place – it had a vital school newspaper that was entirely student-run, one of my students (Victoria) wanted to pursue a career in putting make-up on deceased people at funeral homes, and the principal was allegedly fired for directing school funds to build a planetarium entirely for his child's whimsy (who was also a student).

Students could write there too. It wasn't as affluent as its North counterpart (located in the town of New City). And if Southies got into an ivy-league school or elite institution, it was often more likely due to athletics than academics.

And it was where I taught my first "dedicated" creative writing class, forced to innovate or fail. I had 50 seniors who were counting on me to either (A) give them credit for an easy elective course or (B) teach them how to write – the proverbial last chance for gas on the information superhighway of all things prose.

Warning:

This is not a book just for elites. Or just for those who teach the children of elites. Or just for established teachers working at the top-ranked high schools as outlined in the U.S. News & World Report. Or just for graduate students doing their teaching practicum or field study. Or just for HS English teachers.

No. This is a book for anyone who:

a Wants to write better
b Wants their child to write better
c Wants their students to write better

As for "C" above: I don't see this book as just for the HS English classroom. It's for middle school teachers who want to turn their classrooms into prep schools (in the good sense: prep = preparatory). It's for college Composition professors and TAs who want to bridge the gap between senior year of high school and university freshman. It's for Social Studies teachers who want to understand what English teachers are looking for in an essay, and what their counterparts are doing and not doing. It's for those same Social Studies teachers who want their students to write with voice and passion, in spite of the need for facts and honest accounting. It's for anyone in the humanities or soft sciences wishing to build-out their writing program and curriculum.

Scarsdale HS is where – famously, but also under the radar – psychologist Lawrence Kohlberg conducted his groundbreaking research for his stages of moral development and "community" model.

Within Scarsdale High School (SHS), there's an Alternative (or A) School, which has a small student body and just a handful of teachers working with them. It's a coveted program that many students apply to freshman year but few gain entrance to. The former director (a retired English colleague of mine) Howard Rodstein told me something that even *The New York Times* and Scarsdale's own newspaper haven't covered in print. It's the best kept secret in the 10583:

> Lawrence Kohlberg worked directly with the A-School. He trained the original A-School teachers in the Just Community Model at his summer home on Cape Cod. He visited Community Meeting for several years on a semi-regular basis. Most of the research on students at the A-School was conducted by Ann Higgins-D'Alessandro of Fordham University who studied with Kolberg.

In other words, Kohlberg treated Scarsdale HS (The A-School in particular) as his personal workshop or laboratory, working out some of the most important developments in building educational communities, where teachers lead by consensus. Imagine if B.F. Skinner had based Walden Two on The A-School (well – it would be pretty dystopic, for one)? Imagine if Grant Wiggins had based his backward planning design here? Or Howard Gardner, his work in Multiple Intelligences? And so on.

Kohlberg's work has *that* level of importance, yet – almost no one knows the history that occurred here at SHS regarding Larry (as he's called), save for Howard Rodstein.

While small and insignificant by comparison, my own work (on essay writing) has been going on in my laboratory directly above where The A-School currently exists. My classroom, 207, is the floor to the ceiling where Amanda Filley teaches her A-School students English, Chris Paulison teaches Social Studies, Haley Rauch Mathematics, and so on. I've been conducting my research since 2003, telling students – class after class – "This is just an exercise. It's an experiment. Let's see what works and what doesn't."

I'm asking you to think about your own practice that way.

If you do, you won't just want to come to work until you get tenure, but 20, 30, even 40 years later too.

So, let's begin.

As my good friend Richard Rudolph taught me – and after 50 years of writing hit songs he'd know – to create something, anything, you've got to sit your butt in a chair and start writing.

And to gain what I've learned in 30 years of teaching writing, I'd ask you to do the same: Find a comfortable spot, get your favorite drink or snack, sit down, and begin reading.

Wes Phillipson
Scarsdale, NY
November 2, 2024

PREFACE BY TOBY ROSEWATER, MANAGING SPORTS EDITOR, THE AMHERST STUDENT

The best criticism illuminates something you can't see. It is new – novel – and it disarms you. I've run into this special kind of feedback a lot in the writing world. It's not surprising, though. Writing is an art based on a seemingly endless number of constructs. The more educated a writer you become, the more these constructs seem to multiply. Because of this, even the "best" writers can fall victim to a kind of literary paralysis. A friend of mine, Liam Morrissey, a creative film executive turned Iowa MFA candidate turned creative writing professor, describes this phenomenon particularly well. He explained it to me like this: An "untrained" writer sits down to write, and they write. A "trained" writer sits down to write, and they second guess. For every way you can describe something, there is an alternative way, perhaps a more writerly way, to express it. The result is sitting down to write and writing nothing; you hear so many voices that it suffocates you.

I've run into this phenomenon more frequently as I've developed as a writer. Many times, I've sat in front of my laptop and just felt bad – awful – like my writing is incorrect and inherently weak. In that sense, amid these constructs, it's easy to lose your sense of self, your voice, and your confidence. When this happens to me, I usually take a step back, look inward, and reconnect.

If not clear, I believe the self and its relationship to the outside world defines good writing. Before I met Wesley Phillipson, my self and my writing identity were completely separate. What and how I could write was determined by which information I deemed as "writerly enough." Opposing this, I am someone who has, my whole life, adored "low-culture" things, who has identified with video games, and sports stories, and internet culture, and fun, very 2010s pop-culture stuff. That is how I grew up, and in many ways, I couldn't identify with anything else. Yet, for some reason, I never believed these things could be made "writerly." So, for a time, my writing identity, the way I operated in any academic or professional space, was disingenuous. How I carried myself did not identify me – it never said anything about me – because I never incorporated the things that defined my experience.

The first thing Phillipson taught me, then, was that I could combine the "low culture" I adored with the so-called high culture of art, thought, and sophistication to create not only an interesting, versatile piece of writing but, for me, a more genuine form of expression. I still remember walking into Phillipson's office for the first time, sitting on his blue couch with my Ken Griffey Jr. essay, and looking around at all his movie posters, art pieces, and picture frames. With its white walls and mid-century modern aesthetics, it looked like a set from Columbo. In his white suit, he was, both professionally and personally, unabashedly himself. There is a certain kind of fearlessness that comes with that – sitting in class and pivoting from tapestries to Taylor Swift. You best believe it makes you a damn interesting person and an even better writer. Phillipson teaches that kind of fearlessness – he lives it. By extension, he told me I could, too. He allowed me to combine my inner self with my budding interest in "high culture" to make my writing and perspective not just more interesting but infinitely more sincere.

To that end, there is a reason that unlike my brother – who read in preschool and knew every country by the third grade – I took so long to connect with the world of "high culture." For me, reading is about conquering the mind, changing the way my brain wants to see text, and forcing it to perceive characters. In other words, I am dyslexic. For years, this was a big barrier for me – an obstacle in the way of books and "high culture." A feeling of immense frustration defined my early educational experiences. During my school's quiet reading hour, when every student grabbed a book and read, I laid on the floor, legs spread like a starfish, and looked up at the ceiling. Even today, I recall a shelf in my childhood room where I kept all the books I couldn't read; it was an absurd image, just not outwardly. You'd notice if I had shelves full of torn-up paper or broken toys, but these were just books. To me, though, like my disability, their utility was invisible.

As a really little kid, my favorite book was Go Dog Go by P.D. Eastman. I vaguely remember sitting on my bed and watching my mom flip through the pages, reading it to me. I'd track the colorful dogs as, page by page; they traversed their fantasy land in cars only fit for fictional canines. Years later, I remember trying to read Go Dog Go for myself at seven.

Preface by Toby Rosewater, Managing Sports Editor, The Amherst Student

The book's rhythmic flow of b's and d's hit my eyeballs and flipped in my brain so many times that they became essentially meaningless. The book I once loved morphed into an object of frustration. I loved its contents, but I couldn't decipher them. My psychological report from the time illustrates this: I demonstrated impressive reasoning abilities and even better verbal aptitude, but in multiple reading categories, I placed below the first percentile. Even today, I recall an incident from a rainy morning over a decade ago. As it poured, my teacher asked me to match a word card to its corresponding picture. I grasped the card in my hands and hopelessly surveyed the images laid out in front of me. I glanced over the red house, the duck, the boat, the tree, and finally, the blue bird. I pretended to know what I was looking at – I had no idea – my card could have said "tree" or "red house," and it would have been all the same.

It felt like something was taken from me, and I was deeply frustrated. Because of this, I started to act out. I was angry – it was easy to be angry – imagine going to work every day to perform a task you can't complete. You sit there trying to put the pieces together while everyone around you does it with ease – with big smiles – all day. The same psychological report from earlier described me as "dramatic, demanding, and possessive" and said I had the tendency to "lash out with a fierce temper when [I] did not get what I want[ed]." At the same time, it said I could be "incredibly charming, sweet, and funny." This oxymoronic turn of phrase exemplifies my seven-year-old self's many contradictions. I was a fun-loving, curious kid who wanted to do well but someone who fought for everything because so much felt out of reach.

By some miracle, in the second grade, I got into the Windward School for language-based learning disabilities. I left my friends and started anew. I didn't just start reading books, though; instead, I read specific pedagogical passages – strings of largely nonsensical sentences engineered to get me to read. I had three English classes a day, two hours of homework a night, wrote everything in cursive, and kept a daily agenda. Eventually, it worked, and by the end of my time at the Windward School, I could read.

I mention this all to say that for a while, all the information I independently took in did not come from books but from the world around me: the many hours of Minecraft I played in my basement, the TV shows I watched in the morning with my chocolate milk, and the music that blasted on the bus radio every morning. This – not reading – not writing – not anything – traditionally considered "high culture" was at the center of my formative experience. You can imagine, then, that when Wes Phillipson came into my life many years later and told me that these things were inherently interesting – that they were worth talking about in a serious way, then, in a sense, he was validating me. He was calling me interesting – he was saying

I, the kid who could never quite put the puzzle together – already had the damn pieces to construct my own, more interesting, more genuine puzzle.

With that, Phillipson fundamentally changed the way I take in information. When someone tells you that all culture deserves to be analyzed, how could you not approach the world more thoughtfully? I began to look at all things in a different light. I learned that every work – from Clash Royale to the Mona Lisa – is made with intention and that when we view these things, we must value this intention. Similarly, I learned that every story, no matter how mundane, has a certain kind of intrigue – a unique significance – a narrative we must approach with wonder. In that sense, Phillipson didn't just make me feel good about the culture I loved but pushed me to view it critically.

Under Phillipson, I wrote about Ken Griffey Jr, the Muppets, Latin, liminal spaces, and so on. In each piece, I combined "high" and "low" culture and developed my voice as a writer. I approached each topic with a rigorous thoughtfulness and infused every word with my genuine sense of self. In the four years since I worked with Phillipson, I've excelled further. In high school, I attended both the Iowa Young Writers' Studio and the Kenyon Young Writers Workshop. I won the district's award for Latin, Art History, and Creative Writing, and afterward, I got into my first choice school, Amherst College, where, as a freshman, I became a sports editor for the student newspaper.

At the same time, and more importantly, I've become a more empathetic and thoughtful person – one who tries to look at the world with both wonder and critical awareness. Even though I have a long way to go, looking back on all this, I don't think I could have done it – I don't think I would have done it – without the lessons Phillipson taught me. As much as I think a traditional liberal arts education can enable someone like me, I believe the eclectic, singular, and deeply thoughtful approach outlined in this book – at least something like it – will come to define the next generation of writing education.

Phillipson's ability to merge the accessible with the avant-garde is something I've never seen before and haven't seen elsewhere. As a dyslexic student from an unconventional background, I know that pedagogy is complicated, I know that it is not always right, and I know that it is always, always changing. In that regard, I encourage readers to traverse this book with attention and awareness – to embrace it in all of its nuances and to be open to the unconventional methods of a brilliant pedagogy that changed my life.

Toby Rosewater

ACKNOWLEDGMENTS AND SHOUT-OUTS

My Editors Megha Patel and Pakhi Pande at Routledge/Taylor & Francis. They were tireless advocates for this project from its inception.

Illustrator Angela Chiang who provided the pen and ink drawings for inside the book, and inspiration for the cover art. Graphic designers Louis Basso and Safiya Rahman for helping create book cover mock-ups.

I missed James Treadway by two months: He was a graduating senior at Scarsdale High School in June of 2003; I was a rookie (Scarsdale) teacher in September of that same year. James provided me with two key concepts that I fully embrace in my teaching: "wordsmithing" and "super-power."

Beth Raymer has worked with my senior English classes for years, helping them navigate her memoir Lay the Favorite, and – all while developing an F/X series on the opioid crisis, writing her debut novel Fireworks Every Night, and raising her son – Beth was my peak-performance coach and cheerleader.

Colleague David Sherrin introduced me to the Routledge editorial team. David's own excellent book on Authentic Assessment in Social Studies (published in 2020) made me believe that I had a book in me that could be coaxed out.

Deerfield (Chicago) English teacher Jeff Berger-White who understood everything I was trying to do with my classes and offered unwavering support by email and phone.

English teacher Amanda Filley whose acknowledgment and adoption of many of my writing assignments for her own classroom has sustained me in my teaching practice.

English teacher Stephen Mounkhall taught me that students could *call on each other's raised hands* in class discussions. Stephen has helped me refine my thinking about what an essay should and shouldn't be.

English teacher Kathleen McGreal's superpower is her ability to get students to tell stories worth hearing. She has adapted NPR's "Moth Radio Hour" into a series of prompts that she assigns freshmen. That, along with her curricular use of Anna Deavere Smith's one-woman show, prepares students for *what's next* as well as anyone in our Department could. When meeting a new student-writer "with chops," it's never a surprise to learn that their previous English teacher was Ms. McGreal.

Natalie Farina was the first teacher I met at SHS as the least senior member of the English Department hiring committee (of four people) who gave me the chance to teach at one of the best high schools in America.

Seth Evans was my assigned mentor for my first three years at SHS. He's brilliant and is a gifted drama and writing teacher. We shared nearly 20 years as colleagues and regularly helped each other refine our respective writing programs.

Dr. Karine Schaefer is the current English Department Chair of Scarsdale HS and has been one of four I've had since 2003. Christopher Douglass was my first – and he gave me immeasurable structure. Christopher Renino was my second – with a gentle hand he reminded me that I wanted to commit myself to SHS. Ann Liptak was my third – and she was a fun but "no nonsense" leader. Under Karine, however, our Department has the chance to change the tempo and pace of the school itself – maybe even its very culture. At SHS, an English teacher runs (or has run) just about every major club or activity there is, and Karine never misses an opportunity to acknowledge those above-and-beyond contributions at our monthly meetings. Far beyond that, she leads with compassion and empathy, advocating for our continued autonomy in the classroom, never asking for more than we can give, and forever connecting with her charges by way of TED Talk worthy anecdotes that begin and end the year's Department meetings in grand fashion.

My parents, Brainerd and Pamela Phillipson, were classroom teachers. My father was an HS English teacher in Newton, MA, and my mother a third grade teacher in Framingham, MA. From my father in particular, I saw a compelling future in education. My first inkling came when I picked up the phone in my parent's kitchen in 1984 and spoke with a man on a Navy base in Hawaii. It was Bill Rollins, who'd been my father's student in 1975. He wanted to send his former teacher his Iron Man comic books to show his appreciation. I was hooked. Later, it was my mother who encouraged me to earn my Post-Baccalaureate in Education, and it seemed likely the only clear path forward at the time. Still does.

INTRODUCTION BY JAMES TREADWAY, CEO OF GROWTHWISE TUTORING

As I sat in History class as an 11th grader at Scarsdale High School in 2002, it hit me with an uncanny resonance: What called so many high school teachers to their work was an unconscious desire to heal the pains they experienced as teenagers.

What?! I didn't know where this came from. I didn't have any evidence it was true for my History teacher at the time (was it, Mr. Maguire?) – nor do I have evidence to suggest it drives Wes Phillipson.

It might've just been a premonition about my own path in life.

I've spent over 20 years working with teenagers, and healing my teenage self has definitely been driving my life's work.

Through the hopefully inspirational Scholastic Aptitude Test (SAT) tutoring that I did from 2005 to 2023, to the on-line class I now teach called Social Skills for Life, my every waking hour is driven by a passion to help teenagers with the problems that made me a once-quasi-suicidal teen.

Why do the teenage years so move me? It might be the rawness. Newly arrived in adult bodies pumping with hormones, these kids, only a few years back, were still running toward a playground when they saw one, or asking to cuddle with mom or dad on the couch.

Insistent on experimenting with activities you wish they'd wait five more years to even think about, they return each night to stuffed animals or athlete-homaging posters by their bedside.

When I was 15, I woke up each morning with a NEED to discover, in the shower, who I was before I could emerge for the day.

I had no idea who I was. And God did that pain me.

"I'm funny!" I'd insist to myself. OK. That was it. I'm funny! I've got it. I'd head out into my school day, excited to settle into my identity as "funny." I'd make a joke in the car when my friend picked me up, try out a few more at my early morning class government meetings, and by first period had probably made about ten different jokes to people.

But some of them weren't working – cracks in the armor of this identity I'd finally found – the armor I was sure would protect me from the vulnerabilities of teenage life.

By late morning, I'd begin to realize that "funny" was not who I was, and it was exhausting to always have to be that way! I just wasn't funny enough, anyway.

So who the hell was I?

For two years or so, I returned to each morning's shower insistent that today was the day I would figure it out. I'd arrive at an identity, try it relentlessly that morning, and be utterly exhausted, defeated, and depressed by afternoon.

Somehow, amid all this, I managed to win president of my class all four years as well as captain and MVP of the soccer team, be named an editor of the school newspaper, and gain acceptance to Harvard by the end of it.

I was clearly doing everything right, wasn't I?

Or was I doing everything wrong?

Despite accumulating so many of the accomplishments that achievement-obsessed teenagers think will win them eternal stature and fulfillment, I was depressed, bereft of self-confidence or any idea where I wanted to go in life.

By my Harvard years, when a Boston or New York City subway came my way as I stood on the platform, I had to walk in the other direction as it came – afraid the part of me that wanted to throw myself in front of the train was going to win the argument.

At 20, three weeks into my junior year of college, I realized I could not do school anymore. I had a 12-page paper due on the Cuban Revolution, and despite how fantastically engaging my professor was, I could not get myself to write that paper. Rampant perfectionism rewrote the introduction 50–100 times, and I could not make my way to the second paragraph. The paper was never going to get finished.

Nothing worked in my life anymore. I had chronic pain in my hands and knees, and I was way too young for chronic pain. My "friends" would bully me over video games and "forget" to invite me to parties. I'd never had a girlfriend despite so desperately yearning for one.

My family insisted that my two older brothers and I pursue a career path of investment banking into private equity or hedge funds, and I just couldn't put together why.

Yes, it made the most money. But, so what?? I'm supposed to work how many hours a week re-reading investment pitch books for proper commas and correct page-numbering? And care what a company's bond structure looked like?

But it seemed like that was the only respectable path for my life. My brothers had already trodden it, and most of my peers at Harvard seemed intent on doing the same.

How depressing was all of this.

Three weeks into that junior year, I took a year off from school. Embarking on my quarter-life crisis, I was surely spinning out into loserdom, with no idea where to go in life.

From that tender age of 20 until now at 39, I have spent just about every dollar I've earned (well into seven figures) on learning to heal and grow myself out of that predicament.

I've gone to more Tony Robbins seminars, communication workshops, hallucinogenic plant medicine ceremonies, and therapy and coaching sessions than probably anyone you've met. I read about and experiment with these topics endlessly.

And I feel so, freaking, happy, and blessed now.

I do work I absolutely love (yes, helping teenagers). I'm getting better and better at it. I experience zero procrastination issues anymore, nor social anxiety. The friends I have seem to relish my uniqueness – all the things my teenage self feared made me too weird to be lovable or respectable.

There simply are not enough hours in the day for all I yearn to do and experience now. I'm coming home to a sense of peace and presence – and even an embrace of life's pain as truly the greatest avenue to whatever it is I'm hoping to become (feel it, and let it go, I've learned).

And I get to share these gifts, ever more, with teens. Nothing makes me happier than to see my students learning the key lessons of my Social Skills for Life course: How to make others feel seen and heard, navigate out of anxiety and into their better selves, make a game of rejection and failure when going after what they want in life, and recognize and relish the unique gifts they each have inside.

No wonder Mr. Phillipson jumps at any chance to have me speak to his students: He's driven by the same mission.

"The problem with student writers," he writes in one essay assignment, "is RARELY: 'Can I dial this person DOWN?' It's almost always: Where is the ON switch? How can I CRANK UP this dude, dudette, or other?"

He's dying to help students find their voice. He's dying to HEAR their voice!

"It's so wonderful to see students come into my English class and have no idea that they COULD be good – even truly great – writers," he says. "Students who think they're math and science kids. Students who can only think of writing as a chore, punishment, or utter waste of time. Students who think they want a very traditional English teacher and are horrified or nonplussed by the man who stands before them in September. THOSE are the ones I can – perhaps – help transform."

I've never met a better hype man than Wes. When he describes you to others, he doesn't just sing your praises with enthusiasm – he does it with clarity, celebrating things inside you that you'd given up hoping others would see or notice.

I've seen him do it when he introduces me to his classes, and I've seen him do it every time he describes one of his students to me.

"My singular educational goal," he tells students: "I want to be your producer. Jack Antonoff doesn't 'grade' Taylor Swift. He brings out the best, creatively, in Tay-Tay. Mark Ronson doesn't 'grade' Bruno Mars. He unleashes BM."

In another assignment he adds, "A Chinese proverb states, 'the friend who understands us," creates us.' That idea is no fortune cookie gibberish, it's raw truth."

Wes shows up to class each day looking to understand his students – to inspire them to understand themselves – and in so doing, to create themselves. A teacher who wants to be his students' producer. Wow.

With the diversity of assignments he gives, the plethora of examples he offers students of how one can write and express themselves, and the conversational-grading process he's pioneered, he's arrived at a form of English teaching that is a clarion call to each person in the room to unearth the gems of authenticity inside.

To share them with the world in all their blazing glory!

Did you know that Wes assigns his papers to himself? He writes each paper alongside students and then shares it with his class, his vulnerability laid bare on the page before this room of teenagers.

He asks students to take risks in their writing. Express themselves. Tell the fucking truth, and let their humor sing. And he leads the way.

If all this isn't what's taught in the typical "five paragraph essay" that's taught throughout the world, then that's exactly why it's needed.

He offers a bastion of raw, real, and supportive. Take those risks you're thinking about – try out these varied models of writing, video-making, and poetry – and let's see what sticks!

When ChatGPT offers to write teens' thoughts and papers better and easier than they ever could, and we run to our cell phones hundreds of times a day to assuage our own anxiety at the uncertainty of being alive, students are losing touch with whom they are and can be.

They're opting out of life's risky voyages – no matter how small: Should they try to talk to the kid next to them in homeroom whom, if they're being honest, they're at least a little bit curious about and impressed by – or just bury their face in their phone and not risk showing interest in someone else?

A total of 99 times out of 100, teens – all of us – are choosing to put our faces in our phones. It seems safer in there.

But then we never discover the person next to us; what the two of us might share; what we might like and dislike about each other. What we might learn from the other person's experiences or their responses to ours.

In daring to explore, to try things, and to look stupid or unrequited in our interests, we find ourselves.

But somehow, the "anxious generation," as author Jonathan Haidt describes today's youth, seems incredibly fearful of stepping out of their own box and just plain getting messy with life.

So get messy, Wes' teaching says. "Your thinking is messy, your writing should be messy too, just less messy than your thinking," he urges.

Dare, dare, and dare some more. Listen in. And every step of the way, he will have your back.

So behold: the English class I wish my awkward, anxious, and incredibly insecure 15-year-old self could have taken.

Watch Wes inspire students to try every form of writing and expression they can, to sing each other's praises as they read their work aloud in class, and to collaborate with him in grading conversations that make A's and B's an avenue of reflection and connection with their teacher, as opposed to the source of judgment and anxiety it is in 99.9% of classrooms.

Whatever the pain and uncertainty that shapes our high school years, Wes uses his classroom to guide students toward finding the voice, inspiration, and courage that will lead them out of their teenage abyss and into an identity and life that they will love.

James Treadway
La Jolla, California
November 30, 2024

1
THE WAX PACK
Breaking Wax

As I am writing this chapter, I'm not 100% convinced that my Wax Pack essay prompt was a success this academic year, but I wouldn't go back and change much about the assignment.

I am not a man who lives without regrets. There are countless things I would have done differently in my life if given the chance, but not regarding the start of academic year 2024–25: I created a new prompt based on a nonfiction book of the same name (The Wax Pack – by Brad Balukjian), bought $500 worth of "junk wax" from various eBay sellers as well as the brick-and-mortar shop SMR Collectibles in Amityville, NY, and – thanks to that – had hundreds of 80s and 90s unopened packs of disparate trading cards fanned out atop my classroom's HVAC system as if a pop-up collectibles store.

So in early September 2024, students filed into Room 207 at Scarsdale High School to the technicolor display of vintage rectangles depicting sitcom families (ALF, Growing Pains, etc.), NASCAR racers, satirical stickers (Wacky Packages), Craftsmen Tools, Midwestern soccer leagues, Desert Storm villains, Return of the Jedi heroes, Super Mario Brothers associated characters, Christian Bale's Batman, NBA ballers courtesy of Fleer's 1991 update series, Pokemon ('nuff said – they went fast), and everything else ranging from O-Pee-Chee Canadian hockey stars, 1990 Topps NFL players, to 1981 Donruss PGA Golf's heavy-hitters. (I had no idea that golf was big enough to warrant its own trading cards.)

At that moment, junior Stacey Liew remarked, "Ooooh, free stuff! Mr. Phillipson, you've already won me over," as she scooped up two silver-foil packs of Looney Tunes "Comic Ball" trading cards, a commercial orange sticker announcing their 75 cent sale price (per pack) affixed to the wrapper,

DOI: 10.4324/9781003600565-1

showing what I'd paid in hopes of inspiring someone – anyone. Maybe lighting-up Stacey was enough, as everyone else seemed in a daze, or on high-alert – terrified of choosing the wrong pack, simultaneously unaware of what I'd even be asking students to do with the cards once selected.

I could hear sophomore Kaya Williams outside my classroom before the bell rang saying, "How do we have an essay already? It's just the first day?"

Someone, upon exit, had tipped him off.

Brad Balukjian is really into exotic insects, professional wrestling, and baseball. He's a Science professor and author who inspired me to transpose the premise of his warm and engaging road-trip memoir in search of living MLB legends, underdogs, and commoners, into an essay prompt for my students.

His story: Brad took an unopened pack of 80s baseball cards and hunted down every single living player represented on the cardboard inside. He spent a summer traversing the country to get to the bottom of the questions: What happens to your heroes when they've gotten older, and what is life like post-professional-baseball? Brad had collected sports cards as a kid and wanted more than just that "hit of nostalgia" that breaking wax can give the end-user.

My story: I'm eight years older than Brad, but I was raised on wax too. We seem to have this compelling, parasocial kinship: He loves underdog players and so do I. In 1980, when Brad was born, I was buying up all the early-series Wacky Packs (stupid-funny satirical stickers that attack retail products in unclever ways) that I could find at comic book and card shows.

I was listening to a story about Brad's newly released book Breaking Wax on NPR when it struck me:

> What if I gave my students the same experience I'd had as a kid opening wax-paper-wrapped bundles of trading cards, stickers, puzzle-pieces, and powdered sticks of pink bubble-gum? And, what if I layered on top of that a meaningful challenge? Brad had traveled thousands of miles to ask (oftentimes) reluctant retired major-leaguers questions that would satisfy his inner-child, fanboy, and aspirational adult. What if I got my hands on hundreds of random genres and subject matters from the 80s and 90s – that had been frozen in a wax time capsule – and had my students open them in real time, in front of each other? In front of me?

What Kind of Nostalgic Riptide Would Carry Them Away, and Where Would It Take Them?

My first essay for any English class is typically a musical one. Everyone loves music and has a distinct, intimate relationship with some recording artist, group, band, or musician. And music is something we often listen to but rarely unpack and decode, so there's an opportunity for anyone to participate (low bar to enter), and it's often the first time underclassmen are analyzing a "text" that they care passionately about, delighting in spending time with the source material. How many students will read Of Mice and Men more than once? Ask them to take a deep dive into their favorite song or album, and you'll get the music-critic equivalent of Harold Bloom: Their track playing on repeat, copious notes jotted down fast and furious – at least, for the moment, they become a graduate student in attitude and posture. Ask a 9th grader to explore Steinbeck's thinnest volume and you'll get the complex equivalent of a SparkNotes-entry written by someone who half-read the book while simultaneously scrolling through social media.

So I often kicked things off with *that* essay for *those* reasons.

But I had gone through a Renaissance of sorts during the 2023–24 school years that helped me realize two things:

1. As an English teacher, I have a duty to my students to differentiate each essay prompt I assign. I simply cannot give a formulaic, thesis-driven five-paragraph essay twice a quarter (or eight times a year) and feel like I'm adding value to their lives, or offering them a meaningful challenge. English classes are often static rather than dynamic: We keep asking them to do the same kinds of activities and assessments over and over again. Students aren't so much "grade-locked" by teachers as worn down by the monotony of read this, take notes, complete this reading quiz, write a prescribed essay, make a poster, write another prescribed essay, here's another reading quiz, present your poster. Repeat.
2. *If I don't innovate*, then how can I ask my students to do so? Every so often, I need to fold in a brand-new essay prompt that surprises students and forces me to teach a new skill-set in service of that essay.

But I suddenly wondered if this "Breaking Wax" essay assignment was going to be style-over-substance, or – perhaps – gimmick over grand narrative.

Would young teens even care about trading cards? Outside of Pokemon, would they even know what they are?

And what would I have done as a 10th grader with a pack of Topps football cards, or O-Pee-Chee hockey cards, if my teacher had said:

Use these cards to write an essay about your relationship with nostalgia. Or – even more broadly – as I articulated to them during that first September class: **Write about how you intersect with these cards.**

My English class is a bit like reverse-bootcamp or anti-basic training. I'm taking people who've been soldiers their whole lives and turning them into civilians.

To achieve civilian status, they must learn how to live without strict rules, a commanding officer, or the structure that had previously given their lives rhythm and meaning.

That aside, the Breaking Wax essay was due in two weeks from opening day. During that time, they could schedule office visits with me through my on-line booking site to brainstorm, or simply review a draft. Many students did just that. When meeting, very few of them presented a kind of analysis paralysis or writer's block to me – which was surprising. I had never given such an open-ended prompt before with so little context and so few parameters. Initially, I thought about changing gears, maybe abandoning the topic (or what was starting to feel like a gimmick). I wasn't – early on – seeing many great ideas emerge from my students' minds on laptop screens, nor was I seeing the sharpness and clarity of writing that normally happened at that stage.

My ethos as an English teacher is that writing is cathartic, and it's best when shared with a community. So I try to accomplish both with each prompt – determine how you figure into the essay (you're your own mental-health patient), write it so that you come to a logical or illogical conclusion (that's the time spent on the psychologist's couch), and let as many people as possible read it (hence: community or – perhaps – group therapy). Don't create pieces that "get you the A," make ones you enthusiastically want to share. And that rarely happens when you spend your time writing what your teacher wants you to write.

So, I was worried. But then I got to Edward Chen's debut essay in sophomore English.

He reflects on the experience here:

"After this piece, I finally understood why people enjoy writing about themselves so much: it's a way not only to describe, but also to explore. Instead of simply listing and explaining parts of myself, I was able to pull narrative details from both my conscious and unconscious mind, realizing I am so much more than I could have imagined."

Here's an "alternate way" into the assignment:

Right now many of you are wondering – do I have to source (and pay for) 100 packs of vintage trading cards to do this prompt with my own students? No. Having wax packs definitely made it more tactile, experiential and playful, *but any teacher could adjust the assignment to read*:

Google image "trading cards" and one specific aspect of American popular culture of great interest to you personally (if you're teaching American literature, for example).

Start with your childhood "favorite things." If you loved watching the TV show Full House, then Google "Full House trading cards," and you'll find – among other things – this eBay listing for 1991's LAFFS cards (featuring sitcom stars of that time). There are over 2,000 search results for that card series alone.

Once you find cards that give you a pure, unadulterated shot of youth-juice, then physically zoom-in on some details of each card and determine: What information is provided on the backs of any cards that you can read up-close-and-personal? What images are chosen for the front, and how do they promote the piece of media, sport, TV show, cartoon character, celebrity, or pop-culture category you've focused on?

Thereafter, consider how these cards make you feel. What moment (or moments) are you reminded of from your past? What is your current relationship with the subject matter or hobby? What had your relationship once been? Are these cards, you once owned, have stashed in a container in your parent's attic, or are they an entirely new way for you to engage with this category of interest?

The idea here is: What do these cards say about you, or let you explore who you once were, who you aspired to be, or the dividing line between your childhood and young adult selves?

Here's the prompt:

Essay One: The Wax Pack of RANDOMNESS   Assignment Write-Up Phillipson/English

Wax packs are just like they sound: Inside is a thin stack of trading cards with pictures of athletes or celebrities, wrapped up in a piece of waxed paper. Oh, and there's usually a stick of powdered bubble gum in there, too. It's often fractured into many pieces because the gum is hard, old, and just a little less flavorful than actual cardboard.

The trading cards themselves are *randomized*. My understanding is that they are cut from large sheets of cardstock or cardboard (100 or more individual cards to a big sheet), shuffled, and put into packs through an entirely automated process. There's no intentional pattern to their order in a pack, or who ends up where. No sequence that I know of, anyway.

That means: you have no idea which baseball or basketball player's card is inside ANY ONE pack. You could go through 30 packs of 86/87 season NBA Fleer cards and NOT find a Michael Jordan rookie card. But to buy that ONE pack would cost you $2,500–$5,000, and there's a very good chance: NO JORDAN CARD. Because it's random. And because these packs have sometimes been "searched" (a euphemism for "sneakily gone through and sealed back up – no one the wiser").

Brad Balukjian is an entomologist (insect scientist) and evolutionary biologist, and he's also the author of one of my favorite books: *The Wax Pack – On the Open Road in Search of Baseball's Afterlife.*

I'm not a baseball fan. I'm a tennis fan (and former seven day a week player). But I did collect, trade (and sell) baseball cards when I was a kid (even into my early 20s). I grew up just outside Boston, a hardcore sports' town, and I invested in the rookie cards of heavyweight slugger Mo Vaughan and four-seam fastball pitcher Aaron Sele. I lost money on both players.

For Balukjian's *Wax Pack* book, he does some things that resonate profoundly with me, *in this order*:

1 From a storage locker, he pulls out a wax pack of – still sealed – 1986 Topps baseball cards that he's been holding onto like a time capsule since he was six years old.
2 He opens the pack, lets some fresh air in, and blows the powdered sugar off.
3 He personally tracks down each and every retired player who is still alive from the pack (only two are dead, and only two refuse to speak with him directly), driving a total of 12,000 miles to interview them all in one summer.
4 He writes a book about his experience that is both poetical and practical, making himself the central part of the story. He's a baseball fan. He loves baseball cards. He appreciates how players' statistics (printed on the backs of cards) tell an intricate story about the man (on the front) who wears the uniform. So – he manages to tie all of that together: His own fanboy dreams coming true, his work as a Science professor in California (and how that connects to stats and his intellectual curiosity), his magical (and-not-so-magical) childhood memories, his summer road-trip logging 12,000 miles, the tale of the two retired players who rejected him, but then connecting with his all-time favorite player (then Philadelphia Phillies') southpaw Don Carman.

So – what are you doing for your own Essay One? Well, **you've chosen** a sealed wax pack from my personal collection of disparate trading cards **for a reason**. Some chose athletics, entertainment media, or historical subjects. But you reached for ONE particular, specific pack for SOME reason. One of them spoke to you. Why? In a moment you're going to open your own vintage pack (to take with you, study, use, and keep). The next step you take is entirely up to you, but you must meaningfully use the pack of cards to write a 1,250 word "analytical personal essay" – due two weeks from today.

Not allowed: No cliches, no two- or three-word phrases that exceed 100,000 results in a Google search, no generic statements or claims, no non-essential summary, no stock transitions, no five paragraph essay structure, no topic sentences that break into two, no two examples in your paragraphs, no thesis restatement, no summarizing in your conclusion, and no "telling the reader things they already know."

Mandatory: A title, subtitle, image/picture, caption for image, byline (your name), personal motto, and signature graphic (internally and at the end of your piece). Also mandatory is: engaging voice, world-building, intersecting personally with the topic, and meaningful (to you) analysis. And: It must be the essay you WANT to write, and it must be the essay that ONLY you CAN write. In service of that, you must add something new to the conversation. Your essay should embody my maxim: Your thinking is messy, your writing should be messy too, just less messy than your thinking.

2
THE PHILOSOPHY OF YOU
Your Students Are Deeper Than You Think

It was October 2023, and I badly wanted this year of teaching English to be different. For me, and more loftily, for my students. I had never been bad or negligent in my work, but I didn't always feel that my writing assignments had real gravitas or an intelligent design that would also inspire sophomores and juniors to "create art versus just get it done for the grade."

I was a bit of a fraud or an imposter working at Scarsdale High School, just in the sense that there were these rock-star teachers in my department, as well as in History and Science, that students took seriously – if not worshiped. *And then there was me.* Yes, I had positively impacted several hundred students since 2003, and they'd come back to visit long after my time with them, but I didn't really know what I wanted to do with my essay assignments, which (as an English teacher) meant I didn't really know what I wanted to do with my students, either.

Scarsdale HS had turned out prize-winning writers of all kinds (Pulitzer, Tony, Oscar, etc.), but I was beginning to wonder if I had what it took to launch students on a path of that magnitude. And this was after fifteen years of my first being there, so that's a pretty daunting epiphany to have at such a late stage of the game.

But something was starting to happen to me that I'll try to explain.

Since Covid broke, I had spent a lot of my time reaching out to the best writers in the world and – to my sincere surprise – many had responded. More than that, they *wanted* to talk with my students and teach them the tricks of their trade.

I connected with heavyweights like Christopher McQuarrie (who received an Oscar for *The Usual Suspects*) and Dave Barry (who is the most

DOI: 10.4324/9781003600565-2

successful humor columnist in history, as well as a Pulitzer winner for social commentary).

Through those classes with legendary authors, I learned so much about the thought process of great writers that I started to understand it. And if you understand it, you can teach it. So I did.

"Essay Two" of that year was the moment I realized that I was working with a real-live prodigy: Alina Yang. Alina was just 14 when she came into the class and wrote her response to my open-ended prompt called "The Philosophy of You."

Irony of ironies, I had thought that Alina *was very average* after grading her "Essay One." If anything, I'd thought she pushed back <u>too much</u> about the A – she'd received for a piece that took several drafts to complete and a good deal of feedback (from me) to shape into something presentable.

The premise behind "The Philosophy of You" is pretty simple, but it changed my thinking about what a 10th-grade student could create from "simple."

Here's the idea:

> We were reading Albert Camus' *The Stranger* for class, a thin novella that explores hedonism, nihilism and existentialism through the lens of a mild-mannered sociopath named Meursault, when I seized upon the obvious.

Students can't expertly write about a book they've just read. It takes English teachers three years (or so I've been told) to become truly comfortable with a book, yet we demand that students who have barely read (if at all) a book **one time**, to "author" a paper about it. And author = authority, or at least it should.

My thinking became: Why not have students engage meaningfully with their own philosophy? Why not have them take deep dives into their psyche? If Jung was right that "the only way forward is inward," then how could I ask my own students to write an intellectually honest and meaningful paper about The Stranger, when they, themselves, were strangers to the book?

My other thought at the time was, *I need to do this too*. If I'm asking them to be vulnerable and write their most intimate thoughts on the page about how they think and feel and why they believe what they do, then I must be the first across the pond's thin ice.

So, I wrote about the most personal thing that was happening to me at that moment: my family's masseuse was leaving for China to visit his own family and stay for the New Year. It may not sound that powerful a tale, or just a first-world problem, but it was downright devastating at the time. I locked myself in my office for two hours and wrote my own "Philosophy of You" and *decided that I would never again assign an essay that I also hadn't written and shared with my students first.*

The method to my madness behind assigning writing prompts is simple:

- Don't ask your students to do anything that you aren't currently doing *yourself*.
- Write (yourself) the essays that you want *them* to write: be vulnerable, explicit, raw, and real, modeling for them the things you value (and grade) in their writing.
- Read your own essays *aloud* to the class (create a culture where they see sharing their own works as central to "the English classroom experience").
- Get the class' feedback: Do not fear criticism. Ask them to talk about what they liked and didn't like about your essay. Make sure they have printed copies, so they can mark them up with red pens or highlighters. You want to engage them in a different kind of conversation about writing, so put yourself in their shoes. Usually, they are the ones being graded by you, so you must be willing to be graded by them first.
- Have high standards but low expectations: Students are going to resist this process, but they will come around to it (trust me – most do). It's going to be bumpy at first, and it's going to take a lot of your time to have them unlearn past habits.

So, I wrote about Mr. Kang's departure from my life, read it to the class, got their feedback and ... then sophomore Alina Yang writes this and my life has never been the same:

* * *

But then Luka Li busted a move I'd never seen a student pull off.

Luka is a current sophomore as of 2024. He did this odd thing where we graded his essays out of sequence. Near the end of quarter one, with four essays under our collective belts, Luka came to grade his Essay Two: The Philosophy of You.

In his case, it was a paper about the intense nostalgia induced by Taiwanese garbage trucks' perpetual theme song (think American ice-cream trucks). My wife's parents are from Taipei and Kaohsiung, but I'd never traveled there and knew nothing of "garbage truck culture" (and that said trucks repeatedly played a maddening yet comforting song on a loop as garbage men made their rounds).

A few days prior, I'd read and graded Luka's Essay Four about the TV program Poirot (the Agatha Christie detective series made for the BBC). It was sharp. It had elegant wordplay. It made an impression on me. We also had the shared experience of performing it aloud and putting a grade on it jointly – when grading it together.

But his Essay Two? Sitting together in my office and hearing each word roll off the tongue like vintage Jamaica Kincaid – the piece didn't feel one millimeter like a student's essay. It had the kind of epic, sweeping nature of a foreign correspondent embedded in a city among the locals. It felt no less worthy than Truman Capote's searing travel essay about Tangier. It was as penetrating as anything Anthony Bourdain had ever written to use as voiceover copy for his TV shows No Reservations or Parts Unknown.

When you're in Luka's hands, seeing things at the ground level in Taiwan, feeling the full-court press of local color permeate, you understand what evocative writing is. In that moment, it transcends writing, becoming cinema, or the opposite of a sensory deprivation tank. It is an all-immersive carnival of delights.

And there's effortlessly embedded wisdom and – somehow, someway – distance and perspective while simultaneously feeling immediate and intimate. How does someone who's 14 or 15 pull off that magic trick? In 1987, when I was a sophomore, I wouldn't have known how to world-build like Luka (or what world I'd have wanted to construct) or how to structure such a fluid yet anchored piece.

Here's Prompt Two

Essay Two: The Philosophy of You English 10 – The Stranger Unit – Assignment Write-Up

Essay Two will be due in a few weeks. Please start thinking about it. Please read my own response to the assignment. You will have pre-writing to do for it soon.

If you haven't graded your first essay with me (and still wish to), then you have until the end of next week to do so. The thinking here is something I said the first week of school: those who want feedback will seek it out.

Essay Two is about "the philosophy of you." What is ONE aspect of the world, life, and/or human nature that you have come to understand in your own, unique way? What is one specific story or subject through which to express that "unique take on humanness?" For me – it's my weekly appointment with the family masseuse, Mr. Kang. And it's that we – as humans – are seeking two things really: (A) Relief, and (B) More Time. That's "my philosophy" – not yours – not your parent's. But mine. In my essay, I wanted to explore a problem that I'm facing over the next four months: the absence of Mr. Kang, a guy who administers medical massages for a living but who is also someone who brings relief and affords his clients a greater quality of life. (As my Bikram Yoga teacher once told me, "The quality of your health is determined by the quality of your spine".)

Why this essay topic? Well, we're five chapters into Camus' The Stranger, an entire novella about one man's personal take on humanity, separateness, strangeness, otherness, the pursuit of pleasure, self-negation, apology, and the meaning of life (or its antithesis).

Assignment Specs:

- *1250 Words (+/- 75 words)*
- *Explores an aspect of your philosophy that is wholly unique to you*
- *Unpacks at least one meaningful distinction that you've been grappling with*

3
CONSIDER THE LOBSTER

When it comes to teaching writing, I find that David Foster Wallace is not so much the elephant in the room but the live lobster click-clacking stove-side before being submerged in a pot of scalding water.

Wallace is the G.O.A.T. of creative nonfiction and long-form journalism. He's transformed the banal act of boarding a cruise ship into something both stark and deconstructivist, made watching Federer strike a forehand into a study in dumb luck and untold grace, and a trip to the Maine Lobster Festival into a meditation on hypocrisies, tourism, animal rights, and white privilege.

As I write this chapter, I am coming off a lively day of teaching in which I argued both for and against the merits of postmodernism. My junior class was the last period of the day, and there was a fair amount of pushback from my students: Why are we studying postmodernism, why are so many aspects of it contradictory, and why is some of the writing so laughably bad?

I found myself defending The Bluest Eye by Toni Morrison, White Noise by Don DeLillo, and David Foster Wallace's place among the pantheon of essay-writing gods. A student had attacked the simplistic writing at the start of Morrison's debut novel, not understanding that Faulkner's Sound and the Fury was being riffed on, and that Morrison was mimicking the Dick and Jane readers of mid-century America to set up her narrative of abject poverty and the kind of trauma that causes permanent developmental paralysis that many Blacks suffered from in mid-century Ohio.

I made the claim that about one-third of postmodern works were of reasonably high quality and was challenged on that assertion for it being (A) non-scientific and (B) seemingly made-up. The truth is: there is no definitive definition of Pomo (as it's known in colloquial shorthand), and – given that it's a movement that rejects absolute truths – it (accordingly) has no fixed rules or tenets that govern it. There's also no official – final – arbiter of good taste. How readable, really, is the prose of Thomas Pynchon (I've never finished even his slimmest of novels, The Crying of Lot 49). Yet Pynchon is hailed as the Dean of postmodern literature. Do the conceits of postmodernism – temporal distortion, flattened affect, intertextuality, metafiction, pastiche, and the like – get in the way of storytelling or enhance it? With Vietnam postmodernist Tim O'Brien's novel In the Lake of the Woods (a murder mystery without a corpse or direct evidence of a crime committed), the answer is clear: his form choices (footnotes, alternate theories, chapter titles grouped together by theme) "marry well" with his content choices. It's good matchmaking.

And that's my metric for whether a postmodern work is successful: Is there evidence of intelligent design? Does the *form* work harmoniously with the *content*? In the timeless neo-noir Memento (by Christopher Nolan), the film's lead character is a former insurance investigator who can't make new memories because of a traumatic brain injury sustained in the undefined past. Nolan tells the story backward *not* as some style-over-substance gimmick but to powerfully place the viewer in Leonard Shelby's shoes: Leonard doesn't know where he's just been – or what he's just been doing – and neither do you. It creates empathy, if not sympathy. It makes both the viewer and the main character co-conspirators and co-unreliable narrators.

As for David Foster Wallace?

His use of footnotes is legendary. His 1996 novel Infinite Jest is 1,076 pages of pure metafiction. Even his two-page suicide note has been openly speculated about on Reddit and elsewhere (but never released to the public).

And Consider the Lobster was supposed to be an innocuous bit of reportage for Gourmet Magazine back in 2004. You know, just a hipster – a self-styled nerd who favored bandanas and makeshift-pillow-cases for headwraps – traveling to Maine to capture some benign details about how to best butter-poach lobster tails and discover what constitutes a world-class lobster roll? That kind of stuff.

If you've read the article (CTL), then you know it's far more *loaded baked-potato than simple French fry*. It's also no lazy man's lobster, either. **That** was a dish that I first had as a child at a gourmet restaurant: The chef had scooped out all the meat and left it – drenched in butter – atop the excavated, autopsied shell. I was happy. My mother thought it began my journey of entitlement.

But Wallace takes an editor's basic assignment, his girlfriend, and his parents (one is from rural Maine) and heads straight to the MLF (Maine Lobster Festival), but what he submits to Gourmet Magazine for publication thereafter is nothing short of what I aspire to write myself and – more importantly – to have my students write.

CTL is a hardcore metanarrative – Wallace takes great pains to pull back the cheesecloth on the festival's appearance-vs.-reality framework: It's marketed more aggressively than events at the Grand Ole Opry and the Las Vegas Convention Center combined; it's not representative of the state (per se), as it's the Disneyfied version of Maine (even Wallace's native father doesn't really recognize or identify with Rockland); there's a profound cognitive dissonance with the hippies, greenies, tree-huggers, Earthy-crunchies, Greenpeacers, and PETA types that populate the event – the oceans are being overfished; what was once a flourishing protein source is drying up; and – most saliently – lobsters are literally boiled alive, but no one seems to care.

There's lots of raw real estate in his essay given over to a semi-pedantic history lesson on Maine's chief-crustacean-export. Wallace wants to bring readers up to speed on how undesirable, cheap, and vexing lobsters once were. They were the original American prison chow of the early 19th century. They were once considered storm detritus. Pilgrims could hand-fish them out of the shallows by the wagon-loads. Moreover, their stinky remnants became a kind of default fertilizer for crops.

Beyond the rich, layered, meta nature of CTL is the way Wallace weaves a pastiche of purple prose, reportage, feature article, analytical essay, and rant into one cohesive and (largely) readable piece.

CTL covers the kind of ground that only an investigative-journalist-meets-food-critic-meets Consumer-Reports-tester-meets-music-critic-meets-historian-meets-philosophy-major could conceivably author.

Here, Wallace taps into what the best nonfiction writing does: It's exploratory, dense, free-ranging, messy, all-encompassing, passionate, cynical, contradictory, and distinction-driven all at once.

And it's the argument I (sometimes) have with colleagues: I draw no distinction between personal and analytical essay-writing. Further, I'd submit that any teacher who argues that only essays about books can be analytical has it backward. Occasionally, the least analytical essays I find in the communal faculty printer are thesis-driven papers written about core-curriculum novels that teachers assign by grade level. If these print jobs are abandoned after several days, I'll read them and find genuine surprise in two things:

1 They often feel like book reports, featuring plot summary and little more.
2 The kind of prose these prompts inspire often feels downright uninspired.

I am well acquainted with 1 and 2 above because I have – in the past – assigned and graded work that felt more SparkNotes than spark ignited.

So I'm writing this with the benefit of hindsight. For many years I'd taught "thesis patterns" such as cause-and-effect, stages-of-development, appearance-vs.-reality, compare-and-contrast, and other cookie-cutter essay structures. When I did, I often graded papers that were plug-and-play: essays that blindly followed the novel's trajectory (plot structure) or some argument that was not really the student's but a regurgitation of the prompt itself, something I'd said in class, or a consensus my students had reached after days of discussion.

What Wallace accomplishes by writing and publishing CTL is a kind of English teacher fantasy composed of ink. It's proof that readers will hang in there with you, waist-deep in your bisque-like verbiage; they'll forgive your contradictions (Wallace promises not to deliver a "PETA-like screed," but he most certainly does), they'll endure your self-indulgent digressions and detours, and they'll delight in your *nerding out* on the history of – things like – lobsters.

That readers opened Gourmet Magazine for a food festival review but got something more on their lobster roll than meat, mayo, and parsley – and not just ate it, but relished every bite…well, that's what all us English teachers want for our customers too.

Wallace's essay is the antidote to incuriosity. He prophetically and ironically said – in his Kenyon commencement speech – that "the mind makes a wonderful servant but a terrible master" and was a tortured soul who took his own life in 2008. Part of what made Wallace so remarkable was a mind that couldn't shut off, tune out, or power down. But it could focus like a thousand surgical lasers when inspired. His ruminations likely brought him the kind of circular thinking that most of us (under these circumstances) can't break out of. But he *could* – for long stretches of time – and was able to use his postmodern-wired brain to anatomize and deconstruct the minutiae of his world in a way that was fresh, brave, and compelling. And like a great journalist is wont to do, he didn't follow orders (so – thankfully for readers – his editor at Gourmet got something far different than he bargained for; it's akin to ordering lobster and getting langoustines – a first-class upgrade).

As my junior class was writing a "consider this" style essay based on DFW's legendary meta-review, student Maddie Lee brought up (in class discussion) a Jabberwocky submission they'd received the day before. Jabberwocky is the long-running literary and arts magazine published twice a year at Scarsdale HS. My friend Stephen Mounkhall is the club advisor who lures students into weekly editor's meetings with the promise of unlimited Capri Sun pouches and six Container Store tubs filled with bags of Smartfood, Doritos, Cheetos, Ruffles, and all the mainstream bite-sized candy that would easily weigh down a trick-or-treater to the point of muscle failure. They'd likely drop their plastic pumpkin and beg for tricks.

Around that time I'd found Frank Waldman's personal copy of Jabberwocky (then called "The Jabberwock," after the Lewis Carroll work) for sale on eBay. It was from 1936. In the 60s, Walman co-created The Pink Panther franchise with director Blake Edwards. There is a rich legacy of SHS alums working in stage and screen (Liza Minnelli, Linda McCartney, Aaron Sorkin, and so on).

Today, the magazine is going stronger than ever under Stephen's thoughtful leadership.

Each week, Mounkhall photocopies the latest Jabberwocky submissions after removing the students' names for anonymity's sake (in hopes of maintaining a neutral editorial board). The staff sits and reads, critiques, and sips Capri Suns. One spit take later, they'd opened an envelope to find a photography submission that gave pause, raised eyebrows, and brought out unlikely defenders.

As Maddie Lee recounted to my junior class:

"It was a photo of a ceiling tile," she said – nonplussed – with her back to the large windows that look out onto the organic garden outside Room 207. "Just a corrugated tile, no caption, no title, no context. The editors and staff spent the next thirty minutes talking about it, considering it, justifying it, arguing against its very existence, shooting it down, talking it up, but it was what it was."

And when it comes to our essay prompts, what do we ask our students to "consider," really and truly?

What I've discovered is that we English teachers are really gifted at getting students to read and engage with texts, have them create lots of deep-thought questions, ask them to pair and share with books in hand and mouths open, and encourage them to speak in large groups about subtext and author intent. We're successful at teaching them how to annotate and journal. We regularly push them to present their literary analysis through slideshows.

But when it comes time for them to write the essay about the book we've spent half a quarter unpacking together, *that's often when the real consideration ends.*

It becomes a fait accompli.

Why?

It's because we ask students to figure out everything they're going to write about – in advance – before they even put pen to paper or keystroke to Google Doc. We say – *Guys: make a thesis outline, write a rough draft, conference with me, make some edits, and then submit the final copy to Turnitin.com or Google Classroom.* But that leaves little room for contemplation, messiness, taking detours, or the spontaneity that meaningful consideration actually requires.

Instead, the essays we assign are often exercises in "proving the thing true that our students already know is true." I often warn them, if you've got your paper all figured out before you've begun writing – *stop*. Do not go any further. If you write *that* essay, it's nearly guaranteed to be stiff, unfulfilling, uninspired, and insipid. *And those may be its best qualities.*

The way I see it, and why I place such importance on students modeling an essay like CTL is:

> Through CTL, Wallace provides a public service. He teaches us things that we didn't even know we wanted to know. In this case, it's things about lobsters (but it could be anything, right?): in Chinese restaurants, or any fish section of your local supermarket, they gather in the darkest part of the tank. I hadn't realized that (or the 1,000 other insights into something I like to eat that I was blissfully ignorant about prior). Moreover, Wallace adds something new to the conversation about food festivals, sharply redefining what a critic's role is even supposed to be.
>
> Instead of a "standard food review," it becomes a clinic in how to enact voice and execute non-linear thinking (it's ADHD with the properly calibrated medication). That's what CTL captures in its own lobster trap and doggedly refuses to release back into the wild. Wallace wins the attention game in spite of all the essay's complexities, pedantic asides, field notes, and footnotes. He won't catch-and-release because he's trophy hunting for your complete and total submission and engagement. And by the article's end, he's claimed his prize.

* * *

So much of what lights me up about David Foster Wallace's work is that he was a cultural critic with a big brain and lots of ways into an essay. It's what I ask my students to become: free-range cultural critics, not teens writing five-paragraph essays.

It's a brutal slog to assign "essays" all year long – ones that focus on whether or not George's mercy killing of Lennie was justified, if Holden Caulfield was a metaphor for The Buddha, or if Atticus Finch suffered from a White-savior complex.

At the very least, mix some personal essays into your course – but please stop calling them "personal essays." Wallace's CTL has personal *content* in it: he's the protagonist of the story, and the pain and sentience of the lobster is precisely what *HE HIMSELF is* "considering." But is CTL a "personal essay?" No. It's a cultural critique that the author powerfully intersects with.

When I ask students during the second week of school to "investigate their former selves in essay form" (which is what I call that particular assignment), they go back and look at their old Google Doc essays from 8th and 9th grade English class. You know what they discover? The essays they feel good about are the "personal" ones (with very few exceptions). Why – as English teachers – are we pedantic and Procrustean about having students "stick to writing about the book they've just read?" Looking back on 30 years, I can point to only a dozen or so "pure literary essays" that meant something to me – or the student. Those 12 papers are statistically unaccounted for when compared to the tens of thousands of essays that have slipped through my fingers (and mind) since 1994.

And I think I know why English teachers adhere to the five-paragraph essay formula so intently, largely assigning book-specific prompts: **it's fear.**

There are innumerable ways to assess a student's understanding of novels, plays, short stories, and poems – other than requiring they write essays about them.

So why the obligatory "book-essay?"

Why don't we assign "creative nonfiction" instead, allowing students to intersect with the primary source material – more reader responder and cultural critic than summarizer or regurgitator?

It's that we fear our colleagues will say we're not being rigorous enough. That our own students won't take the course seriously. That we don't know how to teach memoir writing or cultural critique anyway. That it opens up a Pandora's box of sensitive, vulnerable, and potentially explosive topics. That we already have clear rubrics with which to evaluate five-paragraph essays, *but not creative nonfiction*. That we will be moving away from our dearest value – assessing literature through writing – but as Stephen Mounkhall has said at our English Department meetings many times:

Why do we teach fiction but ask our students to write nonfiction?

That's a question that few can answer thoughtfully. English teachers as a group must acknowledge that approximately 3% of all college and university degrees in our subject are even issued each year – yet English teachers give more than 20% of the HW students receive. (Just think about how long it takes your typical student to read two chapters of The Scarlet Letter, take notes, and answer guiding questions; oh, yeah, and there's an ongoing essay they're simultaneously working on.) A former student of mine, Masashi Kawabata (who went on to get his business degree at the University of Rochester before returning to Japan), would often spend four or five hours *each night* on his English homework. That was due to two factors: he was a native Japanese speaker, and he was dyslexic. But I have a number of dyslexic students each year, and many of them do not "present as such" (despite their comprehensive IEPs announcing it). So – the next time you assign a "30 minute reading," know that it's far more than that for a number of your students. It has taken me many decades to become sensitive to the reality that few are doing the kind of work we require in the limited time allotted.

We often ask so much from our students but – in the end – get so very little back (in terms of measurable productivity and engaging product). And when that happens, it's our fault. They submit that Scarlet Letter essay, but how enthusiastic are *you* about reading it, marking it, putting a grade on it, and returning it? How many "remarkable Scarlet Letter essays" do you collect and return each year, delight in, and celebrate by sharing, giving public shout-outs to the student-writers, and posting exemplars to your Google Classroom feed?

If you're confused by my questions, I can only tell you that I regularly challenge my students to make work that they enthusiastically want to share. That's the default thermostat setting in my classroom. If you have set up your own classes so that students are writing for an audience of one (namely you), I'd encourage you to think differently.

And based on that 3% statistic from above, we are clearly not preparing students to major in English Literature or become English teachers…and most certainly not English Lit Professors and book reviewers.

So – as Stephen asked – Why all the fiction teaching and nonfiction writing? What's the logic there?

Many HS Math and Science classes have direct applications to the vast majority of college and university majors in STEM. Yes, *writing* is important; I'd never argue against that statement. But it's the *kind of writing* most frequently being assigned that feels disconnected from "what's next" or "aspirational" for many students.

Sports writer and Chief Editor for The Amherst Student (Amherst College's newspaper), Tobias (Toby) Rosewater, once gave me a career-defining compliment that affirmed what I was doing: "Yours is the class of the future."

Toby also wrote the foreword to this book. He is – in many ways – the second coming of David Foster Wallace, yet when he was in elementary school, there was genuine fear and concern for his future self. His parents and teachers wondered: Would Toby ever be able to write a single, coherent sentence? His dyslexia was debilitating. Windward School in White Plains, NY unblocked him. He came into my life as a sophomore in high school – open and ready.

And what Toby meant by "class of the future" was that my courses are designed to challenge students to – well – consider. I don't know how many other English teachers across the country are most interested and invested in that one simple thing – considering – but it's really all I care about.

There are so many "C" verbs that I use in class that all circle back to the same basic idea: **Consider. Contemplate. Connect dots. Cogitate. Curate. Confess. Contradict.**

The SHS senior prank a few years ago required the unleashing of hundreds of live lobsters all over the building: bathrooms (toilets and urinals), well-traveled stairwells, the auditorium, gyms, and select classrooms. It was the one year that I was a fully remote teacher, stuck in the Zoom-scape of remote Hell, but happy to be protected from the politics of desk-shields and the uncertainty of Covid infections. So I wasn't there personally to wrangle crustaceans like a low-rent, unadventurous Steve Irwin, but I did hear about the lobstrosities' havoc in real time.

And my first thought, and my first words in an email to a colleague who was on campus at the time of the coordinated attack?

"We should teach those seniors Consider the Lobster by David Foster Wallace, not as a punishment, but as a way to make them more thoughtful before they go out into the world."

And that's what cultural critics show us how to do. They don't write "screeds" per se; they don't outright lecture. No. The good ones "contemplate in real time" (as student Rishi Shadaksharappa once said about my writing, giving me a way to express the very thing I had no clear directive for but wanted so badly my students to do). Noted pop-cult critic Chuck Klosterman writes (in Perpetual Topeka) about things he hasn't yet resolved (why he hates LeBron James but wants him to win). Seminal Black author James Baldwin doesn't have the answer either at the end of Stranger in the Village when writing: "This world is white no longer, and it will never be white again. People are trapped in history and history is trapped in them." Klosterman is thinking on paper in real time – examining his motives for liking a disgraced rapper while worshiping an NBA legend but (inexplicably) wanting the former to lose and the latter to win. Baldwin is articulating a problem that he has no solution to, and one that might even be unsolvable, but still he *considers*.

Many English teachers **don't** want students to write book-essays that contain contradictions, stray from their topic sentences, resolve messily, bring up new information in the conclusion, have equal parts assertion and concession, ask too many questions without answering them, or fail to follow a logical-sequential order.

But if I were to strictly follow that advice in my own nonfiction writing, I simply wouldn't want to write at all.

And our students (largely) "don't really want to write" either. No offense. Not really. Just listen to the sounds they make the next time you announce a new essay project. I know this to be true from over 5,400 days of on-the-job experience.

Over the summer of 2024, I tried an experiment for myself: Write 30 essays in 30 days. I started a blog called "The Anti Essay Writer" and committed to creating and posting at least one finished piece per day. To be clear, these were not small "puff pieces," but bold adventures in dot-connecting. At least half the time I'd sit at my computer in July or August and have no clear sense of how or when (or whether) the piece would take shape.

I'd often start my day with nothing more than a feeling, an opening line, or the kernel of an idea. But by 10 AM I was off and running. But two essays in particular were exercises in profound discovery for me. One was about the late filmmaker Ted Post, who took Clint Eastwood from the TV show Rawhide to Hollywood heights (Hang 'Em High and Magnum Force).

What did I figure out (while researching and writing) about Ted Post that no other "critic" had ever noticed? That nearly all his films involved a pivotal scene set in a basement: The catharsis or transformation always happened at the subterranean level. After I wrote it, I made a second discovery: Post has a son, he's alive, and he's highly literate (the trifecta!). I emailed a copy to Robert Post, a former Dean of Yale Law School. He was delighted with what I'd unpacked and touched by the tribute. He thanked me for writing it.

I also found, while researching for my second essay, that humorist David Sedaris had been a student at The Art Institute of Chicago when David Mamet's profane play about timeshare salesmen (Glengarry Glen Ross) world-premiered there. I don't think – in the history of the internet – that any critic has ever connected these dots or put these two men in that same place at that same time. And why is that important? It's because my argument in that blog-post-essay was that Mamet's endless profanity and decided lack of a filter (and his generally pushing the envelope of good taste, political correctness, and decorum) had corrupted a young and impressionable Sedaris.

Now do I *know* this to be true? I do not.

But here's what I do know: If a HS English teacher or college Composition adjunct professor had insisted – as teachers have required me to do in the past – that I present my fully formed thesis to the class, tell everyone why I was arguing that, and provide some distinctions I intended to make in the paper, then (once approved) create an outline for my intro, body sections, bridge paragraphs, and conclusion...I would never have made these two discoveries that became my two favorite essays.

David Attar (SHS '21) once said: "Yours is the only class that gave me room to breathe."

Having room to breathe? That's everything. It's not serendipity that Wallace's editor trusted him to bring back something robust and compelling from the Maine Lobster Festival – it only happened because that running room was built into the process.

Each day that summer while working on my blog, I trusted myself to find dots to connect, despite not knowing – for sure – what the graph even looked like or whether coordinate planes even existed.

But we're so afraid that our students will take on essay problems that they can't solve, ones that we don't have "ready advice" for, and the cost of that fear is incalculable.

* * *

It doesn't matter if you use Consider the Lobster as a text to engage students in your classroom or not. You could use Klosterman's Perpetual Topeka, Baldwin's Stranger in the Village, The Elevator Ride by Nathan McCall (all the essays from What's Going On? are excellent), anything from Draft No. 4 by John McPhee, the longform nonfiction of Ian Parker, Tad Friend, Hua Hsu (check The New Yorker archives for the previous three writers), Joan Didion's The White Album, excerpts from Bill Bryson's A Walk in the Woods, Gay Talese's Frank Sinatra Has a Cold, or anything and everything from Truman Capote's The Dog's Bark.

No matter what: teach more nonfiction. After all, it's what you ask your students to write.

At all costs to your larger curriculum: Spend more of your class time asking students to consider, contemplate, connect-dots, cogitate, curate, confess, and contradict.

As SHS '21 alum Vivian Guo offers: "Mr. Phillipson's class brings to life the art of pure humanities, journalistic rigor, and creative exploration. My junior year with him was my most formative – a world of postmodernism, and cinema theory that shapes my college studies to this day. Mr. Phillipson is eclectic, playful, and deeply thoughtful: a teacher who not only pushes intellectual boundaries but also inspires belief in one's own potential."

And that's why I:

a Have students read, annotate, and discuss Wallace's CTL. Warning: it's not an easy article for students to get through. I've used it with 10th and 11th graders. It may go over the heads of some sophomores, but you'll be pleasantly surprised by the results.
b Have students model CTL in service of writing their own "Consider The..." essay.
c Write my own "Consider" essay each year, and share my fresh contemplations and confessions with current students.

Here's Prompt Six

Essay Six: Consider the...Lobster? Assignment Write-Up

You may know the character David Wallace from *The Office*. He's Michael Scott's boss at Dunder-Mifflin's NYC headquarters. **What you might not know** is the show's creators are huge fans of David Foster Wallace, so they named the character after him. Why does that matter?

David Foster Wallace (**called DFW for short**) once said at his Kenyon graduation speech: "The mind is a terrible master, but an excellent servant."

He DID, however, often use his mind to "consider" things in our world more deeply than most of us might ever hope to. That cuts both ways. Foster Wallace was often depressed. His life ended by his own hand. His wife had to cut him down off the balcony of their deck after his hanging. DFW is considered by many the single-greatest writer (fiction and nonfiction) of his generation (living from 1962 to 2008).

He wrote many essays, articles, profiles, a memoir, and some novels, including **Infinite Jest** (which is 1,079 pages long – and has been read – cover to cover – by VERY FEW people, despite selling well over 1 million copies; I only know three people who finished it).

One of his most famous essays is **Consider the Lobster** – for which DFW attended the Maine Lobster Festival in 2003 for **Gourmet** magazine, where he was supposed to report on the food, do some people-watching, and write a review, but he turned it into a meditation on animal rights: the ethics of boiling a creature alive for the consumer's pleasure.

In 2021, SHS seniors used live lobster (a great many of them) for their "senior prank." I remember teachers telling me they walked into the boy's bathroom and saw lobsters snapping at them from inside the urinals. From what I hear – there were lobstrosities everywhere (I was fully remote, where I was doing nothing remotely interesting on Zoom, so I wasn't on campus). Clearly, these seniors hadn't read David Foster Wallace. They hadn't considered the lobsters, let alone the custodians, the hungry and homeless, the underfed, the sensibilities of others, the faculty, their fellow students, or the "net" effect of their misdeeds. I didn't know how to work the word **trap or pot** in here, so I'll use an unrelated fishing term to try and get lexically close.

David Foster Wallace was sent to the Maine Lobster Festival in 2003 by the biggest food magazine in the world (Gourmet) to get some recipes, capture a few anecdotes, and write about the main protein attraction.

But he didn't, really. He did so much more than that. He wrote a philosophical, sociological, and ethical exposé. He – in many ways – shocked and angered the readers of the magazine he was writing for.[1]

And so – he didn't "review" the festival – instead, **he reviewed us: the human race:** Why hedonism is more important than humanity. Why we don't care that animals feel pain when we prepare them for our consumption – and if anything, why we enjoy it; that pain becomes part of the "street calculus" that factors into our pleasure. Maybe. Maybe not. But: WOW. {By the way – I happily eat all kinds of animals}.

So, what's your Essay Six about then?

You will have two class periods **to start and finish** an in-class essay, your "Essay Six: Consider the…" (**finish that thought**).

Between now and then, please do the following things to prepare for this "entirely written in-class essay."

1 Read and annotate Consider the Lobster by David Foster Wallace. What is annotation? Print out the PDF of Consider the Lobster. Read it carefully (a few times), and – with a pen in hand – do your best to dissect what DFW does to make you think and feel. How does he use form choices? How does he put words together? What kinds of sentences does he favor or utilize for maximum impact? What are specific moments he does something interesting (to you) as a writer, and how does he do those things in those moments? How does he use data, facts, or history? What purpose does his title serve, and does he come back to it throughout the essay in direct and indirect ways? How does he begin his essay? End it? What parts cut through you OR just pass over your head? **WE WILL DISCUSS DFW'S ESSAY AND YOUR OBSERVATIONS IN CLASS.**

2 Do something in this world outside of your house. Go to Costco. Go to McDonald's (inside, not the drive-thru). Attend a piano recital. Take a Bikram Yoga class. Go to a hotel if you're traveling for school or family reasons. Journey to another state (Yes – New Jersey and Connecticut do count). Get your teeth cleaned. Find a Friendly's Ice Cream restaurant that's open somewhere and eat there. Go to The Westchester Mall, The

American Dream Mall, or Ridge Hill in Yonkers. Shop at Whole Foods, Trader Joe's, or Wegmans.

3 Take notes during your "doing something in this world outside of your house." Take pictures when you're "out there doing." Take notes on your phone. Take a notepad. Write down observations. Jot down impressions. Take notes when you get home. Start writing down some conclusions. Some considerations.

4 Figure out what you are CONSIDERING beyond "the trip, event or activity" itself. Shopping is an "activity," as is taking a tennis lesson or getting a root canal. But there's "the activity," and then there's "what the activity might allow us to consider."

If David Foster Wallace went to look at lobsters as a reporter but ended up changing the way people thought about eating lobsters (forever), then what will *you* do? Brittany Stinson wrote a college essay about her trip to Costco. She "got into" all five ivy-league schools and Stanford with that essay (which just isn't true; a college essay does NOT get you into college). What does Brittany's essay leave you thinking and feeling? Does it feel like a 17-year old's voice or sensibilities? Is it intellectually honest? Does anyone, from the age of 6, have philosophical conversations with herself, or political conversations with her dad while shopping at Costco?

But **your goal** is to create "one consideration" about your activity, trip, event, or place you went to (**if only for 30 minutes with your parents or a Scarsdale deli with your friends for lunch**).

When Katerina Rvacheva (Kat) went to the theme-park-level supermarket Stew Leonard's last year, she returned home and wrote for two hours straight about her trip. She sent me the essay that night – which had embedded photos and phone-screenshots of messages to her mom. It was a wonderful piece because Kat had "considered," and got us to "consider" why Stew Leonard's is both terrifying, electric, and a place that makes her feel whole.

Today 9:54 AM

Kotya can you please drive with me to stew Leonard's some time after school? We have no food, and with Kay staying with us we need extra

Ok can Kay come

Sure

Ok

So your #4 is: What are YOU going to consider about the place you went, the thing you did, or the activity you took part in?

For Brittany Stinson, it was: Costco made me consider that anywhere can be a classroom, a laboratory, and a literary salon. For Katerina it was: Stew Leonard's made me consider that the places we love are often profoundly weird and alienating, but we wouldn't have them any other way.

For David Foster Wallace it was: Lobster Festivals are reminders that while we come together as humans to celebrate ourselves as social, gustatory, and hedonistic animals, we're not very kind to actual animals. What will you consider? What will you have us consider about some ordinary, everyday, all-at-once, thing?

5 Once you've figured out what you're going to "consider," start by writing some bullet points to yourself to consider. Create a kind of "thought outline" *for yourself*. I'm not going to collect this outline. I'm not going to grade this outline. It's just for YOU. Want to come and see me about your idea before the in-class essay? Please do. Want to email me something to look at before the in-class essay? Be my guest. *I'm here.*

6 Write the in-class essay, start-to-finish, in 100 minutes over two class periods. You will use Google Docs, and I'll need to see the entire editing history when you submit it to me.

Sean Hotchkiss, an acquaintance of mine who's a professional journalist (who has written for some of the biggest magazines in the world), has the same approach to pre-writing that I take: WORK OUT THE ESSAY, PRETTY MUCH IN ITS ENTIRETY, IN YOUR HEAD FIRST, and on paper SECOND. I often speak my essays aloud, edit them in my head, and then sit down to write them. And sometimes I don't. But I find this approach to be useful when I do use it, so you might try it too. For this in-class essay (per usual), you'll need: title, subtitle, image, caption, byline, and slogan/motto. 750 words (+/− 15).

Note

1 You don't become a legend by writing a restaurant review that does nothing more than review the restaurant.

4
WHEN THE HITMAKERS KNOCK, YOU ANSWER

There has been one constant in my teaching since I got into a classroom in 1994: having students write about music.

But I'd never asked them to **write songs** until academic year 2023–24.

Back in 2020, #1 songwriter, producer, and recording artist Mario Winans (I Don't Wanna Know was a #1 hit in multiple countries) Zoomed with my classes about how he uses the concept of Signifying in his sound-design, sampling, and lyricism.

I was convinced that his production of "Spend Some Cheese" (for the rapper Shyne) had been a tribute to NWA's 100 Miles and Runnin, so he spent an hour with my juniors talking about – among other things – sampling (taking part of another artist's song) – and how he'd appropriated Sting's haunting Shape of My Heart for his brutal break-up track – Emotional – for R&B singer Carl Thomas' debut solo album.

When Dan Piepenbring was the last journalist to work with Prince before his death – co-authoring his comprehensive memoir The Beautiful Ones – I wanted him to speak with my students about: (A) how to write a longform profile, and (B) what listeners can take away from Prince's body of work. And Dan obliged.

Richard Rudolph has Zoomed with my classes for years, oftentimes for back-to-back sessions, talking about his work with rapper J. Cole, the creation of his timeless neo-soul music with late wife Minnie Riperton, and how he sustains himself creatively into his late 70s (working with the up-and-coming artist Maejor, who wrote many of Justin Bieber's hit songs).

Recently, my classes worked with rock historian Greg Renoff, who wrote the definitive text on the hard-rock band Van Halen and a comprehensive

DOI: 10.4324/9781003600565-4

memoir with producer Ted Templeman. Renoff – a former history professor and exhaustive researcher – had dedicated his life to committing to public record the moments when significant popular music was born and nurtured, and the producers and engineers who made everything from Eddie Van Halen's Eruption to the Doobie Brothers' Takin' it to the Streets possible.

And I've been obsessed with song lyrics since childhood, listening to Billy Joel's Glass House album on 8-track-cartridge-repeat-Heaven until the tape rubbed against itself and burned out. Everything Joel wrote seemed to be an argument or directive about the state of the world today:

You may be right; I may be crazy.
Everybody's talkin' bout the new sound funny, but it's still rock and roll to me.
Don't ask for favors; Don't talk to strangers; Don't ask me why.

So when I learned that legendary songwriter Sam Hollander had moved-in right down the street from me in Mt. Kisco, NY, I saw it as a sign. As an English teacher, I already taught poetry, so why not pop music too? I have my sophomores write a "poetry forgery" (see Chapter 13) each year, studying various poetic forms in the process – so why not extrapolate that to a medium they're already facile with? And one they're actually enthusiastic about? One they want to share with each other?

In 2019, Hollander sold his 499-song catalog to Hipgnosis – a company that buys up music artists' oeuvres faster than Alexander Hamilton wrote (he was – after all – running out of time).

Hollander penned hit songs for Katy Perry, One Direction, Carole King, Panic! at the Disco, Wheezer, Gym Class Heroes, Train, Daughtry, Def Leppard, Kelly Rowland, Tom Morello, Walk the Moon, The O'Jays, Tom Jones, and even Joe Cocker.

Once in my SHS classroom, I asked Sam if he were ever mistaken for the actor Nicholas Cage – his voice has the same nasally quality, and his delivery is (with eyes closed) *vintage Cage*: Andy Samberg could even take notes for an encore SNL performance on Weekend Update.

He regaled me with tales of Johnny Depp leading an impromptu game of handball at Sam's son's preschool (when he lived in Beverly Hills), and of his time with One Direction (they're all lovely guys – and he's still in frequent touch with Louis, by the way).

Far beyond these superficial trappings of fame, fortune and industry relationships, Sam Hollander is just a mensch. He came to my junior honors English class to make 20 students feel seen and heard, to validate the songs they'd written and performed, and to give them a sense of where creativity's wellspring exists – how to tap into it – and that one need not "be special or gifted" to write a song that the whole world might someday sing.

Hollander lacks perfect pitch. He can't even really sing, per se. But he's a hitmaker. He's a "vibe" in human form, who can write one-syllable words for Katy Perry, fully aware that she'll stretch them into three, four, even five iambs.

He is the music industry's equivalent of Quentin Tarrantino – taking "old acts" (Cocker, King, and Jones), and making them fresh and relevant again.

Moreover, the guy has written and produced more number one hit songs than The Beatles, The Rolling Stones and Billy Joel (ten in total).

And Sam breathed new life into my teaching too, as he – along with Richard Rudolph – showed me that one can be creative and relevant in their 50s and 70s (respectively).

A little context if you care to listen –

Picture 20 high-achieving, risk-averse Scarsdale HS students in a top-level English class. Each one of them would view anything less than an ivy-league acceptance-letter as abject failure. Each has been raised on a steady diet of five paragraph essays and thesis outlines. Each student knows that taking intellectual risks does not (usually) pay off or pan out. They've been trained to give the teacher what he or she wants – to please them at all costs – because the price of not doing so means earning a B, B+, or A–.

Of these 20 kids, 2 ran for class president, many others for lesser school government positions, 1 started a blog (called Hypothetically Speaking), 1 is a Latin scholar and Sci-Fi nerd, 1 is the niece to the president of a major Middle Eastern country, 1 is a gifted social commentator who is also terrified of not getting into Cornell or Columbia, 1 is a Ukrainian-Jew who writes like an angel, 1 is a stand-up comedian inspired by Seth MacFarlane, 1 always goes her own way and possesses a highly-articulated rejection system and strong internal frame of reference, and 1 is...I think you get the picture.

This is an actual snapshot of one of my recent English class sections. But my room is *often filled* with people possessed of outsized ambition and brains to match (or brains that will soon catch up to said ambition). The greatest barrier to unleashing their creativity and having them write from a place of abundance and meaningful self-exploration, rather than the fear of being penalized (or exposed), is – well – having them trust the process.

But What Exactly Is My Process?

So much of it is rooted in the workshop model. I taught "Writer's Workshop" in a West Nyack, NY school for three years (before coming to Scarsdale). It was a senior elective that was just "all kinds of creative writing thrown at the wall to see what would stick." It's where I worked out some of what I use today, but it was really my time at Chappaqua's Greeley High School during three consecutive summers (teaching the enrichment program) that helped me figure myself out as a Composition teacher.

Those Greeley summer class sections (I had three a day) were small and intimate. My last one was 23 years ago, but I still remember one student (Scott) who had been in and out of rehab for most of high school. We were working on college essays one July afternoon in a conference room right off the library – 15 of us sitting around an oblong table – 15 different niche narratives expressing something metacognitive and vulnerable about eating disorders, drug abuse, death, and other musings. A clear memory is when Scott and Esther (who'd written about diet pills being her undoing) looked around the room and said, almost like they'd rehearsed it, "We've never felt this comfortable writing this stuff, or sharing this stuff with anyone – let alone a teacher and a bunch of classmates – until now. This is kind of special."

In all ways, I suppose, I've been trying to perpetually and perennially recreate that Horace Greeley HS moment ever since. And bringing in Sam Hollander and Richard Rudolph is in service of: (A) Making students feel like there are worthy challenges and legitimate stakes to what they do in my class, and (B) exposing students to not just "professionals" – but some of the most successful creatives in their respective fields.

My first attempt at getting someone "legit" to work with my students was Rupert Holmes (a long-time Scarsdale resident); the man who wrote The Pina Colada (Escape) Song, had some minor radio hits (namely "Him"), and wrote successful Broadway shows. Despite Holmes being initially receptive to my request, and living just ten blocks from the HS, his help never materialized. (By the way, his email address at the time was something like ETPhoneHolmes@. It's refreshing to meet a hitmaker who doesn't take himself too seriously.)

My thinking behind everything I do in the classroom is: you should be writing for "the marketplace," not for Room 207. And most importantly: not for me, your teacher.

And since I'd never written a successful pop song, it made little sense for me to dispense advice on the subject. Richard Rudolph (Dick, or Double R as he's known to his friends) was eager to impart some wisdom, and he had the bona fides to make an impact: #1 hit song (Lovin' You), co-produced an album with Stevie Wonder (Perfect Angel), was president of his own label with actor Michael Douglas (Third Stone Records imprint under Atlantic), had his music sampled by J. Cole, TuPac Shakur, Nas, and countless others, and – most impressively – has written and produced music every single year since 1969. Most recently, he released a song called "Feels" performed by Nissy and Saweetie. The music video has garnered tens of millions of YouTube views.

Richard is also Maya Rudolph's father (named for Maya Angelou), a Saturday Night Live alum, and star of Apple TV's adult comedy Loot. Most saliently, she was a member of The Rentals, a rock band with Weezer's Matt Sharp.

Richard was married to one of the most prominent Black soul singers of the 1970s (Minnie Riperton) and – currently – to one of Japan's most influential female jazz singers (Kimiko Kasai).

So with two hitmakers on standby, ready to offer their steady, guiding hand to my junior class, we set out to write some pop music.

And that included me.

I hadn't "written a song" since my college days. The last one I'd tried my hand at was a hair-band "formula song" called Vixen that would give second-hand embarrassment to (even) the surviving members of Great White.

After shrugging off that former, failed version of myself, I sat on my living room couch on a Saturday over Christmas break and wrote a song about "Old Hollywood" called The Battle for Dresden. It was a homage to the days when the Rat Pack-era celebrities would often enter restaurants through the kitchen's back door. I conjured up the image of a young Clint Eastwood in Carmel-by-the-Sea, fresh off the set of Rawhide, slipping past the line cooks with a kind of silent swag. For inspiration, I looked at vintage photos of long-ago shuttered Beverly Hills and Los Angeles eateries and supper-clubs once haunted by Hollywood royalty.

"The Battle for Dresden" – by Wes Phillipson

Old Hollywood only used the back door
Young Eastwood pushing past back of house
Nicholson a joker, Polanski a louse
Line cooks gave side-eye — hard squint —
To the man with no name, Saint Clint.

Dan Tana's not for the Eric Banas
Dan Tana's not for the Eric Banas

New Hollywood prefers the *trap* door
Young Spelling in the pumpkin patch with the paparazzi
Old Spelling spinning like a Sands' Lucky-7-cum-Masertati
Britney's bodyguards dropped a dime on the once-perfect ten
Jolie-sold-out-Pitt-to-jettison-Anniston-off-Kenya's Seine

Dan Tana's not for the Eric Banas
Dear John's was made for the James Caans

Tam O'Shanter so damn Wiliam Shatner

Sinatra left his drawers on the hotel suites' floors
For the interchangeable whores who exhaled j'adores

Dan Tana's not for the Eric Bana's
Bob Taylor's entombed with the Elizabeth Taylors

Bob Taylor's entombed with the Elizbeth Taylors

There's no seat at these oak-stained tables for the MCU
To be stark, these hacktors in costume are just so see-thru
They can't check-out because they never checked-in
Henley's homily a reprise for these table-cloths worn-thin

Dan Tana's not for the Eric Banas
Mark Ruffalo's best suited for the Wild Buffalos
Mark Ruffalo's best suited for the Wild Buffalos

* * *

While I didn't sing this song for my juniors, I did perform it with some degree of rhythm and precision. They gave me a sincerely lively round of applause. I was surprised how quickly the lyrics had come to me on that lazy Saturday.

Next, I asked students to form groups of up to four and choose an existing instrumental backing track to "set" their lyrics to. The tracks needed to be from songs they weren't familiar with, as not to influence their thinking on an unconscious level. I chose hits by Groove Theory, Eric Clapton, Minnie Riperton (and others) that they were likely unfamiliar with.

The write-up for the assignment was as follows:

Songwriting Challenge: Note – much of the wisdom articulated in the "steps" below comes from a conversation I had with Richard Rudolph. For the benefit of this class, Richard "codified" his songwriting process. I did my best to faithfully capture and represent it here.

Step One: Form a group of up to four students. You are welcome to work as a *true* solo artist on this one, but collaborators can do more than just lighten the load.

Step Two: Listen to and select from these eight instrumental backing tracks, and go with the one that speaks to you most primally, that gets you to feel something you weren't feeling before you began listening, that moves your blood or stomach acid (in a good way). It should be music that "makes you see words, colors, shapes, and other worlds" –

1 Cocaine by Eric Clapton
2 Tell Me by Groove Theory
3 Les Fleurs by Minnie Riperton
4 Every Time He Comes Around by Minnie Riperton
5 Say Yes by Floetry
6 Just Breathe by Telepopmusik
7 Cause We've Ended as Lovers by Jeff Beck
8 Rambling Man by The Allman Brothers Band

Step Three: Go into your jungle. Once you have your backing track, play that song on repeat while you "go into your own jungle, forest or exotic landscape" and "visualize the song." What is the music saying to you? There's a jungle cat in that tree over there: what words does it whisper in your ear? There's a friendly, foot long baby Burmese that's singing to you: what words escape its pursed lips? What words "appear" or "materialize" from the music? In the music? Maybe there's a story in that jungle, an Odyssey, or a hero's journey? Maybe a story of pain? A celebration of humanity? A commentary on the state of the world? Maybe it's the story of you? Or the narrative of a single flower?

In your jungle, you're "trying to make the invisible, visible." You have your music provided for you, but the lyrics to your song have been written in invisible ink. Find the chemicals that will uncover those words that the whole world will someday sing.

Step Four (a): Write the story that you dragged back to base camp from deep inside your jungle. If you're Aristotle, a story must have a beginning, middle, and end: and it must follow that sequence. If you're Christopher Nolan, not so much: you can distort time, flashback, flashforward, even invert the beginning and the ending (your story could literally go in reverse chronology).

Your music's story will reveal itself to you. Tell that story. Choose a narrator. Make the narrator disembodied (spectral), first person, 3rd person, or even a flower. A fly on the wall. Maybe even let the narrator be you. Regardless: Have a story to tell.

Step Four (b): Make an argument inside of your story: My experience studying pop music since 1978 (this is Phillipson, not Richard Rudolph speaking) is that the most commercially-successful songs have a "compelling argument" at their centers. Why does "Call Me Maybe" resonate? It's because it's the story of a woman's search for true love in a world of shallow flirtation, but it's also an argument that Carly Rae Jepsen is making to herself that she's deserving of something real and lasting, and that she can be comfortable being the pursuer vs. the pursued.

Step Five: Use your English class "superpower" to write this song: We've done a great deal of skill-building and writing this year. We've looked at how to use chiasmus, tautology, pun, strategic ambiguity, figurative language, taboo language, imagery, pacing, titles, subtitles, captions, mottos/credos, big fat claims, concision (ABC = always be cutting), distinctions, docent (tour guide), white space, wordsmithing (Google-Zero), framing, the Six Human Needs, voice, vulnerability, juxtaposition (purposeful contradictions), violation of expectation, layering, points of connection, adding something new to the conversation, Chekhov's Guns, whispers, questions, and much more. What qualities do you want to "bake into" your song lyrics? What are you already good at? Great at? Use that. Find each group member's true superpower and unleash them on the lyric-writing process.

Step Six: As a group – write your finished Lyric Draft One (the story and argument your backing music is telling you to write), as only your group could write it. Write what you know? Sure. Write what the music is leading you to write? Even better. Don't think your way through this; Feel your way through it. Don't do "Step Five" until you've "felt your way through" Steps 1–4.

Three pieces of advice that may (or may not) serve you:

1. Sit your butt in the chair (or on the floor, or on the edge of your couch) and just write. You can't "theoretically write" or "hypothetically write" or "write later." You need to write right now. Get it done and then make it look pretty. Don't let perfect be *acceptable's enemy*.
2. Use serendipity and keep your ear to the ground: This assignment is about "words" and "writing." When someone in your group says something – randomly – that "just fits the mood of the song, the song's story, or the song's argument" – use it. When I assign students to make documentary films, the best content comes when they think the camera is off.
3. Don't make the song "more than it is." We've already spoken about this phenomenon. Don't make an essay more than it is. As Steve Madden said about his own memoir: "The truth is always more interesting." Don't force it. Don't be a try-hard. If you have a simple story to tell, then tell it simply. If you want to write a song entirely made up of questions because it's a song about questioning faith or love – then do that. If you want to teach us about human nature but you haven't "lived much" – don't do that (or – at the very least – go out and "live first" and write that experience later).

BONUS ADVICE: WORK WITH ANYONE AND EVERYONE: Richard Rudolph once said to me, "I may have more literary references than the people I write songs with," but, at 77, he doesn't ever think about his age, and he never thinks in terms of how age might limit creative productivity. He refuses to be intimidated: when he was an unknown, Richard wrote songs with Stevie Wonder (in the 1970s), and in his (literal) 70s, he's writing songs with Bieber's main collaborator named Maejor, he writes three-way songs on phone calls with people in different countries, he writes with a teen girl in New Jersey who's an up-and-comer, a young Korean artist, a 30-something in Flint, Michigan, and so on. His philosophy is – more or less – "I'll write with you." He doesn't ever think: I don't write Punk. I don't write Country. If you're from Brazil and you want to make a Brazilian song – let's do it. If you want to make a pop-punk song – let's try that. If you want to make a Christmas song – and Richard is Jewish – sure. He'll write with anyone who's interesting and interested. Who has something to say. Who's "up to write something." He collaborates with anyone, anywhere, anytime, often with multiple people at once. Sometimes he's writing five songs a week, and he's been working this way since 1969. And everyone from J. Cole to The Jackson Five to Nissy and Saweetie has worked with Richard in one form or another. He's worked with Rod Temperton – the main songwriter for Michael's Jackson's Thriller. He's worked with Quincy Jones – Thriller's producer. But none of that has gone to his head, nor gotten in his way. When he sits down to write – he's just passionately invested in the *pursuit of the song*.

Here's Prompt Four

The Lyric Essay Assignment Write-Up

In 1974 Billy Joel had been touring clubs and theaters, opening for The Beach Boys, leaving him little time to write new songs, but he was under pressure to put out a new album after Piano Man. So he wrote an entire album's worth of material in a weekend or two between gigs, despite the fact that "he had nothing to say lyrically." Again: he had nothing to say, but he said it anyway.
Keep this in mind: Billy Joel has 3 number 1 hits. Sam Hollander has 10.
The greatest songwriting team in rock history (Mick Jagger and Keith Richards of The Rolling Stones) had to be locked in a kitchen for two nights by their manager, Andrew Oldham, who Confirmed: "Don't come out until you have a song." Richards didn't think he could do it, but they came out with "The Last Time." That song reached #1 and #2 on all of the U.K. singles charts. Richards said, "Once you've written the first one, it's easy. At least you know you can do it." Jagger would write his "lyrics in a book" or make them up as he went along. Mick would write with a drummer in

the room. He'd later use computers. "The more ways the better," he would say about his own process. Allegedly, from the Tall Tales of Wes Phillipson's memory, Keith and Mick were at a party in 1964 with John and Paul (meeting The Beatles for the first time). John and Paul had writer's block. Mick and Keith (called The Glimmer Twins) went off to a corner of the room and wrote Satisfaction in a few minutes. In that moment, they'd taught the greatest songwriting team in pop-music history (Lennon-McCartney), *how to write a song*, saying, "It's just songwriting, it's not brain surgery."

For Perspective: The Rolling Stones Have 8 Number 1 Hits. Sam Hollander Has 10

We have nine classes from the day we get back from break until Sam Hollander comes in person to work with us. What to do between now and Sam's arrival?

ONE: Explore Sam's music. His catalog. Some of my personal favorites are fast becoming:

Say Amen (Saturday Night) - Panic! At The Disco
Cupid's Chokehold - Gym Class Heroes
Waiting for Superman - Daughtry
Miracle Pill - Goo Goo Dolls
If You Can Afford Me - Katy Perry
Love Makes the World - Carole King

Now – to be clear – these are not my favorite songs. These are 6 songs from Sam that I just encountered for the first time (except for 2 of them).

But – if Sam understands three things – better than anyone in music – I think it's:

a What is commercially viable
b What moves people emotionally
c What it means to be collaborative

TWO: Explore one songwriter who truly speaks to your heart and to your head.

For me, it's one man: Richard Rudolph. Dbl-R (as he likes to be called) is Maya Rudolph's father. He is the widower of Minnie Riperton. He wrote and produced a #1 song called Lovin You that has constantly been on the radio since 1975.

Richard will (also) be doing a songwriting class with us in Jan or Feb. He has written with Stevie Wonder (yes, that Stevie Wonder). He was written and produced for Whitney Houston, TuPac, Maejor, New Edition, and his music has been sampled by Kanye West, Dr. Dre, J. Cole, Q-Tip, Old Dirty Bastard, and used in films by Jordan Peele (Richard's song was end credit scene in Us), and Quentin Tarrantino.

Richard – today – is 78 years old, but he is making musical movies for Netflix, creating a series of graphic novels with The Beach Boys, Metallica and Slash, and – among other things – producing music with Beiber's songwriter Maejor, creating original television for Hulu, and is NOT slowing down (thanks – in part – to his intermittent fasting).

If I could write lyrics with the clarity and beauty of anyone in history, it would not be Lennon, Mccartney, Richards, or Jagger. It would not be Joel, nor Cole (Porter). It would be Rudolph.

5
THE UNICORN COLLEGE ESSAY

Can you be trusted?
Are you special?

After thousands of hours logged advising students on their personal statements for the Common Application, I have boiled down everything to those two questions.

You're welcome. No, really, *you – are – welcome*. Because it has taken me forever to come to that conclusion (we're talking 30 years), to strip away the (oftentimes) superfluous advice of college essay doctors, and my belief that *"the* college essay" was this sacred thing that only some of us had cracked the code on.

I used to teach all kinds of acronyms to get students to remember the innumerable, intangible qualities they'd need to communicate (implicitly) in their allotted 650 words. I used to give my seniors 30-page packets in September that articulated my intricate philosophy about "the most important essay they'd ever write in their lives."

Now I tell students: **Never make the college essay more than it is.**

The irony, right? *That's all I ever did come fall* – try to convince my students that their personal statements factored heavily into the admissions process. That the college essay was a matter of life and death.

It's not. Yes it matters – somewhat. But how much it matters depends on the size of the school, your GPA (Grade Point Average) and course levels, and your USP (unique selling proposition) – point of difference – as a candidate.

I once told students that this really brief piece of writing is a lie-detector test, personality test, writing test, and psychological profile. To admissions officers (or the graduate students who earn pocket money reading them), your students' college essay is either a "loving response or a cry for help."

Again, what I tell my springtime juniors and fall seniors is:

> Your Common App personal statement must communicate to your *potential school* that you are special, you can be trusted, and you are not someone who makes things *more than they are*.

Exactly what do I mean by this?

Special

More often than not, the same admissions officer at Cornell, UVA, Duke, or Syracuse reads all the personal statements and supplemental essays for a particular region or state. My knowledge of this practice is anecdotal but has been confirmed by a few sources. For example, I worked with Mitchell Thompson for 22 years (he was in admissions at The Cooper Union), and Aaron Mooney (who was in the same role at Miami University in Ohio). The head of Yale admissions gave a lecture to same physical space (SHS) teachers back in 2007 about the art of writing recommendations. Because I teach at a school that is a high-pressure, college-admissions driven environment, I tend to engage Deans, Counselors, and Officers in these kinds of conversations when I can.

So, to the extent that I'm correct about my "one reader" theory, let's apply some common sense to this small sample size – or microcosm of the country:

> There are roughly 375 graduating seniors leaving Scarsdale HS each year. Cornell is a popular choice for many of my students, and has an overall acceptance rate of 8% – but those odds improve if you're a Scarsdalian. I often call Cornell "Scarsdale the sequel" for that very reason. Since 2003 even my English Department has contained at least a half-dozen colleagues who attended Scarsdale HS then Cornell University, after which they returned to teach here.

If we take Cornell as the standard-bearer of ivy-league aspirations at SHS, it's the same woman in admissions there, reading all of the lower-Westchester-County applications and essays.

Top colleges have made it clear to Deans at SHS (the academic counselors) that they "don't want well-rounded candidates." That message started getting broadcast (or whispered?) about ten years ago. That means your students' personal statements have to – essentially – communicate that they're unicorns. Which is another way of saying "I'm special" without directly saying it.

It reminds me a great deal of the opening scene from the film 21 – about MIT students who take down casinos with their covert card-counting before getting banned. It's based on a true story.

Here's the conversation between the film's protagonist Ben Campbell, and a Dean for Harvard Medical School. It's the movie's frame story. Ben has been admitted to Harvard Med but he needs the financial assistance of the coveted "Robinson Scholarship" to stay. I'm paraphrasing here from the Steinfeld and Loeb screenplay:

"We have seventy-six applicants this year, only one of whom will get the scholarship and most of whom have résumés just as impressive as yours. But The Robinson Scholarship is going to go to someone who dazzles. Somebody who just jumps off the page. Ben, last year the Robinson went to Hyum Jae Wook, a Korean immigrant with only one leg. Have you considered cutting one of yours off? That was a joke. Ben, it's all about the essay. You really need to explain to us what makes you special. What life experience separates you from all the rest. Life experience. What can you tell me, Ben, that's going to dazzle me?"

The movie 21 was released in 2008, and while I only saw it once on a small screen, it was something that consciously influenced my teaching of the personal statement.

But I was all wrong about the notion of what "special" truly meant. I was using an idealized, Hollywood extrapolation of the concept.

It turns out that *special* just means differentiated, vulnerable, human, fallible, thoughtful, reflective, or sincere.

It also requires that your students be the sole author of their personal statement. A colleague of mine said to me recently (he's about my age) that "During conferences, students come right out and tell me now that they used ChatGPT to help them write their college essay. It's pretty shocking how up-front they are about it."

My response was: "A tutor? ChatGPT? It's all the same. Students have been admitting to me that a parent, tutor, sibling or college essay advisor pretty much wrote the entirety of their college essay since I got here in 2003."

In other words: ChatGPT changed very little about student cheating at Scarsdale HS. Tutors in our community charge upward of $250 an hour for English support and test prep. Advantage Testing (in Rye, NY) charges (at its uppermost level) $2,500 an hour – and no – that's not a typo. If a student wants to work with Arun Alagappan (Advantage's founder and CEO) then their parents must shell-out a "Mercedes Benz car note" (to quote 2 Chainz) to do so.

It's just – I suppose – that ChatGPT is more egalitarian than Advantage Testing: it's a paltry $10 a month for the basic add-on. Anyone in the 10,583 could swing that.

And you can't communicate your "specialness" to a college if you are using generic language and cliches to create *the snapshot of you*. A college essay is the ultimate selfie: do you want yours to be vintage VSCO-girl (ask your daughter), artistic headshot, or something with gravitas – a Richard Avedon portrait, perhaps?

Demonstrating that you're special means you've seized upon a story that only you could possibly tell. You've told it with great specificity (again – separating yourself from 85% of college essays that are the sentence-level equivalent of black stretch pants and beige UGGS). Most college essays are literally interchangeable.

What that really means is you could just change the implied subject of most essays from "Costa Rica service trip" to "Habitat for Humanity build" (or swap out "when I joined the chess club" for "robotics club"), and it would work just fine. *But it shouldn't.*

Most college essays I've read are written (or greatly influenced) by private tutors. When I meet with my seniors to review their personal statements, my singular focus is on stripping away the ubiquitous, fragrant voice of a 50-year-old White lady who attended Columbia – or some variation of that highly-educated hired-gun. Why? Well – one – I can't abide by plagiarism, and two – I know what colleges are looking for. One can't possibly be special if one is co-opting a homogenized, stylized voice that can be readily purchased on the open market.

Special does not have to mean, "I helped prosecute war criminals at The Hague as a rising HS senior" (which is what former student Emily Yankowitz actually did; she's now a TA in the Department of History at Yale).

And yes, Yankowitz is not just special – she's extraordinary. Her college application CV was four pages long, single-spaced, size 10 font. She was my student during all four of her years at SHS (if not in my class, then working with me on independent studies) and was the first historian to connect a court-case between Alexander Hamilton and Aaron Burr in Westchester County. Emily attended both Yale and Cambridge and made her accomplishments seem effortless.

Special can be as simple and straightforward as, "My mother once told me that we are not white. We are Ashkenazi Jew. I poked fun at her for that, yet now I see the wisdom behind such a statement" (as junior Isaac Tiomkin wrote for his college essay).

The truth is always more compelling than a contrived fantasy.

Trust

Can you be trusted to not go on academic probation, to be your most authentic self, to be a process and not a project, to assimilate into campus life but maintain a sense-of-self, to not go on mental-health leave, to respect your peers as much as your professors, to conduct your affairs with integrity, to be an upstander and not a bystander, to self-advocate, to have the capacity for self-reflection, to keep your ego in check, to love, to self-love, to view yourself as a work-in-progress, to walk the talk of self-improvement, and to see yourself as you really are?

In other words, a college essay must implicitly communicate that you are solid and dependable: that your essay offers a resounding YES to at least one of the above questions.

And that matters because colleges and universities are becoming increasingly stuck with students who are loose-cannons, activists, emotionally fragile (or downright unresilient), mentally unstable, clinically depressed, perpetually anxious, entitled, and woke (the opposite of sincerely socially conscious).

"Campuses are facing what many experts call a mental health crisis. For example, 70% of students said they have struggled with mental health since starting college, according to a recent U.S. News/Generation Lab report, which surveyed 3,649 college students in March 2024."

Secondary institutions have become full-blown businesses, fund-raising machines, and land-annexers (NYU and Columbia own "14 million square feet across 100 properties apiece" – as Elo and Farence reported for The Read Deal in 2022).

Places of higher education care mainly about two things: (A) The students they admit can pay their tuition bills on time, and (B) That those students graduate and donate generously.

The college essay must implicitly whisper: I am not a risk; I wave no red flags; I am healthy; I am already a successful member of one community, so I can easily recreate those human connections elsewhere; I can assimilate into your campus culture; I regret some of the things I've done in life, and if I could do them over again I most certainly would; I'm self-critical, but not self-effacing; and – among other things – I know enough to know there are things that I still don't know, but I'm eager to learn them at your institution.

Never Make It More than It Is

I worked out this concept with one of my favorite two-year-in-a-row students named Daniel Gray. It came from an idea that I had: *Never make an essay more than it is.* Say, for instance, you're asking your students to write about an episode of Seinfeld that you watched in class. You paired "The Voice" (S09E02) – about George being ousted from his desk job at Play Now, Jerry's girlfriend being ostracized because of her stomach noises, and Kramer's ambitious NYU intern all colliding with a giant ball of oil by episode's end – with Albert Camus' The Stranger.

The problem with essays (generally) is also the problem with college essays (specifically).

In the past, my students would have tried to make the Seinfeld-Stranger essay a deep meditation on existentialism vs. hedonism and served up some "grand" closing statement that was both entirely generic and simultaneously absolute. They'd try to make a show and a book "about nothing" into something far, far greater than it actually was.

Seinfeld is famously a show about the "nothingness" of our everyday existences. It's a show about the minutiae of life, simple human observation, and one that picks apart social dynamics. It's a show about reprobates and misanthropes who are closer to our actual selves than we'd like to admit.

The Stranger is about the cost of seeking pleasure and comfort at the expense of everything else.

To make either work "into something more than that" is to commit the crime that most students transgress when completing a college essay draft.

That "Costa Rica service trip" was "the moment my life changed forever." No it wasn't. It really wasn't. It was – perhaps – an experience that opened you up to new possibilities. Sure, I'd buy *that*. Maybe it helped you understand that you don't like flying in airplanes, or eating Gallo pinto, or being stared down by giant tarantulas who've climbed up your mosquito net to disturb your slumber.

And when I'd meet with Daniel Gray to grade his essays during sophomore and junior years (and there were about 20 essays we pored over together), he'd often call back to that lesson. "I really tried to work quietly within the world of the essay," Daniel would say with a wink. "It doesn't make sense to make it something it's not, right?"

In the Tony Robbins documentary I Am Not Your Guru, director Joe Berlinger captures the six-foot-seven giant, whisper-barking at an even taller Swede who is on the edge of a nervous breakdown at Robbins' Date With Destiny seminar. The Swede is skeptical about Robbins' intent. He's guarded about letting the motivational speaker inside his head and violates his personal space. Robbins uses his words like a padded battering-ram:

> "I know f-ing people," he coos, alluding to his nearly forty years as a pseudo-therapist and phobia-buster.

Well, after 30 years, *I know college essays*. Most of them contain "charged" phrases and "absolutes" like:

That's when I decided to pursue medicine; I was never the same after that day; This was a transformative experience for me; I truly found myself that summer; Never before had I known such pain; Tennis will always be my life; A great weight had been lifted from my shoulders; and - It was the event that made me realize that I couldn't live in my comfort zone anymore.

These are all cliches that I have seen hundreds (if not thousands) of times since 1994 in personal essays. They're – essentially – the greatest hits, a Spotify playlist of blunt and non-thinking phraseologies. They're insulting to the reader because the writer can't be bothered with specifics. And – *here's the kicker – specifics are always more powerful than generics.* "Store brand mouthwash" is never equal to Listerine. At every turn in this book you're reading right now, I include the names of the actual students who wrote my favorite essays, and the names of colleagues who agreed or disagreed with my approach to this or that. Could you imagine a politician's stump speech that didn't call someone out by name? Could you imagine a rap song that talked about handbags and luxury cars – but didn't name-check the brands?

A great college essay also explores a brief moment in time. Nathan McCall's The Elevator Ride is a three-page personal essay about a Black man and a White woman sharing an elevator. It's 15 seconds of "real time" hijacked (by McCall) and subverted into a rant about race relations and the long history of Blacks suffering from what he calls "white fear."

It's a remarkable essay that would have made a *terrible* college essay. Why? Because he turns an innocent, innocuous elevator ride into the WWIII of racial disharmony and discord. Yes, it's about a singular event that requires a stopwatch to track (so he gets points for that), but it's an exercise in cognitive distortion the likes of which is rarely seen in print. He "gets inside" the mind of the White woman and ascribes the worst kind of Karen-ism to her every breath and blink.

When I began tracking the rise of the "viral college essay" – you know, the ones that "got the student into all the ivies" and took TikTok by tornado? – I noticed a common theme: they were either (A) written in a way that made me dubious about their authorship, or (B) outright terrible.

It was inevitable that even personal statements would "go viral" (as everything in the future will be famous for 15 seconds – to reframe Warhol's maxim), but what these Insta-famous or TikTok-friendly college essays told me was that the students in question would have gotten into Stanford, Harvard, Yale, or Penn even if they'd written exclusively in Pig Latin.

Brittany Stinson was an overnight sensation with her infamous "Costco" essay (with over 1.6 million people having clicked on it at least once). Abigail Mack claims – herself – that her "Letter S" personal statement got her into Harvard (as articulated in her own Refinery.com reflection). Stinson doesn't feel that way and claims the topic of Costco was forever a running joke between her friends (as told to the blog "Essay Hell").

Regardless, it was a student (Gabby Weiner) who brought up the Mack essay during a class on college essay writing. *She loved it.* It's rare that students – on their own – like an essay enough to share it, talk about it, consider it, and even vigorously debate its merits. I wasn't impressed by the "Letter S" college essay. It was a good idea that couldn't really sustain itself over 650 words (at best it was repetitive). But I was impressed with the impact it left on Gen Z readers. I didn't find Stinson's composite trip to Costco an authentic or engaging read.

But both are unicorn college essays, and we can learn something from them.

Prior to 2016, what academic type would have deigned to write about her intellectual exercises inside of a big-box discount retailer?

Before 2021, were students being (almost) lipogrammatic with their college essays? Treating their Common App prompts like word-games to be solved? I have to – at very least – tip my chapeau to Abigail Mack for not writing something basic or tropey. There is clear value in the legacy of these two overnight college essay celebrities. Being unique, clever, and even gimmicky (at face value) pays off big.

I don't fully embrace Stinson's piece because it does make a trip to Costo "more than it is." I use it in my classes as a model of both what to do and what not to do. There's voice and layering that works pretty well and sustains a narrative that I don't really believe happened as it's told, but it's still there – as redolent as any college essay I've read. That it turns Costco into a think-tank, as well as an allegory for every intellectual and academic accomplishment Stinson has ever racked-up, definitely chafes against my sensibilities.

Each year, many of my former juniors get into at least one ivy-league school – several of them multiples, yet there is a sea change happening: many more deliberately don't seek entrance to those once-hallowed halls. Increasingly, I see students choosing places like Duke, Vandy, and UMich.

I teach real-live unicorns five days a week, 180 days a year. Could you imagine being the top of your class and not even *considering* attending an ivy-league institution?

That's a unicorn if I've ever seen one.

That's what students need to represent on paper in the "most important snapshot" they're likely to take during their high school career.

* * *

My in-class college essay workshop begins with a simple prompt: What's a story you'd like to tell someone not-yet close to you that will create instant intimacy, familiarity, and vulnerability?

Resources

Table of Contents

- The Write-Up for The Unicorn College Essay Assignment
- Teacher Model: The Vest, by Wes Phillipson
- Student Model #1: Krokodil Gena is a Liar Isaac Tiomkin
- Student Model #2: Anonymous Student Submission – Academic Year 2024

The Unicorn College Essay Assignment Write-Up

The Personal Statement (The College Essay for the Common Application)
YOU CAN TRUST MULANEY'S COMEDY SPECIAL WILL BE SPECIAL

John Mulaney's a master of metacognition and metabolism: the *funny* lies in the joke's autopsy and its digestibility.
John Mulaney's SNL sketches are far from funny. They're awkward and abstract. They're duds. Or dogs. Or dull-as-dishwater. But not his stand-up comedy. That is a masterclass in four things:

1 Metacognition: the ability to think deeply about your own learning and thinking, and to understand, express, and explain it to yourself and others. The consciousness of how you think, and how you learn.
2 Vulnerability: the ability to reveal a part of yourself to your audience that is raw and real, painful and/or personal, emotionally honest and naked. It does NOT have to be "bad" (whatever that means). It should NEVER be a pity party. NEVER EVER. It SHOULD BE that Kelly Deng "leave a piece of your heart on the writer's table" that Chloe Liu spoke about (when discussing her good friend's essay-writing habits).
3 Trust: if your audience cannot trust you to be a reliable narrator, cannot trust you to be emotionally available, to be truthful, to be healthy (even about your emotional ill-health), to be present, to put yourself into the piece, to be engaging, to be alive and connected, to be a human being

they would want as a friend, a roommate, a classmate, a student, a significant other, or someone they'd want to hang with: then you're done.
4 Specialness: the essays that have resonated most with me (and please stop saying that "You resonate with something" because that isn't possible) are the ones that make me say – "This person is special." This person is "terminally unique." Only sophomore Zirui Zhou can express the world like a scathing fashion critic. Only junior Jackie Kershner can turn the everyday into a magical world-build. And so on.

There are ONLY TWO things a college admissions officer is interested in about your candidacy (once you've cleared the "Naviance" or "Scoir" hurdle) –

ONE: You can be trusted –

- To not go on academic probation
- To not self-harm or harm others
- To not have a psychotic break (or a nervous breakdown)
- To be an active + contributing member of their academic and social communities
- To be a dependable roommate
- To attend classes
- To pay your tuition, and room and board (to pay your bills)
- To be thoughtful and considerate
- To be open minded

TWO: You are special in the sense that –

- You are "not just like the other Scarsdale kids" (don't talk about the bubble, and don't talk about religion or town culture if you can help it – unless you have something (ah hem) "special" to say about these things).
- You have an area of expertise or something "niche" that sets you apart.
- You are not one dimensional: being "a great student" is not what they're looking for. Being well-rounded is also NOT what they're looking for. And being "well-rounded" = you are good at one thing (a jack of all trades = a master of none).
- You have a distinct voice (in writing – and in speaking) that is uniquely yours.
- You defy stereotypes (or – perhaps – subvert them).
- You have accomplished something that no one else in Scarsdale has – or experienced it in a way that no one else has.

- You possess humility, self-consciousness, and self-reliance and can metacognate well.

In-Class Essay Parameters:

- Two periods to write 625–650 words on a "topic of your choice" that will (ideally) become your Personal Statement for the Common Application next year ("topic of your choice" is ALWAYS a choice on the Common App).

Rubric:

- Word economy = not a wasted word: every word can be justified and is needed 25%.
- Wordsmithing = not a cliche to be found; the words that ONLY YOU could write 25%.
- You're Special = communicated indirectly through intangibles and tangibles 25%.
- You can be Trusted = communicated indirectly (intangibles and tangibles) 25%.

6
EMILY'S WAY AND HOW TO WRANGLE A GUEST SPEAKER

How often do you get to argue the merits of The Night Manager with the first person in history to win the Pulitzer Prize for TV Criticism?

When Emily Nussbaum came to my classroom in 2016, she had just won the most prestigious award any cultural critic could hope to claim – yet I had no idea who she really was, what she'd accomplished (namely that Pulitzer), or even that she'd once attended Scarsdale HS.

I had invited her because she'd written a review of the Breaking Bad finale "Felina" that entirely changed my perspective on the episode, if not the series. Moreover, I loved Nussbaum's regular contributions to The New Yorker magazine, and I was assigning my junior class to "write like Emily."

So who better to help them with that prompt than – well – Emily herself?

Nussbaum is larger than life, opinionated, and an effortless talker. In our hour together, there was not a moment of silence: no breaks, pauses, or rests in the conversation. It felt like catching up with an old friend (but one who knew everything about television and had already thought through her arguments all the way to the end). Our first exchange was about how my wife had recently befriended our (then) neighbor Alexis Bledel (Rory Gilmore or Lena Kaligaris for the uninitiated), and Nussbaum seemed to know about the series The Handmaid's Tale filming in Toronto (for which Bledel earned her first Emmy).

As the students filed in, Nussbaum turned her attention to them, asking, "What are you watching these days?"

Before I get to their answers, I want to take a moment to acknowledge that critique of "Felina."

DOI: 10.4324/9781003600565-6

Great critics rarely tell you if a TV show is good or bad; they're much more likely to hypothesize or make the invisible visible.

Nussbaum took Breaking Bad showrunner and writer Vince Gilligan to task for making the finale of season five about the *salvation* of meth-kingpin Walter White. In that episode White, as his alter-ego Heisenberg, is able to launder his drug money through a charitable foundation directed to his son (Walt Jr.), confess his true motives for getting into the drug trade to ex-wife Skyler, spring Jesse Pinkman from a literal dungeon, exact brutal revenge on a gang (one that ruined his business, stole most of his fortune, and slaughtered his brother-in-law), and – last but not least – get to die on his own terms (not from Cancer, but his own gun) on the floor of a meth lab that he indirectly helped set up.

To quote Georgina from Jordan Peele's horror film Get Out: No, no, no, no, no, no, no …

Nussbaum wasn't having it either.

Her New Yorker review from September of 2013 entitled The Closure-Happy Breaking Bad Finale was a profound upending and reimagining of Walt's swan song. Instead of righting his wrongs in spectacular arch-villain-turned-anti-hero fashion, White becomes a block of ice, dying inside his clunker of a car, impotent, succumbing to Cancer, the cold, or both? What if everything the viewer sees once Walt gets behind the wheel, determined to head down the mountain and into town, is a fantasy that plays out in Walt's head?

I watched every moment of all five seasons of Gilligan's dark and sinister series, and then ate up – what can only be described as a slow-cooked meal – all six seasons of its prequel Better Call Saul.

As for "Felina" specifically? I couldn't have been more satisfied with the final shot of Walter White face-up, bleeding out on the concrete floor of a meth lab, the dulcet tones of Badfinger lead singer Pete Ham (and his song "Baby Blue"). The irony of the song initially lost on me. After some research, I pieced some things together that may not be common knowledge: (A) If you Google image Pete Ham you'll see that his hair and beard look oddly similar to actor Bryan Cranston's in that final scene (who plays Walt) and (B) Ham committed suicide, just as White's kamikaze mission to free Jesse and exact revenge on the gang was a fait accompli.

My reaction to Gilligan's ending? Yes! You got it precisely right. Walt can't have it both ways: he can't leave his money to Walt Jr. and reconcile with him too. He can't treat Skyler like his priest at confession, telling her that his descent into crime had been for purely selfish reasons and not for the good of the family, and be absolved. He can't liberate Jesse from unspeakable torture and certain death and be acknowledged. He can't remotely unleash an M60 machine gun on a trailer full of thugs (himself included) and walk away unscathed.

So, I was happy with how Gilligan wrote Walt out of the world. It was no cop out.

But after reading Nussbaum's review, I realized something about myself as a consumer of media: I'm really not that critical. I'm not that discerning. I'm not nearly as engaged as I thought I was – I'm just mindlessly watching.

And that's okay. There's that fine line I try to walk between letting my brain rest and watching TV that makes me think, but TV (as a medium) had gotten so compelling that I'd started losing the ability to distinguish between really great, from great, from very good.

Or I'd just blindly accepted what Gilligan had served up for Walt's final meal: your finale is perfect, no questions asked, no critical faculties engaged.

Nussbaum showed (or reminded) me in just one short New Yorker article what a critic's job is: to not just criticize but improve upon; to not merely delight in but to push further; and – among other things – to not just write but redraft.

During her class visit, Nussbaum brought all of that sharpness (and more) while engaging with me and my students about TV. We went back-and-forth about Tom Hiddleston's limited series The Night Manager (I'd felt that the show failed to suspend my disbelief – but Nussbaum had no issue with that shortcoming; unsurprisingly, she was focused on other issues).

Nussbaum also weighed in on the controversial show about teen suicide, 13 Reasons Why, and how she herself had done some research and reporting on mental health, eating disorders and self-harm among that demographic. She'd even previously returned to her alma mater Scarsdale High School to speak with Deans and Counselors in service of that.

We discussed a term she'd coined, "prestige television," and how American society was fully ensconced in its Second Golden Age of TV. No, in 2016 we hadn't yet reached peak streaming, but we did have Hulu, Netflix, Amazon Prime Video, and Peacock was just four years out. Both the guest speaker and myself could remember a time when there were just three networks and Public Broadcasting Service (PBS), then Fox in 1986, and basic cable thereafter.

Through it all, Nussbaum listened to students' TV essay pitches, engaged in debates about Game of Thrones, Breaking Bad, and Gilmore Girls.

There was no mention of her recent Pulitzer Prize.

So how does this apply to your English classroom? If you're a Composition teacher, what's the relevance?

There's a stark truth that we need to lean into as educators: we're not really teaching students how to write. At best, we're exposing them to ideas, models, strategies, and enthusiasm that they positively respond to.

I brought Emily Nussbaum into my class because she'd written something that changed my thinking. I did the same thing with brilliant novelist and critic Oindrila Mukherjee, who wrote – for The Bleacher Report – about how Andre Agassi's memoir Open had revealed more than the retired tennis star had intended.

I'd been an Agassi fanboy since the late 1980s, then growing my hair into a mullet, switching from a black Prince Graphite racket to a flaming yellow Donnay frame as he did. I'd read a chunk of his personal account in Open, but my sense of Agassi? He was a victim of his own success, a young man who feared his Olympic boxer father, and someone who'd fallen under Nick Bollettieri's Svengali-like spell.

But after reading Oindrila's think-piece on Agassi, which was a critique of both the memoir and the man, I suddenly found myself seeing Andre very differently. He was no longer my hero, but a profound narcissist who needed to vilify everyone around him (Jimmy Connors, Pete Sampras, Nick Bollettieri, and Brooke Shields) to feel whole.

And these thought-leaders are out there. They can come into your classes via Zoom or FaceTime (or – if you're really old school – Skype). Or – if you're a traditionalist who appreciates the human touch – in person.

Nussbaum is a big get, I know. She's the most influential TV critic working today (other than Wesley Morris, who also won a Pulitzer). She's written two bestselling books on the medium (I Like to Watch and Cue the Sun!). She's the smartest person in any space she's occupying.

But so is Oindrila. She isn't (yet) as famous, but she's also a Composition professor and novelist who can walk the walk. And so is Meg Lukens Noonan who's written my favorite nonfiction work The Coat Route (about a $50,000 vicuna topcoat and its journey from fields to finished product).

Meg has worked with my students. She's a world-class journalist and ghostwriter.

Meg's not a critic, per se. Oindrila is. Dave Barry is. Jon Caramanica is. Dan Piepenbring is. Saul Austerlitz is.

And speaking of Saul, he's written the definitive book on the TV show Friends. He's visited the set of Gilmore Girls to write about the show's legacy. He's married to my wife's friend from high school, and he was more than willing to give my classes some of his time, attention, and cumulative wisdom.

When I'd contacted the other critics above – Dan, John, Dave, Oindrila – I had no real connection to them, no favors to call in, no self-evident common ground, nor leverage over them.

If you decide to reach out to a public figure whose work "speaks to you" (and you're hoping it will also resonate with your students), I'd start with a very simple email, DM, letter, or phone call.

Here's how I engaged Oindrila:

Hi –

I hope it's you who wrote the Bleacher Report review of Agassi's book, Open.

I was (and am) a fan of Agassi as a performer and a remaker of his own image (he who writes the history, wins the war, kind of thing) …

But I was utterly blind (I think) to his narcissistic injury – now I see that it's like a Harry Potter scar across his forehead, without the heroism.

I read the book when it first came out, but I don't think I saw (or understood) much of what you review – you psychoanalyze Agassi in a profound way – you're not star-struck, and you call him out for his self-interest at every turn.

It's a masterpiece.

I'd love to have you Zoom with my students someday – primarily about the notion of reader response, and how that is (perhaps) the most useful lens to apply when reading or viewing anything (a lens of one's own).

Thanks for making the invisible, visible for me.
Wes Phillipson

* * *

The secret sauce to connecting with a writer, artist, or public figure is – wait for it – *sincerity*.

I once made the mistake of inviting someone into my class based on a recommendation from a student. They'd said to me, "I took this summer course at Harvard, and I think you and my professor have very similar approaches to teaching Black studies. Do you want his contact information?"

I took it, reached out, sent the professor some materials and heard back: "I'm not interested in coming to speak as it seems we have antithetical approaches to the subject matter, but thanks for the opportunity."

As the teacher, you should consider reaching out to those who have moved you, not moved someone else.

Another approach that often works is appealing to the writer's desire to be appreciated and more deeply understood. And – again – you can't fake this.

Before hitting send on an email or DM to an author I ask myself, "Is the answer to this question available on-line or in print? Have I looked at enough interviews to know that they haven't addressed this question elsewhere?"

That's another way of saying: don't waste their time.

What's in it for them if they come to your class, virtually or otherwise? Can you give them (in advance) a sense of the class' format? Is it going to be a series of self-evident questions and answers, or have your students meaningfully engaged with something the guest has written, filmed, produced, recorded, or edited?

A noted TV and film producer, whose nieces and nephews attended Scarsdale HS, was eager to Zoom with my classes from his Los Angeles home about a show of his we'd watched several episodes of (in anticipation of his virtual visit).

While he – initially – showed enthusiasm, in the weeks leading up to his guest lecture, he was unresponsive to my emails. I was trying to get him to preview my students' questions about a pilot episode of an Emmy Award winning limited series he'd produced. I wanted him to (at least) be familiar with the topics and nuanced queries coming his way.

It was radio silence until 30 minutes before the class when my guest demanded to see the questions, read them, then told me he's bailing because he can't find a single question he likes or one that is appropriate. The visit was off. He was in a huff. I was left scratching my head.

But it was a lesson for me: If your guest speaker shows hesitation or trepidation, just forget it. Don't push it. Don't even sweat it.

In the words of the most overrated song in the history of karaoke: *Let it go.*

Because it's really funny: the more you want it, the less they want to give it to you.

I actually canceled on Oscar winning screenwriter Christopher McQuarrie because he'd canceled (previously) on me. I thought he was going to flake again, so I booked a different guest speaker in his place. But McQuarrie hung in there and delivered a masterclass (with a robust Q&A) on the last day of school.

The irony with that TV pilot producer who was ejected from the plane minutes before class time?

All he wanted to answer were softball questions. He was only comfortable addressing topics and subjects that had already been addressed in public interviews and articles.

The greater irony? Earlier, I'd emailed him a question about the historical research that had gone into his historically accurate series (and period piece) and he responded, "That's in an interview I gave somewhere; I'm sure you can just find it if you look for it. I don't have time to answer you – I'm getting ready for the Emmys."

And that was exactly my point. Why would I bother you, waste your time, and use up your precious resources, having my students seek information that is already public record?

Speaking to the process of soliciting classroom visitors more broadly, I'd say one more important thing: it's not always easy, and it's not always worth it.

But many times it is (worth it).

And it's not always a straight line between two points. Sometimes I slide into Instagram DMs, other times I email literary agents to get to the author. And you must get creative and be resourceful: I'll find out if they teach at a college or university and see if they have publicly available contact information; I'll use on-line people-finder tools like Zaba search to track down a known address; or I'll do the most blunt and non-thinking thing like search up their official website (which almost never pays dividends).

The good news about this practice?

I've never had a disastrous experience and most speakers who get on your calendar deliver the goods (or at least show up and try).

My most memorable example is bestselling author, color commentator, and top tennis coach Brad Gilbert, who Zoomed with my classes from Mill Valley, California at 4:30 AM (Pacific Standard Time). He and his wonderful agent wife Kim had tech issues, but kept trying to get back on the video conference call, experimenting with different lighting attachments, refusing to give up.

Because of technical difficulties, it was a short conversation with my sophomore class, but Brad was in great spirits and 100% present with us. Kim even emailed me later to tell me Brad hadn't seen some of my questions (it was a huge packet in Doc form that I'd sent him) and told me he'd be happy to return for a follow-up, despite the time difference and the early start to the school day.

Covid lockdowns affected many things, but they also changed the immediacy of public speaking (that includes, I suppose, Tele-Medicine, too).

The intense isolation touched everyone – especially public figures who, understandably, missed their public.

Since then, as frequently as possible, I've tapped into that changing zeitgeist. Out of necessity and to meet the basic human needs of love and connection, the very private have become increasingly public, and the public figures have pursued intimacy in the form of private Zoom rooms.

* * *

Here's Prompt Six

Emily's Way — Writing about TV like a Pulitzer Prize winning television critic

There's a four-step process for this essay:

Step One: Watch some television. Well, we're doing some of that in class. We're watching what Nussbaum coined as "prestige shows" (high cost, big name, high gloss TV). Specifically dramas. Even more specifically pilot episodes. We began with Fargo, then Yellowjackets, followed by Homeland, American Crime Story: The People v. O.J. Simpson, Mad Men and we're ending with The Americans.

You can't become a critic by just watching what you want to watch (or what makes you feel good). These are WEIGHTY shows, with potent metacommentary on American culture.

Step Two: Read some Emily Nussbaum TV reviews and cultural critiques.

- Her entire body of short-form criticism can be found in the archives at New York Magazine, The New Yorker magazine, and Vulture.

Step Three: Pick a show (or shows) that you wish to subject to a meaningful cultural critique. It does NOT NEED TO SOUND like Emily Nussbaum, but it needs to do the kinds of things she does in her essays about television. What are "those things?" You've got to do the intellectual heavy lifting here, and appreciate the following:

- Success Leaves Clues. Nussbaum won The Pulitzer for TV Criticism, and she's the only one in history to have that honor. How did she do it? She – single-handedly – transformed "being a TV critic" into an art form (and a science). What does she do? What kinds of things does she talk about? Reference? Make sense of? Ask of us, her reader? How does she begin a TV essay? End one? What kind of language does she use?

Step Four: Write a TV cultural critique with the level of attention to detail, intricacy of thought, and – to the extent that you can – "voice" (or attitude, swagger) of Emily Nussbaum.

Specs:

- 1250 words
- You should explore ONE SHOW as the main focus of your essay, but you are encouraged to bring in other works of TV
- You are NOT limited to writing about the shows we've watched and discussed (throughout this unit)

- Your Job Is No Different than Other Essays: you must be the "expert" on whatever topic you choose. You cannot write about a TV show that you have not watched at least twice (that episode or season). Emily Nussbaum loves watching TV. That doesn't mean you have to. But you have to commit to an essay topic that is "something only you could have written," and "something that you OWN."

7

MY LIPOGRAM

The no "E" paper

There's little known about the man who died in 1939 – the same year his fourth and final book was published – Gadsby: A Story of Over 50,000 Words Without Using the Letter "E."

Gadsby vs. Gatsby

Ernest Vincent Wright may (or may not) have been attending a cocktail party in California when he was bullied into writing an entire novel without the most common letter in the English alphabet.

Wright was a huckster. Perhaps even a literary conman. So much of his mythology is – ironically – reminiscent of Jay Gatsby himself. Did Fitzgerald's titular character attend Oxford University? Not a chance. Was Wright a graduate of MIT? There's no evidence that he ever earned a college degree from anywhere (his obituary says one thing, while the public record suggests another). Was Gatsby a decorated war hero? Did Wright actually serve in the Navy? There's an open question about his citizenship, so, who knows?

Even Wright's death was used to sell copies of Gadsby. His newspaper obituary states, "The book was off the publisher's press here the day Wright died," but The Village Voice journalist Ed Park's research has dismantled the rumors of his death occurring "within hours" of Gadsby's first printing.

But it was marketed as if the very moment Wright dipped his toe into his long-neglected swimming pool, he was mowed down by a metaphorical George Wilson. *Yes, Wright died that year, but not that day.* There are

DOI: 10.4324/9781003600565-7

rarely meaningful coincidences in life, but there are often sloppily plotted conspiracies concocted to move product.

And I get that you might be confused by this point.

Everyone knows that classic American-dream-reinvention-novel by F. Scott Fitzgerald called The Great Gatsby (published in 1925). But who knows Gadsby (with a D and not a T)?

Fitzgerald was best friends with my great-grandfather Thomas Boyd, whose only successful work was a war story called Through the Wheat. The only reason Boyd had access to the rock-star editor of his day (Maxwell Perkins) was because Fitzgerald opened that door for him, willing to share his greatest collaborator. It's clear to anyone who reads Through the Wheat that Fitzgerald's voice-and-syntax fingerprints are all over my great-grandpa's novel, and it's likely that he – indirectly – influenced Wright's swan song too.

And just as Wright did, Fitzgerald died a "failure" in California (one within a year of the other). Wright had paid to have his last novel published in 1939, but he'd conceived of it in the 1920s and had a completed draft by 1930. Fitzgerald's Gatsby was envisioned in 1917 when he left Princeton to go to war, but it didn't take shape until 1925. It's really the story of how Zelda wouldn't marry F. Scott until he was a success. So, he writes his first novel upon returning from the front-lines, gets Scribner to publish it, and becomes the Jay to her Daisy, with an equally tragic ending.

By 1940, F. Scott was a penniless alcoholic working in Hollywood, desperately trying to get a screenplay greenlit (pun intended), and died before Gatsby would become a smash-hit among homesick and lovelorn WWII servicemen, or the darling of ivy-league literary critics. Wright died in near obscurity, sitting on a pile of Gadsbys that had been self-funded (vanity publications), the balance of them burned up in a warehouse fire (according to Bookride).

But Gadsby, too, is about reinvention. It's the tale of a middle-aged man who returns to revitalize his hometown (the fictional Branton Hills), eventually seeing its population rise from four figures to five through his good works. And Gatsby follows Jay as he returns not to Louisville when he was a young officer and Daisy a debutante but to pick up where they'd left off – recreating their young love on Manhasset, Long Island. Thomas Wolfe was also a Max Perkins protege, and his book "You Can't Go Home Again" certainly applies to Gatsby, but Gadsby? Not so much.

The intellectual elite have sustained both Gatsby and Gadsby's very existence. T.S. Eliot, Malcolm Cowley, and Lionel Trilling launched the former into public consciousness. Georges Perec and Douglas Hofstadter have done the same for Wright's only "important work." Each man's legacy is really tied to *just one book* and a handful of fanboys.

Each sentence in The Great Gatsby is written at a Spinal-Tap "level 11" – its own July 4th pyrotechnic finale – each sentence a shining example of rarefied beauty and philosophical fleet-footedness told by a 28 year old roving poet in its all-eclipsing, compound-complex glory.

Each sentence of Gadsby is a masterclass in reduction, constraint, and syntactical subversion.

Yet, one is beautifully written and the other is halting, awkward, choppy, and often constipated (through its repetition), but both are grand exercises in style.

Writing even one page of an essay or short story without a single word that contains the letter "E" is a counterintuitive act of foolish bravery or stubborn sleight of hand.

Eliminating a single letter from one's writing is a literary form called "the lipogram." The name of the game here is "constrained" prose. My father, Brainerd F. Phillipson, has been a rare book dealer since the 1970s (and persists in doing so today in a Kindle world). He's owned signed first editions of The Great Gatsby (even a copy with a partial dust-jacket and a tipped-in family group photograph of Zelda, F. Scott, Thomas, and Peggy Boyd), but he's drawn to any book that is truly rare or even scarce. Wright's Gadsby fits that criteria. Dust-jacketed copies can fetch beyond $5,000 but don't often come on the market. As I'm writing this chapter, Burnside Rare Books in Portland, Oregon has a copy on offer in red cloth (sans DJ) for $1,400.00.

That means I first heard about Gadsby – and Wright's parlor trick – when I was a teenager. I saw the book in my father's library and was immediately confused by the title's spelling on the spine. Naturally, I had read The Great Gatsby in Mrs. Smith's English class – but what, pray tell, was **Gadsby**?

When dad gave me the backstory, I thought it was little more than a gimmicky endeavor. By some accounts, Wright had taped down the "E" key on his typewriter to combat the muscle memory of 60 years of writing and speaking English, freely using words with "E." Others claim he'd removed the key altogether as a fail-safe.

Before turning this idea into an activity for my students, I began with a test case – a dyslexic freshman named Jason in 1995. He also had ADHD and a wild imagination. I thought of Wright's novel as an antidote to Jason's boredom. And in just 30 minutes, he'd written a poetic and philosophical musing about an imaginary friend – without the letter "E." That was my proof of concept.

The first incarnation of this class assignment was short fiction. It was a fun writing exercise, begun in class as a kind of "let's get the blood moving" activity. I'd challenged pairs of students to see how much they could write in 20 minutes based on the following prompt: You find a bag of money with a bank's name printed on it. It's the most amount of cash you've ever seen in one place in your life. Tell that story without using the letter "E" – with no unusual abbreviations, extreme slang, or foreign words allowed.

Many of my students like creative writing, and they found this new wrinkle to be a welcome (or near-impossible) challenge. Yes, there were some groans, and even a few gasps. Others gave me looks of disbelief, but it was something no other English teacher had ever asked them to attempt.

Full disclosure: it took me 28 years of teaching to realize that it wasn't a good assignment – *as it stood*. Asking them to write a short story with such austerity measures in place was not a substantive endeavor. I'm not qualified to teach students how to write short stories. Analyze them? Of course. Write about them as armchair critics? Yes. But I'm a nonfiction writer, so during academic year 2023–24, I wondered,

> What would be the pedagogical value of asking students to write an analytical essay without using the letter "E?" *The answer wasn't immediately apparent.* Until I sat down to do it myself. In fifty minutes (during one free period between classes), I completed an essay about Macbeth that revealed the genius of this assignment (thanks Ernie Wright!), and the baked-in skills that get honed by virtue of the crucible that is the No E Paper.

What struck me was: the problems surrounding quote integration are immediately solved when you don't use "E." Why? I found myself (for the very first time as a writer of an analytical, text-based essay) laser-focused and deeply thoughtful about which quotes would sustain my argument. Two challenges arose that were disguised blessings: (A) I had to re-read large swaths of a play I'd taught for three decades and thought I knew cold, and (B) I had to scrutinize each and every word in a passage from The Scottish Play to decide which individual words and phrases could be taken out of context without changing their meaning.

In other words, I had never pored over and teased out the language of Shakespeare at that level (despite having repeatedly taught Julius Caesar, Romeo and Juliet, Othello, Midsummer Night's Dream, etc.), before writing about Macbeth sans "E."

And isn't that what we claim is most important to us as English teachers? That our students grow into these remarkable evidence gatherers and *combine harvesters* who then can – literally – separate the wheat from the chaff? Locate the right quote, create the context, integrate said quote, analyze it thoughtfully, and then repeat that process at least once more in the paragraph?

I used to believe that was my raison d'être. I've come to find that it isn't.

Through the No E Paper, I've found not a "shortcut" to getting students to that place of quote-selection literacy, but a process of constriction that forces them to choose better, more elegantly, and far more concisely than ever before.

Just think about the "Why?" behind that. My students' No E Papers had to have direct quotes from Macbeth. There was no way around that. They had to find text-based evidence for their claims, but they had to go about it at the micro-level, looking for – at best – three consecutive words they could string together (without an E). Gone were the days when they could indiscriminately "quote bomb," taking multiple lines from the Bard whole cloth. Past tense were the times when they could "search it up" (as my Gen Zers love to say), perhaps avoiding having to read the play altogether, leaning heavily on Google and CTRL-Fing inside the digital Folger Shakespeare Library edition.

Crafting a lipogram means far more than having to pay attention to your writing at the sentence level, you must be the steward of each and every single word that you create, or that you borrow. Beyond quote selection and quote integration being literally upended or transformed, lipograms do for students what Mary Shelley's Frankenstein did for active and passive voice.

Something a Princeton professor once pointed out was that – and I'm paraphrasing here – whenever Victor Frankenstein spoke or wrote about the evil that his monster brought into the world and who was culpable, Shelley would use passive voice. But when the monster would tell his tale of woe (and the killings or terror he'd unleashed on mankind), the author employed the active. The idea was simple: active voice = taking responsibility, and passive voice its antithesis.

For over a century (or as far back as I could document), Composition teachers have dissuaded their pupils from using passive voice. I've never understood the thinking behind this. If you go to the "common sense corner" for a moment (indulge me), you'll likely agree that one needs to vary their syntax in a piece of writing.

I'd also argue that passive voice sounds more "poetic" (almost by default), or certainly can produce a kind of lilt, flourish, or disembodied quality that more sophisticated writers so effortlessly expel. Shelley used it as a deliberate form choice that drove the content of her ghost story.

And since students don't read nearly as much as they once did, our job is increasingly less about reciting "Strunk & White's" greatest hits, and more about helping them unleash their voice – passive, active, personal, metacognitive, and philosophical. It matters not which one, just that they have a stake in what they write, and that their personality intersects with their prose.

Not having the luxury of using words with "E" stops student-writers (or anyone) in their tracks. Neo-noir filmmaker and former housemate of mine Tim McCann (he's also a professor at the North Carolina School of Arts) once taught me: "Filmmaking is problem solving." On a movie-set or shooting location, you are up against waning daylight, actors' conflicting schedules, changing weather systems, budgetary limitations, continuity issues, and countless human variables that force a director and their team to solve problems as they arise so the film can (eventually) be completed.

When students are hamstrung or handicapped by "the E restriction," it pushes them to seek creative solutions. And we're not talking about availing oneself of ChatGPT here. As far as I'm concerned (and my own tests bear this out), this assignment cannot be successfully executed using Artificial Intelligence (AI). My colleague in the Scarsdale High School English Department, Dr. Joshua Gaylord both agreed but was also skeptical. He wrote to me in an email:

I just had ChatGPT produce this based on your assignment:

Prompt: Write a paragraph about Shakespeare using only words that don't contain the letter E:

Old William, prolific Bard, wordsmith grand, plays glorious. His works stir souls, captivating all with wit, passion, and drama. His legacy vast, enduring through ag's, inspiring many with art, depth, and insight. His quill, mighty tool, crafts worlds, characters, and plots, enchanting crowds for generations. A maestro of language, his verses soar, igniting minds with imagination's flame.

Yeah, you'd have to replace some words ("legacy" with "impact" or "ag's" with "history," etc. But this gets you pretty close. You're right, it's not great – A.I.I never is. But it seems like it could get you to mediocre. That's the danger.

Which is not to say that your assignment isn't a good one! I really do love it! Have you thought of doing a follow-up, like Georges Perec did– using ONLY the vowel E?

The specter of what Dr. Gaylord raised about AI in June of 2024 increasingly haunts English teachers. Josh is known for giving "15-minute-in-class-essays" written entirely by hand.

"I think my thrust was that ChatGPT really IS a threat to the assignment. It's not a threat in the case of the excellent student, but it IS a threat in the case of the mediocre student (the quality of whose work really CAN be duplicated by ChatGPT)," Gaylord posits.

Others in my Department favor philosopher and social theorist Jeremy Bentham's "panopticon prison design." Danny Zeliger "has students sit in a circle with desks facing the walls. But I'll say that in practice students like it. It gives them privacy and removes distractions, and it allows me to easily and privately conference with them. The panopticon effect of self-policing is an added bonus."

My wife taught English at Bronxville High for several years, and their Department was already heading towards an "all in-class essay policy" years before ChatGPT's existence.

Friend and long-time colleague Stephen Mounkhall views AI as the likely undoing of the English essay as we know it. He began the 24–25 academic season with one thing in mind: teaching students how to think for themselves so they wouldn't need to depend on a machine to do it for them. Mounkhall's opening day slideshow included such thoughtful questions as follows:

"To what extent do you believe the idea that learning to write is about learning how to think? To what extent do you think learning how to write/think is valuable? How would you feel if you put a lot of effort into writing an essay, and the teacher fed the essay into a computer and let the computer give you feedback and a grade? How would you feel if a teacher had Chat-GPT write a college recommendation for you?"

I borrowed the final two questions for use in my own English classes, and the conversations that flowed from them were worthwhile, and (at least) established a baseline of concern and ethical attitudes towards using technology to cheat the human experience and condition.

I get why English teachers are panicking, but I see things a bit differently. Instead of controlling the situation as much as humanly possible, I'd much rather design writing prompts that

a Can't be completed by "aggregating the internet"
b Require – or at least allow – students to personally intersect with the topic they choose C) Demand markedly different skill-sets each time my students write (while building on the previous ones)

And "A" (above) folds into "B" very neatly.

What I often tell students about ChatGPT is based on Stranger Things star Noah Schnapp (a short-term student of mine in my senior English class Words and Images).

I say, ChatGPT's superpower is aggregating the internet. It curates all the information that is publicly available (without firewall) on the World Wide Web, or all the information it's been trained on. Unless you're Noah Schnapp (a public figure who has been interviewed, profiled, fan-blogged, etc.), *you* don't have a rich, on-line, mineable history. *Noah does*. That means that ChatGPT can't "curate you." So, if you're writing about a meaningful experience you've had, or a philosophy you've developed through a specific circumstance, or a way that you've intersected with a character from The Great Gatsby – then ChatGPT can't approximate that for you. If you try, it won't have specificity. It won't have a human soul at its center. It won't have your voice. It won't have your nuanced thoughts. It won't have the kind of world-building that only you could do. It won't contain the kinds of rarefied distinctions that only you could make. And, if you're writing a No E Paper about Macbeth, and your teacher requires direct quotes from the play (that also don't have the letter E), *then ChatGPT is utterly useless.*

ChatGPT can't curate a selection of things, data points, or personal details, if they don't already exist on the internet, or if someone hasn't trained Chat on that information.

In the late 1980s, when I was coming of age, the amount of information in the world doubled every seven years. Today, it doubles every seven months. By the time your current students are parents themselves, it will likely double every seven weeks.

All that is to say, ChatGPT and Generative AI is accelerating that process. But it's entirely mimetic. It can't think for itself. It can only mimic thinking. And it's our job to (as Mounkhall and others are doing), (A) help them think independent of machines, and (B) give them something worth writing about – or at least "worthy challenges."

The No E Paper is an exercise in *how to use a thesaurus with a license*, how to deploy active and passive voice consciously and creatively, as well as how to bend syntax and diction to one's will. As for that quote integration thing: *Insert any novel or play you wish*. If you use The Great Gatsby with this assignment (instead of Macbeth, Animal Farm, or Slaughterhouse Five), it has the same effect: razor-sharp quote selection that is both profoundly economical, and lexically tuned, to the sentence it's being dropped in.

And an added bonus of the No E Paper is: students will be compelled to subvert cliches. Those ready-made phrases and common platitudes most likely contain an E or three. They'll need to wordsmith their sentences by way of linguistic innovation and razing, then rebuilding the trite phrasings that serve as the unfortunate hallmark of any high school student's essay.

Here's Prompt Seven

The Lipogram Essay – NO E's Allowed Assignment Write-Up

A Lipogram Is a Piece of Writing that Leaves Out – Deliberately – One Letter throughout.

There Are Some Famous Lipograms

One of the most remarkable examples of a lipogram is Ernest Vincent Wright's novel Gadsby – NOT The Great Gatsby – (published in1939), which has over 50,000 words but not a single letter E. Wright's self-imposed rule prohibited such common English words as the and he, plurals ending in -es, past tenses ending in -ed, and even abbreviations like Mr. (since it is short for Mister) or Rob (for Robert). Yet the narration flows fairly smoothly, and the book was praised by critics for its literary merits.

Interest in lipograms was rekindled by Georges Perec's novel La Disparition (1969) (openly inspired by Wright's Gadsby) and its English translation A Void by Gilbert Adair. Both works are missing the letter E, which is the most common letter in French as well as in English. A Spanish translation instead omits the letter A, the second most common letter in that language.

The Challenge

Write a 750-word analysis of one passage from Animal Farm, or one stretch of lines from Macbeth (or compare and contrast them), in which you refrain from using the letter "e" at any point. Achieving "Google Zero" and using – for example – kennings, would serve you very well on this assignment. Employing chiasmus and tautology makes sense, too, as a strategy (at times).

The rubric: An "A" paper would need to be ...

- Fluid syntax creation and diction usage
- Extraordinary wordsmithing and phrase-making
- Penetrating insight

8
THE USUAL SUSPECTS

A Dialogue Essay from England with Love

It only happened because of Covid and because Tom Cruise wanted to go rock climbing.

Christopher McQuarrie was on location in the U.K. trying to wrap Mission Impossible – Dead Reckoning when a positive Covid test from cast or crew (or both) allowed Cruise to slip away to Lake District National Park in northwest England – most likely to conquer Scafell Pike.

Holed up in his temporary digs in London, McQ (as he's known) was suddenly in my virtual Zoom waiting room asking for permission to enter. I, of course, let him in.

In June of 2020, I'd slid into McQ's DMs on Instagram, long before his social media accounts were set to private:

"Chris – would you Zoom with my Scarsdale HS English class next academic year to discuss a film that I've shown faithfully for 20 years: The Usual Suspects? I have a theory about the dialogue (it's some of the most quotable in cinematic history – but I think that most of it is irrelevant to the plot). Moreover, I have students with real, burning questions about the film that would love to get 30 minutes with you. Regardless, thank you for writing the greatest neo-noir ever made. Your writing, in many ways, launched my interest in film."

A year later almost to the day, I'd entirely forgotten that I'd messaged McQ when I see *it* in my inbox: "Not sure if you're still teaching, or want me to talk to your students, but I happen to have some free time this week. What about tomorrow? McQ."

He wants to make silent films.

DOI: 10.4324/9781003600565-8

The man who won the Oscar for Best Original Screenplay in 1996 believes that dialogue is the least important thing in his movie-making process. Yet McQuarrie has quite possibly written the tightest script in Hollywood history.

I challenge anyone to watch Edge of Tomorrow and not be completely seduced by the magic trick of start, stop, and begin again that gets sustained with Patek Philippe-like precision for 1 hour and 53 minutes. Groundhog Day is 12 minutes shorter but feels significantly longer. There's waste. Wind-drag. Dead-spots. Too many morals are connected to too many subplots. A haggard Bill Murray who doesn't endear so much as mug.

But Edge? It's the kind of story that only a master of pacing and timing could conceivably get right.

Christopher Nolan's Tenet is far more "ambitious" than Edge (actors learning how to fight in reverse – car chases that move backwards and forwards simultaneously, etc.), but it's always either grandiose action or insipid exposition. McQuarrie's sci-fi LARP (Live-Action-Role-Playing) has no fat to trim off the chop. It's as lean and muscular as Emily Blunt (as Rita) in full training mode preparing to square off against the Mimics as United Defense force leader.

And as I failed in my attempt to recall my favorite lines from Edge of Tomorrow (which I've seen only once), I begin to understand McQ's belief that dialogue doesn't matter and, if anything, gets in the way.

We're in our Zoom session now, waiting for my students to filter into the classroom, when I get a big laugh out of McQ about a shared childhood memory of watching a weaponized steampipe pierce a mercenary's chest at the end of the 1985 Schwarzenegger film Commando.

Arnold plays retired special force officer John Matrix. He's pulled into a foreign president's assassination plot by way of his daughter's kidnapping. The finale involves "sticking it" to the arch villian's main henchman, Bennett, in the boiler room of a private island compound.

"Let off some steam, Bennett," sneers a shirtless and battle-face-painted Arnold, triumphant, posing like he's back on Venice Beach outside Gold's Gym.

McQ remembers that character (played by actor Vernon Wells), and the litany of puns unleashed on an audience of young men growing unable to distinguish action films from comedies, guffawing as they watched Schwarzenegger throw a short guy off a steep hillside somewhere on Mulholland and quip: "I let him go."

We're about the same age (I'm three years younger than the writer-director), so there is a good deal of cinematic common ground between us: from Stallone's Cobra to late-era Dirty Harry. We saw these films in theaters without reserved seating or computerized ticket kiosks, at a time when capes were the exception, not the rule.

"I thought you had this amazing ear for dialogue that you really liked to exercise. Even that moment in Mission Impossible – Fallout when Ethan Hunt (Cruise) is flying the helicopter trying to drop the payload on his nemesis and says to himself, Hold this for me, will you? When it's an epic fail, and he misses, a beautiful subversion of the predictable action hero cliche occurs."

"And has the exact opposite effect of: Let off some steam, Bennett."

"It fascinates me that you've publicly said", "Dialogue doesn't matter."

"I was a big lover of Mamet and Chayefsky – writers who were very much recognized for their overtness. Writers who were known for their voice. And I grew up believing – along with a lot of other myths and suppositions – that it was how you made your mark. And that was one marker – catchy dialogue. I started to realize that dialogue was part of a bigger problem that writers are taught: that information matters, and it's not so much that I think dialogue doesn't matter, it's that information matters a lot less. It's about learning to separate information from emotion, and how to express emotion. It's a big part of what I now observe, which is, you see a lot of films that are praised for their acting and their writing because they deal with a lot of emotional extremes, and we're taught that it's great acting/writing, and my frustration with a lot of that is that I'm not actually feeling anything while I'm watching it except admiration for the actor. Which to me is not a cinematic experience – that's a cinema nerd experience."

"I feel that way while watching The Score (the Robert De Niro/Ed Norton film), there are some moments that make me appreciate what you've just described."

"Yeah, they're acting so hard, and there's a lot to be admired in that craft, and there was an era in which going to movies meant that you went to see a Dustin Hoffman film because of the Dustin Hoffman performance, and Meryl Streep or Marlon Brando, same thing. I'm somebody who cannot invest myself in the artificiality of an experience no matter how technically great it is. So there are a lot of films that come out now that people really admire and have a fervent passion for that I do not understand in the slightest – beyond their technical achievements. I don't feel anything in the slightest, beyond how impressive it is that they actually made that movie. What interests me more is one that grabs me on an emotional level no matter how many times I see it. The Natural is a far more effective movie despite the fact that it has a high level of artifice to it. It's a mythic film, and something of a fable. And if you're watching that and saying – that's not real – I kind of feel bad for you because there's such a great emotional experience to be had, and it works every time. It's so effective, so meaningful and impactful every time. There are other movies that people love, but if I were to give you my analysis and what my criteria are and how I look at a movie and say: this is not a movie I feel and here's why; or here's a movie that you enjoy because you're doing the work and not the filmmaker, I'd ruin a lot of your favorite movies for you."

"No, I think we're on the same page about that. I remember watching The Usual Suspects for the first time about 15 years ago with my girlfriend at the time – she was a film person and I wasn't nearly as much of a film person as I am now. I remember not really understanding what was happening, but feeling I'd never seen anything like it before, and being completely caught up in (of all things) the surprising Stephen Baldwin performance. I think that the story is so compelling, and the temporal distortion works very well to disorient, but to be completely honest with you I still don't entirely understand it, and I think that doesn't matter because it makes me feel and it makes me think. Just as I don't entirely understand Memento. And you spoke about The Natural as a fable, and it made me wonder about The Odyssey being used as a frame story for Fallout. Hunt receives his "mission" inside of a classic hardbound edition of Homer's tale. It seems both obvious – and not – at the same time. I don't know if he's trying to get back to Ithaca (so to speak). If it's a reboot of the franchise. He's kind of an epic character."

At this point in the conversation, McQ relocates to another part of his London home because his wife requires the space he's currently occupying. He checks in with me to ask how long my class period runs for. He says he can give me an hour, which is (technically) more than I need.

But I'm delighted to witness a reductive craftsman sprint through his intimate space – holding a laptop as he broadcasts – to make way for his wife's early evening activities. McQ is both humble and happy to be alive – and good-natured laughter just emanates from him at every literal turn of the corner.

There's something remarkable about an artist who can write the script for a (still) unknown film like Public Access (1993) that never gets significant distribution (it's not currently streamed or available anywhere in the world that I know of), but just three years later beats out Toy Story at the Academy Awards, and – in-between writing Edge of Tomorrow – take complete creative control of a stalled franchise that some of the most successful directors in history couldn't make work nearly well enough (John Woo, Brian De Palma, and J.J. Abrams all swung and missed). And should we talk about McQuarrie (and Cruise) single-handedly saving Hollywood with Top Gun: Maverick?

McQuarrie has become a legit auteur. He wrote, directed, and produced every Mission Impossible film after MI:4. You can't watch Ghost Protocol (MI:4) and Fallout (MI:5) back-to-back without noticing a sea change in the product. It's not unlike how Martin Campbell and Sam Mendes EpiPenned James Bond back to life.

To my knowledge, Cruise won't make a movie at this point without McQ's involvement. We saw what happened when he doesn't – Jack Reacher: Never Go Back comes to mind. It's a near flop with a 38% RT critics' score, while the first Reacher is nearly twice that. In all ways, Never Go Back feels like a made-for-TV movie, in part because it co-stars How I Met Your Mother's Cobie Smulders. It peters out so badly at some point that it's more Adventures in Babysitting than badass tale of undomesticated lone wolf. Put indelicately: Jack Reacher 2 is on par with Amazon's Reacher Season 2.

A year later, when I'd email McQ congratulating him on the tremendous success of Top Gun: Maverick and his putting the twinkle back In Tinseltown, his waxed, "I was just there when the wheel went round," suggesting that his association with Cruise is what has made him what (and who) he is, and that he's not so much talented – as lucky, consistent, and tireless.

* * *

And that "dialogue about dialogue" was the genesis of this essay prompt: The Dialogue Essay. **A week later only cemented things.** I had a protracted conversation with a man who has sold tens of millions of copies of one book series: Men Are from Mars, Women Are from Venus.

It was an unlikely meet-up with John Gray, teleporting in from Mill Valley, California.

It was June of 2021 when I locked in a time to Zoom with the man who had sold 50 million books translated into 50 languages. His personal assistant, Hallina, was gracious with me even after I'd created a mix-up with my Google Calendar invite.

The relationship handbook Men Are from Mars, Women Are from Venus debuted in 1992, but as an intellectual property it has taken on so many directions that it's become culturally rhizomatic: There are sequels applicable to the workplace and the bedroom, a board game by Mattel, the Broadway musical, an ABC News special hosted by Cybill Shepherd, a catalog of "premium" on-line courses, live weekend seminars, coaching programs, and thousands of licensed products (as well as bootleg merch). It's become the Mars-Venus Universe, affording Gray his own private jet with which he can capitalize on his international cache.

I had discovered John Gray through a Tony Robbins Power-Talk episode. With Robbins everything is power-centric: his most popular live seminar is Unleash the Power Within, his self-help program – Personal Power, and conversations conducted with influencers in a variety of navel-gazing genres was predictably: "Power-Talk!"

For what feels like a confab when I listen to it on an old cassette, Robbins spends an afternoon at Gray's home to capture on audio-tape (for what we'd now call a podcast) the universal and predictable patterns of male-female relationship dynamics. Disclaimer: According to John Gray.

Gray lives down the road in Mill Valley, California from the house where my grandmother Eugenia Smith spent her final years. Across the street was Huey Lewis – until he left for Montana in the late 1980s. There have been many of these one-degree of separation cases in my life (often not unearthed until after-the-fact), but I couldn't use my late grandmother as a reference when approaching Gray. They didn't know each other, and I hadn't seen "Ammy" since graduating high school in 1990.

It would be an improbable conversation with the head Martian.

My junior honors English class had been reading the Tennessee Williams play A Streetcar Named Desire – featuring the abusive relationship of married couple Stanley and Stella Kowalski, and the unexpected, destabilizing force of Blanche DuBois. At the time, it struck me that Gray would be uniquely qualified to weigh in on the traditional dynamics between men and women in mid-century America, the extent to which the Kowalski's relationship was an outlier, and what parts of romantic relationships are conditioning rather than biology.

I reached out to Gray. Hallina responded. And just like that I was on a birthday collision course with the man who'd created his own universe.

I'd long ago read Gray's flagship book, so in preparation for our hour together, I explored fresh content, watching two of his Ted Talks. From them, I learned a metaphor that helped me conceptualize a key difference between Mars brains and Venus brains as Gray explains,

"Women have the superior memory. The hippocampus in a woman's brain is twice as big as in a man's brain. The second story is like a library recording everything on the first floor. On the second floor, she records every mistake you ever made."

The tenets of Mars and Venus have become offensive (to some) in a youth culture where the notion of two genders is seen as a boomer affliction.

Men are like rubber bands; women are like waves.

Gray is – indisputably – a doctor of metaphors (as Anthony Robbins called him during their extended conversation).

And these cleverly packaged gender generalizations often seem too simplistic to be accurate, useful, or liberating. If women don't want men to solve their problems, as Gray asserts (they just want to vent and receive empathy), then can only women solve women's problems? Or, can a woman only resolve her own issues independently? Must the resolution occur only after "she's gotten it all out?" And how long does that take?

Moreover, if men want all the credit for a successful date-night out, does that mean women don't crave acknowledgment for choosing the restaurant in the first place?

Gray offered the world a relationship primer in 1992 that was – in its day – a groundbreaking set of easily digestible principles. Had men and women really changed that much?

My students certainly thought so.

It was my birthday when a salt-and-pepper Gray appeared on my monitor, his plaid button-down shirt (semi-open) added a louche air.

For about ten minutes I had John to myself – an unlikely self-gifted birthday present that couldn't really be tried on for size nor returned to the store if it didn't work out.

One-on-one, Gray is easy to talk to. It's his stock-in-trade. As a young man, he was going to be a priest when a cross-country road trip culminating in a one-night-stand changed everything. Since then, he's guided tens of thousands of couples in workshops and seminars, and 50 million people have read his books – so there's that.

And he is a licensed psychotherapist.

While Gray's wife had died a year or two before our conversation took place, he (understandably) spoke about them in the present tense, but sometimes using graphic hypotheticals.

As a fully remote teacher that year, I hosted this conversation from my home library while my students took up various positions in and around the high school on their laptops. Gray was ensconced in his makeshift, pop-up promotional library, his entire catalog of written work on full-display.

I anticipated that, given the societal shift away from gender as binary, Gray's theories might create some pushback. Still, I couldn't have seen it coming.

Nor could I have seen the power of The Dialogue Essay (as I unimaginatively called it). My father Brainerd Phillipson – who taught English at Newton North High School for several decades – reminded me recently that Truman Capote "invented the dialogue essay" with his publication of "A Day's Work," for which Capote followed a housekeeper named Mary Sanchez from job-to-job, tagging along with her for an entire day of cleanings while keeping her engrossed in conversation.

As Capote famously said, "A conversation is a dialogue, not a monologue. That's why there are so few good conversations: due to scarcity, two intelligent talkers seldom meet."

And he's probably right. Capote was a flamboyant showman, ambidextrous flirt, legendary gossip, and – naturally – a gifted talker (probably the gay, 1960s and 1970s equivalent of Mark Twain).

And that's what my classes were missing: Yes, my students often engaged in meaningful discussion. They could build a thriving discourse that meteorically rose to the abstract, but not enough of them wanted to "dialogue with each other." A hand went up, a point was scored, but were they the proverbial trees that fell in the forest without witness?

So many of them wrote evocative pieces of creative nonfiction, and a good chunk of them would let me share them on my teacher page (Google Classroom), or photocopy a class set to distribute.

But how many of them even read the stuff I posted? How many took home packets of student models and pored over them?

McQuarrie taught me that dialogue should not be used as a vehicle to disseminate information. Gray taught me that dialogues are often awkward, clunky exchanges that fail to bridge the generation gap.

Capote (indirectly, through his writing) showed me that anyone and everyone can be interesting "through dialogue," but – and it's a big caveat – most people are not inherently interesting when they engage in conversation. And if you've ever been to a child's birthday party and listened to the adults making small talk, then you know that Capote's spot-on.

The final inspiration for this prompt came from the U.K. edition of Esquire's Big Black Book: a men's fashion and style magazine published biannually in Britain. It's a thick periodical printed with cardstock covers, featuring beautifully photographed clothing, accessories, watches, wine, and automobiles. But – as they once said about Playboy – I read it for the articles.

That's when I stumbled upon noted Henry James critic, professor, and author Colm Toibin. His short personal essay "All a Novelist Needs" documents a conversation he had around Central Park's Lake with a friend's son. They discussed what's appropriate to wear based on one's age, and what one should – and shouldn't have – in their wardrobe.

Now here's the thing: It's not entirely clear that Toibin actually had that conversation with his son's friend. It feels oddly like an interior monologue between his current "elderly" self and his 20-something persona. Maybe he's attempting to answer the question: What advice would your old self give your youthful self? Except here, he's flipped it: the young man gives ruthless and mirthless fashion wisdom to live by.

So I read that and thought: What if my students wrote Dialogue Essays and enthusiastically performed them?

We were in the midst of a unit on the play Glengarry Glen Ross by David Mamet – the same Mamet that had once inspired Christopher McQuarrie to quip and badinage his way through The Usual Suspects. A dialogue essay just made sense in this context.

Toibin's "All a Novelist Needs" was 90% dialogue and 10% exposition.

What if I got students to capture dialogues as they'd happened or recreate ones that had powerfully impacted them, or that they'd entirely made them?

Maybe they'd be fun to read aloud, engaging to listen to, and – in the process – bring my students together in ways I'd not seen in 30 years of teaching.

And it worked, even better than I could have imagined.

When I asked my juniors (at the end of year) to reflect on what we'd accomplished together, most spoke about The Dialogue Essay assignment as being transformational for us as a unit, during which students wrote and performed (in The Little Theater at Scarsdale High School) intensely personal dialogues they'd recreated from memory. Kamila El Moselhy led the way: she stood and delivered a conversation between her and a boyfriend. Belen Burgert's was about a breakup. Rishi Shadaksharappa about alpha-maledom. Chloe Liu's about a conversation on Metro North with a young child. Jordan Knispel's about the fear of not getting into an ivy-league college. And so on.

That moment in The Little Theatre was when we trusted enough to stop judging each other so we could act as a family would: with unconditional love ... with undying support. Cliche in words yes but not in deeds.

Honestly, I didn't know that I could have all that with a class until academic year 2023–24.

It's funny – I had grown up listening to *nothing but dialogue*: The Howard Stern Radio Show, Charlie Rose, Dr. Ruth Westheimer, David Letterman, and so on.

I hated small talk. I loved "big talk." (I'd even hired "small talk coach" Debra Fine who literally wrote the book on the subject [The Fine Art of Small Talk], hoping for a breakthrough. It didn't happen). In many ways, everywhere I went in life I was forever conducting an interview, engaged with someone in the pursuit of meaningful conversation. Becoming a teacher and working with students one-on-one during office hours was a natural extension of that practice.

I'd grown up reading the hard-boiled detective novels of Robert B. Parker, who'd invented a gumshoe named Spenser, and I'd gotten to spend several hours with Parker when he visited my father's school in the early 1980s. Parker told me that sometimes he'd sit in the Ritz bar in Boston and listen to conversations, jot down notes, and build his dialogues from that.

Postmodern novelist Don DeLillo told me – in a series of letters – that his important novel White Noise wasn't a satire of the media or an attack on a liberal arts education but simply the result of listening to the conversations that came out of a Bronxville, NY street, and a neighbor's family home. And while he didn't mean that literally, he meant that the rhythms, vibrations, and dialogue exchanges of real people greatly informed his character development.

That Toibin essay unblocked me like holistic healers (or yoginis) working on someone's theoretical root chakras.

I felt that everyone had a great conversation in them (unlike Capote), and that it would be – by default – performative when it happened. The Little Theater at Scarsdale High School was the site of the first real "event" I'd taken in at Scarsdale High School (SHS) in 2003. My then mentor and good friend Seth Evans was the advisor to The Shakespeare Club. He'd invited me to a Friday night performance of The Tempest. I sat with English teacher Chris Renino, whose wife is Susan Marshall (the Director of Dance at Princeton and one time MacArthur and Guggenheim Fellow). Sitting with the husband of a three time "Bessie" award winner and watching my friend's sound direction of The Tempest was inspiring. Seth went on to study at the prestigious Directors Lab at Lincoln Center, and explore poetry at Yale with Helen Vendler – in the summers between teaching English at SHS.

From very early on, I felt the specialness of that space: The Little Theater.

It's the place that would inspire me to write a letter to my juniors: "English Class – It's a Family, or It's Nothing." And I meant every word of it.

And in that space with a grand piano on casters in the corner, risers flanking stage left and stage right, and 100 or so uncomfortable wooden folding chairs with swivel top desks facing the performance space, I asked my class on its in-school field trip:

Does anyone want to read their Dialogue Essay aloud?
And the hands went up.
And Kamila El Moselhy broke the ice.

Two days later we'd shed tears together, Chloe Liu had volunteered to read the alternating parts for three presenters, followed by more tears, hugs, laughter, and the music of overlapping voices filling the space that I'd returned to for 22 years, but one that had never felt like my own symphony hall with its prized orchestra, and I the conductor, until now.

Here's Prompt Eight

The Dialogue Essay Write-Up

So – we've just finished our Glengarry Glen Ross unit – looking at (more than anything) the "language of Mamet." He trafficks in profanity but also trafficks in characters' "cries for help." Almost everything a character in a Mamet play says is – quite literally – a crying out.

We've also looked at persuasion, manipulation, influence, and power during this unit.

The idea for Essay 8 is "The Dialogue Essay."

What is a Dialogue Essay? It's an essay made up (almost) ENTIRELY of dialogue.

I'm providing ONE specific model for this assignment (as I've never done it before). It's from a noted Henry James critic, professor and author named Colm Toibin. He's a brilliant man, and a major literary scholar.

For the men's fashion and style magazine Esquire's Big Black Book, Toibin wrote a "dialogue essay" titled "All a Novelist Needs," about a conversation he had around the lake in Central Park with a friend's son. They discussed what's appropriate to wear based on one's age, and what one should – and shouldn't have – in their wardrobe.

So – Two Things

1. It makes 110% sense to me at this point in the course to do a "dialogue essay" given that we've just finished a play that is 90% dialogue.
2. I was shocked by how powerful a simple conversation of questions and answers could be so life changing, life affirming, and have the level of depth that it did. I had never EVER SEEN a "dialogue essay" before Toibin's piece in Esquire.

What I'm asking you to do for Essay 8

ONE: Read Toibin's "All A Novelist Needs" dialogue essay. It's a PDF attachment on classroom. It's linked in this assignment. Make notes about

HOW he uses the dialogue he uses, and what he accomplishes through DIALOGUE only. Put in YOUR SHARED DOC.

TWO: Consider one of five things to "write about" (or speak about) for this essay:

a What's a meaningful conversation your present self might have with your past self?
b What's a "fear" you're trying to work out about your present or future self?
c What's an important conversation that you've actually had, fantasized about having, pretended to have (like those recreated conversations we have with ourselves about how we WISH it had gone when we talked to someone, or what we'd say to that person if we had the chance or the gall to say)?
d What's a painful conversation you've had that contained layers of depth to it that you would like to recreate and/or fictionalize, taking artistic license or liberties with in service of writing this essay?
e What is something that you're truly trying to persuade yourself or others (or another) to do, change, be, become, or consider – or BUY, or TRY, or BELIEVE?

Make Notes about WHICH ONE Appeals to You, and What You'd Like to Explore. Put in YOUR SHARED DOC

THREE: Recreate OR create the dialogue (the conversation) – write out whatever you remember (either thinking or actually saying, or thinking about when they were talking, or thinking A when you were saying B, etc.).

Put in YOUR SHARED DOC

FOUR: Edit, polish, and push your dialogue further – whip it into a finished draft. Only ONE small paragraph (at the beginning) can be NON DIALOGUE. The entirety of the essay (beyond that introductory paragraph) MUST BE all dialogue, all the time (except for sparse "dialogue tag" like he said, she said).

NOTE: This does not HAVE to be a conversation between you and someone else (or you and yourself), but it probably should be.

This conversation can be a creation or a recreation; it can be fiction, or it can be nonfiction. But it must be ONE of the following things (a–e above).

Finished rough draft of the conversation is due at the end of class on _____. Complete steps one – three by _____. Make a Doc, share it with me. Name it Essay 8: The Dialogue Essay. See the parts labeled "put in your shared doc" above.

1,000 words bare minimum – 2,000 words maximum.

9
THE LIVING ARTISTS LITERARY RESEARCH PAPER

When I got to Scarsdale High School in 2003, I was handed a paperback called Ten Steps to Writing the Research Paper. It had been a Bible of sorts for a most formidable English teacher – Diane Wrobleski – who also headed up the district's mentoring program for new teachers.

Needless to say, I was not inspired by a textbook on how to write research papers using a cookie-cutter, one-size-fits-none approach. It felt pedantic, because it was.

For juniors, literary research papers are both a rite of passage and a curse beyond measure. Twenty years ago, I began to see some students emotionally crumble during this unit. It didn't matter how many bite-sized pieces you broke the process down into, there were serious casualties (in one case each year – for four years straight – I believe this assignment was a tipping point that made a student take a literal leave of absence).

Today, I don't see my Department place the same intense emphasis on the literary research paper (as it's no longer a graduation requirement), and the consequence of that is twofold:

1 Students are investigating a book or its author (for longform essays) in more non-traditional ways.
2 Students aren't falling apart because of the research paper.

I like number two – a lot. I also understand that (in a post-Covid world) students are coming undone for myriad reasons.

As for number one – the likely truth is that even in 2003 under the most maniacally structured Department Chair I've ever worked for – students weren't (wholesale) conducting meaningful inquiry for their "literary research papers." Yes, my chair would put his students on a Procrustean table, stretch them out within an inch of their lives, and turn them into topnotch outliners, but does that necessarily make for great research papers that students are invested in?

Today, it's still a "high-stakes" assignment. It's the longest paper they'll write in high school. It requires the forced integration of primary and secondary sources. It entails a great many "steps" that – in my humble opinion – can create more stress than relieve. If you are a student who's overwhelmed by the scope of a project, breaking it into many parts will only attenuate the pain and anxiety if:

a The student is legitimately invested in what they're looking into and what they're (ultimately) writing about.
b The student has a genuine interest in gaining the skills that each individual step of the process requires to complete.
c The student has the patience and fortitude to stay with a long-term project that requires them to search and search again (as Stephen Mounkhall points out – it's called research for a reason), despite their efforts often yielding fruitlessness.

For me, the epiphany happened one Saturday in the early aughts when my cell phone rang while taking my first hit off a milkshake in Nyack, NY. On the line was the raspy voice of veteran English teacher Jeanne Cooper who'd been tasked with relaying a parent demand. Essentially, I was to immediately head back to Scarsdale HS, somehow get into my office, and locate a student's stack of 4×6 index cards that had contained a junior's primary source quotes and annotations.

The student had been one of those cases of profound collapse I mentioned above. She'd left Scarsdale High School (SHS) for a period of eight weeks for mental health reasons, but – somehow, suddenly now – needed to get her hands on these cards and work on her research paper.

Listen – therapy comes in many forms, but I firmly believed that the least important thing in that young woman's life at the time was completing work for my class.

If you know anything about being an untenured teacher, then you can guess what happened next. I crossed the Tappan Zee Bridge (now the Cuomo), found a custodian who took pity on me and let me into the building on a late Saturday afternoon, found the cards, and met the girl's father in the parking lot by the baseball field to hand them over. It was just two dozen or so purple and pink pieces of small lined oak tag with a few quotes on one side and some musings on the verso. I can't even remember if, when, or how my student finished that paper. I can't remember her name. I can't remember what she wrote about (or didn't write about). But I have the same strong sensation now, as I type this paragraph that I had in 2004. It was an action signal that told me that this rigid, inflexible, unforgiving "10 Step Process" was no way to go about achieving a meaningful, investigative, reflective, and thoughtful practice.

Now you might say to me: Just have your students make "digital index cards" and they can access them anytime, anywhere.

And I'd tell you: Yes, I did that for years. Back then it was Word Documents (not Google Doc), but it served the same purpose, and it saved students a step: they could copy and paste their quotes and analysis into their draft.

But if you *had* asked me that, and even if you listened to my answer, you'd be missing the point I'm going to make now:

Your thinking is messy. Your writing should be messy, too. Just less messy than your thinking.

That phrase is printed somewhere (else) in this book that you're reading right now because it's that important, it's that central, to what I aspire to do each day in the classroom, that I've repeated it – here – once again.

There's a fatal flaw in most essay prompts, and the research paper is no exception. Most English teachers ask students to write about a book, poem, short story, essay, or subject that they are decidedly *not* the expert on.

I'm a pseudo-expert on The Great Gatsby, Macbeth, The Stranger, Othello, White Noise, In the Lake of the Woods, Invisible Man, Glengarry Glen Ross, A Streetcar Named Desire, A Few Good Men, The Sweet Hereafter, and so on, because I've taught these texts for three decades – that's 30 opportunities I've had to achieve some kind of meaningful familiarity with these works.

But students? The exceptional ones read *most of* the books you assign – once. End of story. The vast majority of students find any way possible to cut corners: Spark Notes, YouTube video essays, ChatGPT summaries. Colleague Jennifer Rosenzweig once relayed that a student told her he'd made it through his entire four years at SHS without having read a single book. Not even one chapter.

Now, of course, that's atypical. The English Department at SHS is one of the best in the country (and I know this to be true from visiting a great many districts and from teaching at six different public high schools over my career – including my student-teaching and practicum). But the question is: Why are we asking students to write the longest, most involved paper about a book they're no expert on, a book they've only read once (if we're lucky), and a book that is – usually – a classic novel or play that has been drilled for oil a million times over by critics, Redditors, and bloggers, and that well has likely run dry?

When will we admit that most literary research papers suffer one of these fates?

a   It's a study in confirmation bias and a regurgitation of the prevailing wisdom on the subject.
b   It's no different from what ChatGPT could accomplish through its own aggregation, curation, and synthesis of your student's topic.
c   It's a prescribed process – which is inherently stiff and formal – so the finished product has all the hallmarks of rigidity, including how quotes and evidence are framed (this quote shows, this proves, etc.), how transitions are articulated (however, therefore, firstly, moreover, etc.), and how voice is largely absent from the final draft (it's like food that's denatured because it's overcooked: there's been too much feedback along the way, too many quotes crammed into the outline, and too many placeholders that negate the possibility of spontaneity or "messiness").
d   It's a "collection of quotes" versus a "deep dive" into a worthy subject.
e   It's a glorified "book report," heavy on the summary, adding little (if anything) to the conversation about the student's chosen book.

The solution?

It was to lean into what was already wildly appealing for me to engage in: **living artists and authors.**

From a common-sense perspective, which of the following is more compelling?

a   To spend an entire quarter of English class looking "deeply" into a book that you didn't enthusiastically choose (or picked from a list of ten works that you – the student – also didn't select), then writing the most ambitious paper of your HS years based on those discoveries?

OR

b   To spend as much time as you'd like (within reason, of course) connecting with a book and its author until you reach your own logical (or illogical) conclusions, then write-up the experience of that journey?

Well, if you put it like that, Wes, it's so damn obvious. Maybe 10% of all students would choose option "A" due to some fear or phobia about connecting with successful adults, feeling intimidated by "meeting their hero," chafing against the alleged lack of structure, fearing their own procrastination, or fanboying out in the presence of their favorite author, but there's no question that choice "B" offers all sorts of benefits and personal enrichment that "A" simply cannot.

It's like asking a potential employee: Would you rather work 40 hours a week for a salary and benefits (health insurance, sick days, a 403B, etc.), or would you rather just have the salary part?

Students require more motivation than just: I'm a really demanding teacher with high standards, (and one size fits all anyway), so, here's my prescription for your research paper. Follow these ten steps (and never deviate from them), check in with me once a week, and – when I tell you – let's go over your full outline with a magnifying glass. I'll mark it up with a red pencil or felt-tip pen, and you'll go away to dutifully make the changes I've laid out for you.

That method definitely worked 40, 30, even 20 years ago. But just as newspapers are no longer run by men with a red pen behind the ear, a visor pulled tightly over the eyes, and a U-shaped table where they'd slash your story with a sullen scowl, classrooms can't be managed that way either.

Enter Don DeLillo

DeLillo is the premier postmodern author still working today. He's nearly 90 and has written offbeat and prescient novels since 1971. His first full-length work Americana follows the jargony exploits of a TV exec. His third novel Great Jones Street looks at the profound isolation induced by fame and stardom. His sixth, Running Dog, is a satire of Rolling Stone magazine and a neo-noir potboiler. Most famously, White Noise takes aim at the relative value of a liberal arts education and the tedium of suburban family life.

His novels have seized upon everything from the Kennedy assassination to 9/11.

It's possible that he'll win the Nobel Prize in Literature – perhaps even posthumously.

When I lived in Bronxville, NY, a vanilla village bordering Mount Vernon just north of The Bronx, Don DeLillo did too. We lived across the street from one another.

I've been in the same room as Don DeLillo, just not at the same time. And "to enter a room is to agree to a certain kind of behavior" (to quote from White Noise). In this instance, I'd set the terms.

It was to happen in the doorman's "break-room" at The Croydon apartment building in Bronxville. It's a half-dozen stories, put up in the mid-1930s, with Art Deco flourishes that begin and end with its lobby. Doorman

John Folkes would sometimes save a parking spot for me (we'd swap cars at the end of his shift; I'd be extra generous come holidays), but between signing for residents' packages and walking a Schnauzer or two, he'd also acted as the go-between for Wes Phillipson and Don DeLillo.

My written appeal to the National Book Award winner (among other PEN nods and a near Pulitzer for Underworld) was simple enough but thoughtfully constructed:

"I have two complete collections of your first edition novels and plays that I would truly appreciate having autographed by you. If you're willing, I'll leave them with my doorman for you to sign at your convenience. We'll never have to cross paths. My understanding is that you live across the street."

There was more to the letter than that, of course, and it wasn't our first time communicating.

I had never heard of DeLillo before coming to teach at Scarsdale. Two colleagues of mine sometimes assigned White Noise to their advanced classes or added it to their research paper book rotation. It's a mid-1980s angsty meditation on how media and technology are undoing us, but it's well disguised as disaster porn and character study. It may be the author at his most prescient – pointing towards a near future landscape dotted with interfering Alexas and Echoes, ambiguous lifestyle drug adverts, and a generalized dissociated way of moving through one's privileged and mechanized world. DeLillo writes of people self-relegated to information silos before "echo chambers" was even a term of endearment.

White Noise follows a Hitler Studies professor through a litany of his worst fears come to pass, as he holds fast to (and literally clutches) a hardbound copy of Mein Kampf as a life-preserver-meets-security-blanket. Jack Gladney is invisible without his uniform (black graduation robe), and adrift without his perverse self-help Bible. The novel is set in the fictional midwestern town of College-on-the-Hill, but it's undoubtedly a proxy for Bronxville's Sarah Lawrence College.

When I tracked down DeLillo's address on a free people-finder website in 2006, I wasn't yet plugged into Google Maps – which had just launched into public consciousness. I'd come to learn that his home was 0.3 miles from The Croydon by car, but a mere kitty-corner on foot. I passed his house each day when returning from work.

A teacher friend told me that DeLillo would "never respond" to my humble epistolary approach and was skeptical even after I'd thumbtacked Don's postmarked, handwritten envelope to his office cork-board.

DeLillo types everything (except when he writes on envelopes). And I don't mean "type" the way we use it colloquially. No. I mean he uses only one machine: an Olympia SM 3.

The letter's concluding sentence to me reads, "Currently, I'm being stalked by a novel day and night, but I'll do my best to respond to your students' questions in the time available."

About two weeks later I'd received five typed pages, half-spaced, with some hand-done corrections. And while I can't quote (or even paraphrase) from those pages because I was warned by DeLillo that "these remarks are for classroom use only and not for circulation elsewhere," I can say that much of what was contained in the letter was both surprising and conceptually abstract. It addressed aspects of White Noise that I was certain satirized American institutions. I was wrong. The five pages contained sentences that were breathtaking or – conversely – life affirming. Phrase-making for DeLillo must be effortless, second nature, or just an internal-set-of-rhythms-made-public.

My biggest takeaway: A future Nobel Prize winner had taken an hour out of his day (while also finishing up writing his novel Falling Man) to thoughtfully engage with my high school students' earnest questions about White Noise. Questions that only he could possibly answer. Answers that would help my students navigate a book they were currently reading, researching, and writing about.

To me, that's no different than having John Steinbeck field questions about Of Mice and Men, or Sylvia Plath entertaining students' queries about The Bell Jar (as they're reading it). DeLillo's five-page letter informed the writing of 20-plus students that year. One couldn't find those answers on the internet (and still – to this day – cannot). ChatGPT can't address the nuances of author intent, especially when the questions that unlocked those answers had never before been asked. We're in the age of "bespoke." It's a cultural craze. There are bespoke suits (naturally), bicycles, coffins, dollhouses, diet programs, retirement plans, training regimens, and bespoke home-builders, yet we fail to offer our students real choice when it comes to something that dominates their year in English class. It's the assignment they'll spend the most time and attention on.

Yes, we give students the illusion of choice.

And that got me thinking about how "impossible" my friend and English Department colleague Stephen Mounkhall had said it would be to reach DeLillo. But it wasn't. It was a Monday in 2006 when I put my letter to Don in a mailbox across the street from the A&P grocer. I just drove my car right up to it, slid it in the slot, and had no idea what would come next. Until I heard back from DeLillo two weeks later.

If a literary heavyweight like DeLillo would take part in my classroom experiment to have students engage with "living artists," then who else would take the bait?

Over the next 20 years, I've seen my students correspond with Arthur Golden (Memoirs of a Geisha), Ernest Cline's literary agent (Ready Player One), Jeremy Eaton (Future Visions), Frank Ticheli (Vesuvius), Russell Banks (The Sweet Hereafter), Dan Piepenbring (The Beautiful Ones – written with Prince), Hua Hsu (Stay True – which won The Pulitzer), and countless others.

What I've discovered is that – at the very least – students writing an English research paper should have the option to undertake a passion project. Because that's so antithetical to the typical experience of: *Hey kid – pick from this list of three plays or ten novels and ….*

Students *can* be enthusiastic about their research papers, and many of them get through it without breaking (much of) a sweat. A small percentage even enjoy the process and the product. But giving everyone *the option* of choosing a worthy text from an author who is still alive and well – and accessible somewhere on this planet – is the kind of enrichment that separates my English classes from most others.

Take Judy Blume for Instance

Blume is one year younger than DeLillo. She's from Elizabeth, New Jersey, and my student "April" had spent bits and pieces of her childhood there. Blume's books have a way of aging with the reader, as there are stories for all levels (from Superfudge to Wifey).

April had grown up with Blume (or at least her books), and when it came time to write a research paper in my junior American literature class, I presented a Google Slides deck entitled: "My search is not your search," to get their creative juices flowing.

In my presentation, I recounted how I'd come to discover that the graphic artist who'd illustrated some of my favorite book covers and dust-jackets was actually my neighbor in Mount Kisco, NY. James Barkley has created over 8,000 paintings, stamps, and book illustrations. He'd designed and drawn the cover for Stephen King's Carrie (the Signet paperback), the detective novel The Laughing Policeman (by Maj Sjöwall and Per Wahlöö), among countless other high-impact, visually interesting pieces.

The pitch I was making to my students was: You need to be a bit obsessed with anything you're going to write 12 pages about. It's going to be that *fixation* that sustains you over an entire marking period to keep searching, questioning, writing, and revising. When you've chosen the right topic, you'll feel both a lightness (of spirit and body) and also a sense of urgency. It's a miraculous dichotomy.

When I discovered that Barkley was living down the street from me, I immediately reached out to him (by snail mail) and heard back within days. He was enthusiastic about helping my students understand his approach to marketing books. After a handful of email exchanges, I started connecting some dots. Barkley seemed a likely candidate to have done the paperback cover illustration for the Stephen King school-shooter book Rage (written as Richard Bachman in 1977). It led me down an internet rabbit hole of my own making, reflexively reinforcing the beliefs I held about what constitutes meaningful research:

> When students at SHS take part in an enrichment program called Science Research (working with a faculty member in the hard sciences as their advisor, and finding a mentor working in their field of study), they do it from a place of pure interest and unconditional investment.

When those student-participants talk about the Science Research program, they light up like idealistic children choosing their own Halloween costumes. If you ask them to tell you what they're looking into and how they came to be doing it, they transform into total science nerds – and it's just wonderful to see.

But – if you ask any junior in a high school English class about their research paper – forget it. Their answer, and their demeanor, will likely depress you. It's often a heavy response, and one that reeks of obligation and anxiety vs. possibility and creative endeavor.

Now that's not true of everyone, and my own "research" here (ironically) is far from scientific or comprehensive, but it's actually the exception to have a junior who is really humming along and finding bliss and fulfillment while in the throes of their literary research paper.

At least, that used to be the case for many of my own students. During the 2023–24 academic year, I did have April working on her Judy Blume paper (without Blume's help, sure, but still), and Isaac Tiomkin exploring the adaptation of Bret Easton Ellis' novel of Wall Street sociopathy (American Psycho) into Mary Harron's film version.

Neither April nor Issac attempted to contact Blume or Easton Ellis, but the former's final research paper was one of the most touching and sentimentally poignant journeys back into one's childhood through the texts of one author that I've ever read, and the latter was an exercise in dot-connecting and stark vulnerability.

If I had been a certain kind of teacher with a certain set of standards, I never would have indulged an honors-level student's request to re-read and reconsider Judy Blume (who is a literary lightweight when compared to much of what we teach in the course). If I were the type of educator who objected to my students choosing mature and indelicate content to engage with, then I never would have gotten the gift of Isaac's American Psycho paper.

Another student in the course, Lucas Heidbreder, did reach out to his all-time favorite author Jeremy Eaton. Dr. Eaton practices family medicine in Lacey, Washington at Providence St. Peter Hospital, but has a secret life on Amazon(.com). He's the author of science fiction novels with a niche following, the most popular being his series called Future Visions. The premise is that aliens will wipe out humanity in 27 years. The open question is: Can they be stopped between now and then?

Minutes after we phoned Eaton's nurse (who told us it was the good doctor's day off), Jeremy called us back. Most remarkably, he couldn't believe that a student wanted to write a literary research paper about Future Visions, a book that was barely his side-hustle. He and Lucas began corresponding via email over the next several weeks (as needed), with Eaton being his tour guide through space, time, and alien invasions.

As a member of the same English Department for over 20 years, I can say that we've had many conversations about "author intent" – and whether or not there's value in asking students to contemplate such things. Some colleagues have said to me: Author intent doesn't matter because you'll never know what they were thinking when they wrote it. Others have said: Just have students stick to the text, because that's all they can prove, anyway.

Well, Lucas had connected with Eaton to gain access to the one man who *could* answer his burning questions. In return, Eaton had gotten his work affirmed by his greatest admirer. In the end, they (collaboratively) produced a literary research paper that is both a document of their synergy and proof of concept of my approach to teaching the research paper as I do.

Who am I proving my concept to? Well, perhaps you, my dear reader, but more so – me.

Finally, my junior Rishi Shadaksharappa wrote about Ernest Cline's Ready Player One (another sci-fi work – this time about a virtual reality world called The Oasis). Cline was then meeting with Mark Zuckerberg on a deal to bring his RPO (Ready Player One) franchise to the Metaverse. When we reached out to Cline's literary agent Yfat Reiss Gendell, we found a responsive partner in helping us gain access to her author.

Rishi drafted some thoughtful questions that Yfat promised to pass on to Cline (who was on a book tour at the time for Bridge to Bat City) that were included in his email:

Dear Yfat Reiss-Gende,

I want to thank you for such a quick response. I'm having a lot of fun writing this research paper about Cline's masterpiece Ready Player One.

Part of my paper will be focused on evaluating the significance and implications of virtual reality. For this reason, I will be delving into Cline's recent partnership with Zuckerberg's Metaverse – the much-anticipated launch of Readyverse.

I have 3 questions that I would like to ask Mr. Cline if possible:

1 I would like to understand your intentions behind the release of the Readyverse. Can you achieve a sort of "happy balance" with VR without having the social and political repercussions shown in your novel?
2 I would also like to understand RPO. What compelled you to write such an impactful piece? Is it a cautionary tale chronicling the dangers of mass-producing VR, or used as a platform to garner support for your future VR enterprises?
3 Lastly, I would like to know if you consider the novel to be postmodern when compared to other YA Sci-Fi/Dystopian ones? If so, will the Readyverse take a postmodern approach compared to other VR platforms? How so?

I look forward to hearing back from you with hope that it will include Mr. Cline's responses.

Thanks again,
Rishi Shadaksharappa

* * *

Ernest Cline ended up being a dead end. It was a complicated cocktail of issues: he'd been overscheduled by his publisher for events surrounding the book release; he wanted Rishi to sign an N.D.A. because of the ongoing negotiations with Zuckerberg's Meta; and he – perhaps – didn't have a compelling incentive to help out a stranger with their schoolwork.

And that is part of the street-calculus one must undertake when thinking about working with a living artist: Can they give my students what they want and need – and in a timely manner? And what's in it for them if they do? (Moreover, it is safe for my students to engage with Author X or Author Y?)

Rishi was more-than-willing to sign the nondisclosure agreement – he wasn't going to spill any secrets anyway, and it was highly unlikely that Cline was going to spill any tea of his own while in conversation with a 16 year old.

During the research paper unit, there were about a dozen emails between myself, Rishi, and Yfat Reiss-Gende – but never Cline. There was hopeful and optimistic language on Reiss-Gende's part. She really pushed for this exchange of energy to happen – a meeting of the minds to discuss future shock, or how to avoid it.

In the end Rishi didn't need Cline. He – instead – wondered aloud (and on paper), how would Cline have answered my queries? What can I learn in the absence of his responses? Why would he be reticent to talk about these things, and how can I grow something interesting from the kernel of that negative space?

Here's Prompt Nine

Part One: Literary Research Project: An Introduction to the Project

The idea here is simple yet powerful:

I've read thousands of research papers and they're almost ALL forgettable. Most of them underwhelmed me. Many over-promised and under-delivered. They're exercises in confirmation bias: A student gets an idea they like, so that student proves it's true. Most of the RP essays I've read since 1995 have been something along these lines:

- I have an obvious idea about something anyone with connected brain cells could (also) see or notice. Let me write about that for a dozen pages.
- I have a "truth" (that is *factually true*). Let me prove that *it is so*.
- I have no purpose other than "I have to write a research paper for you," so, YUP, that's what I'll do.
- I have no ideas for my topic, so I'll come to you – the teacher – and co-opt your ideas, write that paper, and it will disappoint both of us because I have no stake in it, what-so-ever, as you failed to make me self-reliant.

> ONE: So what, then, exactly, am I suggesting you set out to do here for this project? What would I advise you to do for your research paper, as your court-appointed advocate?
> TWO: And what does it have to do with "forgetting" vs. "being unforgettable?"
> THREE: And what – in the world – does it have to do with 1986 Fleer short-print basketball cards (the image atop this Doc)?

> I'll take these one at a time (from above):

1 What I'm Suggesting: You need to be the expert on whatever topic you choose. No literary critic is "not the expert," or "they research *to become* the expert." NO. They are the authority on that niche thing.

Period. Full stop. If you're not "the expert" or "an expert," then you cannot write this research paper in a way that will move or convince me that you should have.

Conducting research is not the same as "not knowing about something." **Conducting research means** "I am gathering my evidence, dot-connecting, and building my case."

2 Be Unforgettable: Junior Jackie Kershner brought everything she had – every memory and color and sensory experience – to her Collins Avenue Miami essay (about "In the Air Tonight") for our class. I will never forget it because SHE will never forget it. You are not allowed to write a research paper that is devoid of color, voice, personality, memory, and sensory experience. Avery Dickstein invests 100% of her intellectual and familial soul into everything she writes. Her essays would disappoint if she didn't. You can't "be unforgettable" following a "sandwich model" paragraph, or framing a quote by saying, "This quote shows..." TRUST ME. I remember, like, four research papers from 30 years of teaching because:
   a I was not a great teacher.
   b I cared more about appearances than I cared about the quality, depth, and integrity of my students' work. I cared more that "other teachers thought I was serious," and "that parents and students would take me seriously," than I cared about the depth and passion of my students' work. And I didn't even know it. And a senior in 2003 – Lauren Gotchman – tried to warn me.

3 1986–87 Fleer Basketball cards (Michael Jordan's rookie card): I was an HS freshman the year history's most valuable and rarest basketball cards were sold in retail stores, stationary, and discount stores, (places like Caldors and K-Mart). In 1986 and 1987, you could buy ONE PACK of these cards for 50 cents. Today, in 2024, an "unsearched pack" sells for (between) $3,000.00 and $6,000.00. Why does that matter to me? It's a mystery that I really want to "unpack" (every pun intended). What sports cards were I buying in 1987, and why – oh why – didn't I ever buy a pack of 86–87 NBA Fleer? Who sold them in my town of Holliston, and what "epic journey" could I embark on to find out: What was I doing in 1987 that made me "miss this chance of a lifetime," and why do I still care to this day? *Now that's a research project worth my time.*

So what "next step" am I asking you to take?

Write 650–1,000 words about your intention for this research paper project. Tell me everything you hope to accomplish, why it matters to you, the layers that organically occur within the framework of your topic's journey, and the ones you'll artificially construct.

I'm doing this project, too, as I've done every single project I've assigned you this year. And every essay I've written for you this year was – literally – for you this year. I didn't recycle essays from last year.

In the end, I don't care what "kind" of "literary essay" you write, or what kind of literature you read, (as long as it's American in one way or another), I just care that this is something:

- YOU NEED to do (vs. HAVE to do)
- You are (more or less) OBSESSED with
- You have a clear "way into"
- You CAN write
- You can NERD OUT on
- You can personally intersect with
- You can add something to the existing conversation about
- You can innovate within the topic.

Some things I'm considering for my own (Wes Phillipson) literary research paper of 8–12 pages:

NOTE: I came up with these six topics in five and a half minutes this afternoon – and I'd be excited to pursue any one of them:

a How my own "profanity journey" culminated in my first time teaching Mamet's Glengarry Glen Ross?
b Where I was in 1987, why I didn't buy 86–87 NBA Fleer sports cards, and how discovering Bulls' coach Phil Jackson's book Sacred Hoops should have been my consolation prize?
c Why I am obsessed with the ultra-violent films of Clint Eastwood, despite having reservations about guns and the NRA?
d Whether the "literature of violence" has a place in public high schools.
e Whether the works of Richard Rudolph can really be considered part of "the Great American Songbook" (as someone who made music with everyone from Minnie Riperton to New Edition).
f Whether "my year on Zoom" was a redefining one for me, or just an exercise in futility. Did what I taught that year make any impact at all? Did it really give me pause? Make me reconsider what I was doing in the classroom? Could it have – possibly – meant anything (at all) to my students? What did – or didn't – The Great Gatsby or Macbeth mean to me or my students that year?

For our next class meeting: have a printed-out copy of your 650–1,000 word Research Paper (Essay Nine) mission statement. Have shared it with me (I'm the editor, you're the owner: call it – "Essay 9: RP Mission Statement").

Send it to me as a PDF and a Google Doc.
Have a working title. A working subtitle.
Have an image. A caption.
A byline.
A credo.
And – above all else – a purpose.

I'm asking you to write 650–1,000 words by our next class meeting. I just wrote 1,442 in 30 minutes. If you've seized upon the right topic, the way forward will flow from you effortlessly.

**

Part Two of Assignment Write-Up: Your Research Paper Must Be Robust and Readable

Above All Else, Your Research Paper Must Be: Robust and Readable

The research paper that you embark on MUST BE:

ROBUST

- There are both broad and specific areas of exploration, investigation, and interest.
- There is a great deal (or opportunity for) intersectionality.
- There are numerous distinctions (or nuanced things) to sustain an argument from various angles and perspectives and layers.
- There are big claims "baked inside" of your idea.

READABLE

- The goal is to make the final draft of this paper engaging, voice-filled, with elegant and seamless quote integration.
- The paper cannot be a "collection of quotes" – quotes must be used sparingly, with "quote-weaving" vs. "quote-bombing" (to use a quote in this essay you must think about its essential nature – it must be NECESSARY – and how you can weave it into the sentence or paragraph unselfconsciously).
- You can't afford to "lose the reader" at any point in the essay: it's an 8–10 page paper (or longer), roughly 4,000 words. The idea is that you must think about things like paragraph length and type, white space,

form choices, information, and exposition vs. personal or illuminating anecdote, etc.

An example of a "worthy" project scope that would likely sustain a robust and readable paper:

From student April:

"Judy Blume has sold 100 million copies of her books, most of which are exercises in worldbuilding her personal, specific version of Elizabeth, New Jersey. My mother grew up in New Jersey, and I often return to visit family. There are copies of Judy Blume books that once were in my mother's library that are now on my own bookshelf. Blume's books have different series for age-specific audiences, there are the Easy Blume books (for children), the YA novels, and the adult ones (like Wifey – her first novel). In nearly all cases, they're set in Elizabeth, examining everything from the banality of suburban existence and extramarital affairs to – in Tales of a Fourth Grade Nothing – the adventures of Pete, Fudge and his pet turtle (also in suburban Jersey). There is even a documentary about Blume's life in, and literary use of, New Jersey that I'll tap into. My Mom's past and present (at times) in NJ, as well as my own part-time life in NJ, as well as the possibility of and desire to attend Princeton, and even raise my own children there (or in Scarsdale) someday in the not-too-too distant future."

Where to begin:

ONE: What "kind of" paper do you want to write? One that involves the artist (like, interviewing the author), or one that doesn't involve the creator, and why?
TWO: What are some "works" that might really engage your thinking and feeling? What work (or works) have you "been thinking a great deal about," or have been "thinking about reading, watching, or listening to for some time?"

And what have you been considering about them?

THREE: Pick ONE work to "commit to" and give yourself a "directive." IT MUST BE A LITERARY WORK: A collection of poems, essays, or short stories, novella, novel, or play.

For instance, my literary research paper is going to be on The Catcher in the Rye and the "at odds" relationship that students and teachers at SHS have with the novel.

Specifically, I want to "get at" why we teach it, what it means that we do, and what students take away from it.

More specifically, I want to explore "teachers' approaches to teaching Catcher" (some teach it as a religious text in praise of Buddhism, others focus on The Hero's Journey, yet others see it as a commentary on the loss of innocence), and whether students "read it for pleasure" or even enjoy it, and how many of them "learned the lessons the teacher was trying to teach," or if it even matters "what we teach or how we teach it."

The goal, in the end, is to write a literary research paper that

- Adds something new to the ongoing conversation about your work
- Is as "voice-filled" as the work you're critiquing
- Is roughly 4,000 words
- Integrates quotes seamlessly
- Is preoccupied with "weighing-in" vs. "synthesizing what's already well known".

Part Three of Assignment Write-Up: Research Paper Mission Statement Teacher Model[1]

Note

1 See https://www.routledge.com/9781032987842.

10

NICE TO MEET YOU AND GOODBYE

7 Intros and 7 Outros

Student-writers would do well to carefully study the introduction and conclusion of Christopher Nolan's 2010 movie Inception.

The opening scene features dream-scammer Dom Cobb (DiCaprio) face down – unconscious – washed up on the shore of a foreign land – possibly an island. It starts in media res (Latin for "in the middle of the action"). No context. Just an assault rifle pointed at him menacingly as his lifeless body is checked for weapons. There's the butt of a handgun protruding from the small of his back, tucked into his pant's waistband. He's taken to the ornate dining room of a man so ancient that he resembles a turtle whose shell has been removed.

The ending scene is infamous for its controversial ambiguity. Dom's totem – a brushed nickel spinning top is set in motion and left on the corner of his family's dining-room table. As the story's antagonistic hero leaves the totem behind to reunite with his son and daughter (James and Phillipa) playing in the backyard, the viewer is left to decide as Nolan abruptly cuts to black:

> Did the spinning top fall over, or is it still turning on that table in perpetuity? If the former is true, then Cobb is back in the real world after escaping his perpetual nightmare. He's Stateside with his children and his architect-professor father. The murder charge has been wiped from his criminal record. If the latter is true, then Cobb has deluded himself into thinking one *can* go home again. And his dead wife Mal – from beyond the grave – still controls his every thought, as he (literally and figuratively) sleepwalks through life.

When students "construct" their essay's intro and outro (their paper's hello and goodbye), there's little in the way of intelligent design. Most English teachers across America teach one or two ways in, and one of two ways out:

In: It's usually some generic or broad advice that sounds like this – do something to get the reader's attention: Ask a question, use an outside quote, or create a hook that will live up to its name (by actually engaging the reader).

Out: It's usually binary advice – either restate your thesis and summarize your paper's main points, or "go book-to-world." Occasionally, middle school teachers introduce the notion of "hook-and-return" (which involves setting up the paper's hook in the intro, then returning to it in the outro, so the paper comes full-circle).

Like training wheels on a Schwinn (thank Heaven for the advent of balance bikes), students (early-on) need formulas and prescriptions for writing. Or at least chain-guards. They need cookie-cutter templates for how to get the bike in motion and how to effectively and reliably brake at the bottom of the hill.

But we can't pretend that "restating your thesis and summarizing your main points in the conclusion" is a good strategy. It's funny: I've had hundreds of students over the years tell me that their History or English teacher insists on this approach.

Yet I've never run into any teacher – in six public high schools, two colleges, and multiple summer institutes – who can explain to me why "restating anything" in one's conclusion is sound practice. Because it's not. An essay is like Bronxville, NY – one square mile of land – where each quarter-acre piece of property is very valuable real estate. The average home price is 1.3 million dollars.

Then why does the typical English teacher who assigns a five paragraph essay expect their students to use 20% of their paper to (more or less) **recap, restate, and reassert?** Where's the wisdom in that? That's like your defense attorney yielding their time to the prosecution during closing arguments at your murder trial. You're ceding that space in your essay to points already made, arguments already hashed out, and thesis statements already on record. It makes for not just bad writing but terrible rhetorical strategy too.

Many HS students write essay conclusions that look something like this:

"After a quick tour of all the interesting buildings at Syracuse University, we got in his car and drove to his apartment. During the ride, he was giving me the usual talk about how college was going to help me discover who I really was. I took this opportunity to ask him who he wanted to be and if he'd figured out who he was. He said, 'How would I know?' How was this possible? He was a senior in college, shouldn't he know who he wants to be? I questioned what others had been telling me for the past year. Unlike Kung Fu Panda's Master Po, I don't know if there'd be a moment of realization when my path became clear. Maybe discovering my path is a process that will take half a lifetime to figure out. Po is able to recognize his call to adventure and discover who he truly is by reflecting on his past and accepting his destiny. Compared to Po, while I am confident in my past and where I come from, I am uncertain about my future; there's no predetermined destiny for me."

The above outro was written by a senior in my Words and Images course. It was the first draft of an essay that explored his favorite line of dialogue from Kung Fu Panda, but it doesn't accomplish two things that all conclusions must:

1 Make the Reader Say: "Damn Son!" (Or elicit some visceral response that approximates the awe, wonder, or emotional gut-punch readers should feel in a paper's final moments).
2 Make the Reader Say (to Themselves) Some Variation of the Phrase: "I see what you did there." What that means to me is – if a reader can't appreciate (to some extent) the artistry and cleverness with which you've ended an article, essay, Op-Ed, short story, novel, play, or memoir, then you're doing something wrong. It's a missed opportunity to make a lasting impression, leave them wanting more, or stir up a bit of dissatisfaction.

My journalist friend Samanth Subramanian tries to end his longform pieces for The New Yorker and The Guardian (among other publications) with an image that he wants the reader to hold in their mind.

That would certainly be in service of number two above.

But I'm getting ahead of myself. To lay it all out for you in black-and-white, I teach seven different ways **into** an essay's argument, and seven different ways **out**. Having this much choice aligns with one of my core essay-writing tenets: *One size most certainly does not fit all.*

Seven Ways In

Strategy One: Violate the audience's expectations
Strategy Two: Build a mystery that the audience (likely) wants to solve
Strategy Three: Deploy a chiasmus
Strategy Four: Create a paradox
Strategy Five: Treat your audience as a frog in a pot of water

Strategy Six: Use forced teaming
Strategy Seven: Commit acts of radical honesty (confess)

Seven Ways Out

Strategy One: End with an image
Strategy Two: End with a juxtaposition
Strategy Three: End with a whisper
Strategy Four: End with a pun
Strategy Five: End figuratively
Strategy Six: End with strategic ambiguity
Strategy Seven: End with a tautology

A good introduction is a form of platonic seduction. You aren't "hooking" your reader so much as captivating, managing, misdirecting, and charming them. Intros should accomplish what great tennis players do so naturally: Get the reader out of position, dictate the pace of play, and – generally speaking – disorient them.

Intro Strategy One – Violation of Expectation (but It's Good for Outros, Too)

Violation of expectation is something I likely learned from watching TV and film. Warning – there are some spoilers ahead, but I'm a subscriber to the theory: If something's been out for a while and you haven't seen it by now, then that's on you. And – how much did you really want to see it anyway? So – there are multiple spoilers that follow:

> The end of the neo-noir thriller The Usual Suspects reveals that disabled, low-level con man (Verbal Kint) is actually the criminal mastermind (Kevin Spacey plays Keyser Soze — same initials, too) who has orchestrated a spectacular harbor heist. For nearly an hour and forty minutes, audiences have been fed a great many red herrings that Verbal (aka Soze) has masterfully culled from a cork-board in Sgt. Jeff Rabin's LDAP office.

But it's the film's opening sequence that truly pulls the oriental carpet right out from under main character and alleged anti-hero Dean Keaton. We see Keaton and a man in black on the starboard bow of a large ship filmed cowboy-shot-style (shoulders to crotch). Essentially, the man in black is headless to the viewer. We're just past the opening credits and Keaton (an older, dashing Cary Grant type) is lying on the deck of that freighter, post mass-shootout. We don't know who Keaton is. We don't know what he has (or hasn't) done. We don't know why he's there, injured (shot?), on this docked vessel. We don't know why the boat is shot-up, gasoline barrels splayed sideways, raw fuel spilled everywhere. We don't even know what Dean figures out far too late, as he looks up at the man about to shoot him in the head at point-blank range. It's the most remarkable violation of them all: The film's poster even advertises it – "It's always the one you least suspect," as the tag-line reads.

Verbal Kint is Keyser Soze. Keaton learns this just minutes into the drama – we can see it on his face. "Keyser," he says to the man in black, gritting his teeth against the dramatic irony of the moment (we don't know what he knows), and against the gruesome violation he's just experienced (the insult-to-injury of his own impending homicide: He's been betrayed by the very man he's been protecting and shepherding the entire time).

If you haven't seen the film, you still should. To be honest, the "spoilers" only ruin the ending while making the beginning more potent. It's really six-of-one, half-a-dozen of another. Either way, the opening scene of The Usual Suspects:

- Violates the Audience's Expectations: We see Keaton "figure out the script's big reveal," the man he thought was Person A, turns out to be Person B. Apparently the man shooting him *is* "Soze," but Keaton clearly knew him as someone else. Additionally, very few movies in 1995 took these kinds of risks right off the bat: using temporal distortion, off-screen space, and in media res (all working together to upend what a typical opening sequence looks and feels like).
- Builds a Mystery the Audience Wants to Solve: Who's Soze (the name that escapes Keaton's lips just moments into the movie)? Why is Keaton dying in such dramatic fashion on the ship? Who's the man in black? Why don't we see his face? Why the need for the man in black to burn the freighter and destroy what's on board? And what's on board, anyway?
- Employs (or Deploys) a Chiasmus: Keaton learns of Kint's true identity at the narrative's beginning, but viewers learn of it at the end (it's a kind of mirror image, front-to-back, reverse syntax idea).
- Creates a Paradox: The entire film is Kint's attempt to convince authorities that Keaton is "**the** Keyser Soze," yet viewers know that it can't be Keaton (because we see him die at the very start), but we are somehow still convinced by Kint that Keaton is the criminal mastermind. It's a kind of cognitive dissonance on our part – we know Keaton couldn't be Soze, but we also let ourselves become persuaded that he is Soze after listening to Kint's emotionally compelling "confession," as told to agent Kujan.

- Treats Watchers as the Frog in a Pot of Water: That opening scene makes us believe that Verbal Kint is a bystander to the carnage at the bay and has only survived it through dumb luck. The movie continues to lull viewers in a false sense of security about Kint's identity (creating empathy for his alleged physical challenges, his low status in the gang of criminals, and his favoring of brains over brawn). By the time we see Kint shoot a heroin dealer named Saul Berg, it's too late: We couldn't have seen it coming. The frog has been boiled alive in the pot of water as the film's writer (Christopher McQuarrie) has turned up the heat real slow on us. Now we're suspicious of Kint the cold-blooded killer, but the other four men in the gang are equally brutal and distasteful (save for Keaton). Suddenly, Keaton becomes the "one we least suspect" (he dresses in cream-colored suits, pushes hard against his own recidivism, acts as a big brother to Kint, and displays tender feelings for his girlfriend Edie – who also happens to be an Assistant D.A.), before Kint misdirects us back to Keaton as the most likely candidate for Soze.

So McQuarrie (the writer) and Bryan Singer (the director) weaponize five of my seven introduction strategies (simultaneously) to ensure that the film's opening sequence grabs the watcher by the throat and doesn't let go.

Intro Strategy Two: Build a Mystery that the Audience (Likely) Wants to Solve

The 2013 pilot for the Netflix show House of Cards opens with another Kevin Spacey character (politician Frank Underwood) snapping the neck of a dying dog. Is it an act of empathy? Compassionate euthanasia? Sociopathy? All three? In that moment, Underwood becomes the riddle we're compelled to unravel over six seasons.

The 2022 Amazon series Reacher begins with a hulking, beyond-broad-shouldered Alan Richtson entering a southern town by coach bus, walking (with equal parts aimlessness and purpose) to a rural diner to eat the best peach pie in Margrave, Georgia. In the parking lot, the 6'3" Richtson (as the title character Jack Reacher) happens upon a couple fighting by their van. Without uttering a single word or putting his hands on the abusive boyfriend, Reacher reduces him to a whimpering puppy. Without even being told to, the man apologizes to Reacher, his girlfriend, the ground, to God himself. The viewer is left to wonder why Reacher cares about the fate of a complete stranger, how he was able to intervene without moving a muscle, and whether he's the show's villain or hero. And that last question gets even murkier when the entire Margrave police force arrests Reacher at gunpoint before he can enjoy even one bite of his pie.

J.J. Abrams' juggernaut series Lost from 2004 captivates audiences from its first seconds by introducing us to Jack Shephard lying prone in the forest. His eyes open, he takes a gaspy inhale, locates a mini vodka bottle in his suit-jacket pocket, sees an orphaned sneaker hanging from a tree branch, then panic-runs until he hits the beach. The camera pans to the right: nothing but crystalline white sand and azure seascape; to the left is utter chaos: the charred fuselage of an airliner with one engine still roaring, men and women screaming in pain and abject distress, as Jack springs into action. At this point, audiences don't know his name, whether he's an alcoholic, how many passengers have survived the crash or what caused it, where the island is located, or how a bunch of people still draw breath after falling out of the sky.

The Flight Attendant's pilot episode (from 2020) features Kaley Cuoco as Cassandra Bowden (a – you guessed it – flight attendant), who wakes up in a Dubai luxury hotel bed with her one-night-stand slaughtered right next to her. What we know about the previous night is compromised by Cuoco's unreliable narrator: She'd been drinking, maybe even drugged, and finds large swaths of her memory deleted or inaccessible. Did she kill her lover? If not did she actually sleep through his brutal murder? Is she being framed? What forces have (potentially) conspired against – of all people – a flight attendant? And why? Cuoco (made famous by The Big Bang Theory) is a bubbly blonde who plays Bowden as a flirtatious, living-in-the-moment, 20-something. In this role, she's instantly relatable and – if anything – we want to protect her, and help her make sense of the vortex she's been sucked into.

I tell my students: We all love puzzles. And while not all of us adore 10,000 piece jigsaw puzzles, crosswords, Wordle, or Sudoku – we all relish solving interesting problems.

My wife (and her immediate family) spent one Christmas break putting together a nearly entirely *white jigsaw puzzle of tiny vintage bicycles*. I was *there in the room*, but I can't say that I helped much, nor wanted to.

But I have read every Robert B. Parker detective novel ever written (even the ones added to his legacy posthumously by Ace Atkins), all the hard-boiled Raymond Chandler works, and many Agatha Christies. And I've yet to meet a heist movie that didn't get my pure interest, begging me to poke holes in its plot, or figure out – before Danny Ocean did – how they were going to take down the casino without getting caught.

I like mystery-thrillers in all their many splendid forms: BBC programs like Killing Eve, The Fall, and Luther; neo-noir films including The Laughing Policeman, The Parallax View, and Magnum Force; and even biblio-mysteries (crimes involving rare books) like Booked to Die by John Dunning, The Storied Life of A.J. Fikry by Gabrielle Zevin, and Overbooked in Arizona by Samuel Gottleib.

So – the million dollar question is – how can your students make their introductory paragraphs "mysterious," and engender a sense of wonder in the reader? Moreover, how do you set up puzzles that are challenges worth solving?

Sophomore Eric Kwon did it effortlessly at age 14, opening his first essay of the year for my class with three relatively straightforward sentences:

Maybe there had always been signs, little cracks and tears visible if you squinted hard enough. But I'd painted over them. I hated how they looked. I guess I hoped they wouldn't spread.

Intro Strategy Three: Deploy a Chiasmus

Wordplay is pure joy for me. And you'd be surprised at how much students love it too. Just introduce a simple, classical rhetorical device called "chiasmus." It's a kind of mirror image within a sentence. Ben Franklin wrote a famous one, "If you fail to plan, you're planning to fail." Taylor Swift stole it for her song "Mastermind."

I collect chiasmuses and have a running list of about 50 that really speak to me. Drake has one in his song "Dreams Money Can Buy" that is so damn clever (but I can't repeat it here).

Motivational speakers favor them for their pithiness and virality ("It's not how many hours you put in, but what you put into the hours," comes to mind).

Just assign some. In my experience, hardcore Science students find them worthy puzzles to solve. My weakest writers embrace them as badges of honor once rendered. Jay-Z spits the bar, "I'm not a businessman, I'm a business, man," which has all the hallmarks of "flipped syntax" or – in that case – violation of expectation.

For me, as the teacher who wants to supercharge students' writing ASAP – I can't think of a straighter line between two points to get them there.

As for why a chiasmus works so well as an introductory "device?" They surprise the reader. When they're done well, they reframe or recast an idea. If it's an original, never-before-seen chiasmus, then it becomes a kind of portal: You're going to be entering the mind of someone who thinks differently, who's playful with language, and who won't bore you with stale diction and lame syntax. It says: You're in the hands of someone wonderfully subversive.

Comedian Bill Maher once wove a chiasmus into his New Rules segment on HBO's Real Time for his final Op-Ed: "Is it defunding the police or de-policing the funds?"

A Fresh Direct flyer advertising its services stated: "Don't settle for food delivery; get food that delivers you."

Businessman Peter Jones quipped on the U.K.'s version of Shark Tank, while questioning whether a business pitcher was serving up a sound business investment: "There's a gap in the market, but is there a market in the gap?"

Sophomore Isabela Braga Figueiredo's introduction to an essay on What's Eating Gilbert Grape began with: "Gilbert dismissing his responsibilities resulted in his brother's near-drowning; now, the burning of his childhood home conveyed an acceptance for what he had to do, and what he left behind to do it." (This seems more "conceptual chiasmus" than syntactical one.)

And what these uses of chiasmuses have in common is that they've remained in the back of my mind, like benevolent earworms, infecting my language and my teaching since I've heard or read them. It seems like a powerful way to begin an essay.

Intro Strategy Four: Create a Paradox – Lean into Cognitive Dissonance

There is no great art without juxtapositions that don't resolve themselves: The Mona Lisa's smile, Stonehenge, Casablanca, and so on.

It's important for students to master the art of intentional contradiction, of creating (and using) distinctions that draw attention to the schism of the mind. Jake Feuerstein wrote in a sophomore paper's intro years ago about the distinction between performer and musical performer:

"I do recognize Travis Scott (the representative of everything wrong in the music industry) as a talented performer, yet I do not recognize him as a talented musical performer. The latter's shows revolve more around the music than anything else: naked of elaborate dances, bright lights, and synthetic music playing from a backing track. Anyone in the categories ranging from the Baroque Era visionaries, to the rock gods of the '90s all focus their lenses finely on music. It is their sole craft. And out of all the great musicians, there is one group of specialized craftsmen – whose art form draws power from a relatively small musical reservoir – that can manipulate audacious, melodic energy better than anyone else. Musicians who play the blues are the most skilled musical performers compared to the personnel of other genres by virtue of the fact that they can captivate an audience with music alone, improvise with intentionality, and seamlessly play along with others."

It's what Scarsdale Middle School English teachers Cara Hiller and Jonathan Hilpert call "the So What?" of their students' essays.

The way I explain it to my students is through some useful examples: We can like the music of Kanye West, without having to like the man who made it. We can believe in climate change, but not in the value of recycling.

I use these "frameworks" interchangeably (cognitive dissonance, contradiction, distinctions), because all I care about is that students start to understand and use contradiction and contrast in their writing. Truth be told, very few of them have consciously used it in their writing before they get to my classroom. Yes, many of them have written "similarities and differences" papers for History teachers, or English essays comparing Gilgamesh to Enkidu, but very few students have more than one way into a paper, or one way out. Most have compared and contrasted using plot and characterization, instead of abstract qualities.

In many ways, I have Jake to thank for this insight. I really didn't believe that tenth-grade essays could be complex and "distinction driven" (a phrase I've coined) before he came along in 2017.

Intro Strategy Five: Treat Your Audience as Frog in a Pot of Water

There's an old wives' tale or urban legend that if you place a live frog in a room temperature pot of water on the stove and turn up the heat very slowly, the frog won't react in time to leap out. Instead, he'll let himself be boiled to death.

Again – not true – but it's a useful metaphor for how screenwriters create that "false sense of security" that leads to audience complacency just long enough to take advantage of it.

In the Netflix original series Bloodline, Todd A. Kessler puts every single member of the Rayburn family in a giant kettle and has its main villain Danny Rayburn (the black sheep and exiled son of the old-moneyed clan) turn up the heat every-so-slowly so as not to disturb the inhabitants of the hottub. By the time the steam clears, one brother is in prison on federal drug trafficking charges, another has lost his wife and his bid for sheriff, the clan's mother has been psychologically decimated and is forced to sell-off the family business, and the surviving sister has literally changed her name and moved cross-country.

Danny Rayburn, ex-con and cynical reprobate, has been at the stove's controls the entire time.

Hitchcock's Psycho is an early filmic example of "frog in water." Marion Crane is blissfully unaware of Norman Bates' potential for psychopathic violence when she checks into his family motel. It's when she's safely ensconced in the room, mid-shower, that she learns the truth about Norman and the Bates Motel. She's also the first main character in history to be killed off in the first 45 minutes of a movie (which is central to the frogicide's success here).

So that's the concept, but why do it? I think it's really about exposing your reader to unpleasant or objectionable things in small doses or muted colors: They can't unsee something truly potent or poignant (just as a jury can't "unhear" testimony, and the judge "striking it" is pretty much useless).

It's a magic trick: to write something that leads your reader to the edge of a bluff and compels them to walk off into the abyss.

My attempt at "frog in water" was an exercise of rewriting NYT journalist Vanessa Friedman's introduction to a Gucci fashion show review from

February 2023. Friedman is the chief fashion critic at The Times, but often (in my opinion) struggles to write strong introductions and conclusions. One fruitful (and fun) exercise I give to students is having them reimagine a Friedman paragraph, as I did here:

"You're sitting in a well-curated room with tasteful-and-sparsely-positioned furniture. Elegant rappers, influencers and TikTok personalities sit stoically, unmoving, unmoved, apathetic, models of potential energy that will unlikely be realized in your presence. Such movements would be wasted on you. You want to scratch your nose. It itches. But that would be crass. It would be, well, inelegant. Your fingernail's scrape against the bridge would be something that they wouldn't, that they couldn't, abide by. By not breathing hard enough to fog up your own glasses, by suppressing that sneeze as not to create a kind of butterfly effect, and by holding in your stomach long enough to let the models pass by without judgment, you have – at the very least – not caused a bottleneck at the intersection of commerce and creativity. But who's directing traffic?"

Friedman was writing about the consequences of Gucci's operating without an artistic director for a season. My goal was to put the reader in the front row of that show – one that lacked both coherent style, and apparent substance. The idea was: By the time the introduction is over, the "truth" or the "paper's main objective" should be silently sneaking up on the reader, still undetected. It's the radon gas in your home that you didn't know was there.

Intro Strategy Six: Forced Teaming

Personal security expert, public speaker, and bestselling author Gavin de Becker wrote about "teaming" in his NYT bestseller The Gift of Fear. It's a book that profiled women who were the sole survivors of serial killers. De Becker was interested in one key distinction: What allowed the fortunate few to escape the clutches of the criminally insane, and what can we learn from what they witnessed to prevent future victims?

The answer starts off chapter one: **it's teaming**.

As de Becker tells it (I'm paraphrasing here),

Serial killers would gently approach women they'd been stalking for days, weeks, or months – making their first direct contact with their intended victim in a public setting. In one case, a man sidled up to a woman carrying a grocery bag on a sidewalk, saw the cat food tin resting on top and remarked that "So, we're going home to feed the cat, are we?" It's a psychological principle rooted in the use of "we" or "us," and accelerates the rapport-building process. By the time they arrive back at her apartment, the man once again invokes the same pronoun: "We've come this far together, let us get that famished cat of yours fed." Or something to that effect.

The World Wildlife Federation (an environmental nonprofit) used teaming in a series of print-ads in 2013 to avoid directly "pointing fingers" at its audience. The most successful one features a polar bear in warming waters, his paws over his eyes in apparent shame. The caption reads, "What On Earth Are We Doing to Our Planet?"

It's often the case that nonprofit organizations use blame and shame (and pathos) to solicit donations. It's easy for a shelter or humane society to make a TV commercial featuring sad-eyed puppies to stir up negative emotions in service of shaking bills loose from wallets; it's much harder to think strategically about copywriting.

But now you know how. And I understand that some would call this practice "undue influence" (if you're a serial killer, you don't need my help on this one), and it is. Successful writing, storytelling, movie-making, advertising, etc. – it comes down to one thing: winning the attention game.

Sophomore Cameron Hersly rewrote the introduction to her essay about the dearth of music course options at Scarsdale High School, using forced teaming:

Original Intro

To step inside the walls of Scarsdale High School as a musician is to confine yourself to a purgatorial fate. The keys become out of tune. The creative life force is sucked out through an intrinsic IV – a convict that feeds off color and culture. The convict becomes the judge in this red masonry corral. The closure culture creates a hypothetical ban on the arts: All attempts to forge a collector's piece are in vain. Musicians are shunned in the face of apparent athleticism and excessive jockery; support is nonexistent, and the ivory halts contact with creased fingertips.

Forced Teaming Intro Rewrite

There's no vitality left in our lactic templates, we've succumbed to the depths of creative seclusion. Why even try to arrange a modern musical masterpiece when we must focus on the future? Why can't that be our future? Why must we prepare ourselves for a life of fortified labor rather than choice? Teachers and friends that we once thought to be trustworthy and consistently supportive either lost the ability to lie to our faces or just gave up.

Intro Strategy Seven: Commit Acts of Radical Honesty (Confession)

Have you been divorced four times? Well, Brad Blanton has. Perhaps when you hear the title of his bestselling book, you'll understand why that is: **Radical Honesty**.

Blanton's approach to life (also) appears to be brutal candor, which is much like it sounds. It's living one's truth at all costs – financial, relational, whatever.

I had come across Blanton's book years ago at a second-hand shop in New Haven, but it seemed too brazen a philosophy to adopt. Enter Lana Weiser (currently an English major at Barnard College). Lana came to my junior honors English class in 2021 but was not immediately impressed with my teaching. And – here's the relevant part – she had no problem telling me everything that she thought of my course, my teaching, as best encapsulated in this final reflection from June of 2022.

Lana writes:

"In the spirit of radical honesty, I'll tell you I did not want to have you as my English teacher. I said something to this extent but not as boldly worded in my oral argument: 'You were the English teacher and class I needed, not necessarily desired.' Don't get me wrong – your class definitely has a reputation for being unconventional and enjoyable – but I wanted traditional. I expected a five paragraph essay, incremental nightly reading assignments, 'So, what was the author's purpose here?' type of class. To my surprise, my junior schedule listed Phillipson: Rm 207 and my phone buzzed with a message from Drew: 'He's the best!' Eh, I wasn't sold.

Then, we spoke. And, the fourth wall broke. For our working relationship and my writing – we had the most substantive of conversations – about my inclinations, personhood and tenacity. The true magic of that exchange lay in our difference of understanding, the gap between what I could verbally express and what could be comprehended, but within this gap I witnessed your incredible willingness to try. I saw that same willingness to try when I read you the piece I wrote about my own nihilism from the backseat of my mom's SUV, when I read you my entire research paper – but most specifically when I read the part written while I was sprawled on my bathroom floor mid-panic-attack, and when I read my realizations about mental health stigmas NOT IN THE PAST TENSE (get it)."

* * *

Lana Weiser embodied radical honesty from her very first writing assignment of the year. She entered my class ready to be intensely vulnerable – and those are the students you owe everything to as a teacher. You can't take that gift they're giving you lightly, because not everyone is willing to be so open, to so blindly trust, and to ride with you for 180 days (the metaphorical convertible top down, regardless of the weather). And as you can see for yourself in the passages above, Lana almost didn't take that journey.

But to focus more sharply on how to "use radical honesty as an introductory device," I can explain it way: **What do you not want** your reader to know, but would make them immediately respect you if they did, if you just told them? Maybe it would put them at ease. For instance, you're supposed to be the expert, but what if you're not, and you're willing to admit it?

NYT bestselling author and pop-culture critic Chuck Klosterman used this technique masterfully in his Rolling Stone essay Perpetual Topeka (it's an excerpt from his book about villainy called I Wear the Black Hat).

"I've obliterated three days trying to come up with an elegant way to write what I'm about to write, but I think the least elegant way is probably best: I like Kanye West. I don't particularly like LeBron James. I do, however, want LeBron James to succeed. And I want Kanye West to fail (at least once). So there it is. There's the concept. Accept it or reject it."

Klosterman admits to a great deal of truths in his short introduction: (A) He's had writer's block for three days; (B) He's being inelegant; (C) He's a hypocrite; and (D) He doesn't care whether you read his essay or not. In fact, he's daring you to read it – to take offense to his odd double-standard.

Introductions must establish the writer as the authority on the subject, or – at very least – a voice that appeals to, or entices, the reader to "read on." With Klosterman, a big reason to "read on" is that he's got bold opinions that he was initially timid about putting forth. But now – out of exasperation or fatigue – he's letting it rip. There's something inherently compelling about that approach.

In many ways, memoir writing is inherently confessional. James Frey was castigated for bending truths and making up narrative details whole cloth in his juggernaut bestseller (and one-time Oprah Book Club pick) Million Little Pieces. Reporter Jayson Blair spent four years at The New York Times fabricating every "news story" or "feature article" he handed in to his editor. Neither Frey nor Blair could ever be accused of radical honesty.

So it's not for everyone – but many of your students will find it refreshing and freeing. At the very least – they'll learn one specific strategy to disarm their reader.

Outro Strategy One: End with an Image

Journalist and "friend of the class" – Samanth Subramanian – who has contributed to The New Yorker, The Atlantic and The Guardian, taught me and my students that he often ends his essays with an image that he wants the reader to keep in their mind long after the piece ends.

In this case, I'm not talking about a picture, photograph, or illustration, but – literally – a thousand words.

Jocelyn "Jocie" Weiss, a former student and University of Wisconsin graduate, sent me a letter last year that was career-affirming. One line she wrote is very relevant here:

Whoever said, "a picture is worth a thousand words," has definitely never met you.

And that is Samanth's "way out" of choice for his own longform nonfiction. He ended a 2000-word piece about the history (and prehistory) of board games for The New Yorker with this sensory "image-like" meditation:
"Where language cannot reveal everything, something may still be gleaned from the silent, ludic routines of a game."
Former junior honors English student Daheun Oh offered her visual take on the geriatric Netflix bittersweet sitcom Grace and Frankie in her conclusion:
"Whether it's Grace and Frankie or The Kominksy Method, the crux of the characters' deepest fears is their increasing irrelevance. Within each microcosm exists a main cast who is simply trying to live, which isn't easy when it seems like the sky is falling apart around them. The eye-opening, life-shattering struggle Grace and Frankie endure also has the effect of bringing to light the extent to which they've shared their lives with their husbands, with regards to family, friends, houses, and credit cards. And with their betrayal comes the realization of the neglect they face, causing Grace to break down at the supermarket: 'HELLO! What kind of animal treats people like this? Do you not see me? Do I not exist?' Frankie tries to make light of the situation, 'I learned something. You can't see me, you can't stop me.' But as they smoke their stolen cigarettes in the dark ambience of the parking lot, the few silent seconds seem to fully conceal them. Because in this hurricane of emotions of hurt, betrayal, hindsight, and frustration, they've seemed to lose their grasp on their sense of their existence and the world has stealthily done the same."
Here, Daheun is a master of drama and tension, elegantly creating a mise-en-scene, ripped tonally from the screen, with only her words. It turns an otherwise basic conclusion into a meditation on mortality and relevance. And it's palpable.
In many ways it's what Johnny Cochran did in his closing arguments at the Trial of the Century, defending the late O.J. Simpson. Cochran called back to the many images he'd presented over the course of eight months: Cochran himself donning a ski mask to prove his identifiability even when cloaked in a knit cap, and Simpson struggling to slip into his Isotoners proving the glove didn't fit (so you therefore must acquit).
What the jury hears last is what they'll take into their deliberations. If you can leave your own jury of readers with an enduring visual impression, then – perhaps – you've already won the case.

Outro Strategy Two: End with a Juxtaposition

The most compelling scenes in The Catcher in the Rye feature striking juxtapositions: Holden chatting up a sour, hardened prostitute ironically named Sunny (followed by her pimp sitting on his chest as his "date" pilfers money from his wallet), and 16-year-old Holden taking money from his little sister Phoebe (dressed in elephant pajamas).

Of Mice and Men works as an enduring story because of the juxtaposition created by Lennie and George (vis-a-vis Steinbeck). One is a human monolith and jarhead. The other is small, wiry and (relatively) smart. The hulking Lennie's last name is – itself – a juxtaposition: Small. The same goes for George Milton, named after the poet and author of Paradise Lost. The two migrant workers will never have their rabbit farm, nor live off the fat of the land. They're seeking paradise (by the tractor's dashboard lights), but we know they'll never get it.

These literary examples – perhaps – provide proof that juxtapositions are inherently powerful. The law of contrast (a rudimentary psychological principle) is not just useful in selling luxury goods: There's a reason why the Gucci store has $200 keychains and passport holders near the front entrance, and $5,000 shearling coats in the back. As you're leaving the boutique, those wallets and small leather goods seem like relative bargains. So you're more inclined (or primed) to buy one.

Daheun Oh wrote five versions of the same conclusion for her cultural critique of Grace and Frankie (starring Fonda and Tomlin). Her approach to juxtapositions is elegant in its indirectness, as it contrasts three things while also comparing them: the ages of the characters, the actresses, and their youthful energy:

"For the past 5 years since the show premiered, Jane Fonda and Lily Tomlin have been 'playing' their real ages (now 82 and 80 respectively), and yet it seems time has been forced to curve around them. Grace and Frankie are still Grace and Frankie, they're loud and full of life. 'Time is a social construct,' is repeated over and over again, but it never felt as real as it did when these limits were defied by these geriatric women. Time is accepted as being both finite and infinite: To each individual it is implemented in the form of a timer – how long until this milk reaches its expiration date, how long until I meet my expiration date – whereas to society, it is the precise framework intertwining individual with individual, past with present. But time is also a function of society to increase productivity, a mindset to make our lives seem a little more meaningful. It's a limitation we consider to motivate our ability to achieve 'full potential,' but simultaneously boxes us in, destroying our connection to the vast exploration of the universe from which time derived. And Grace and Frankie are well aware of this fact, never letting us forget that they don't have eternity, but that it doesn't mean they shouldn't explore the world. Even if it is through an industry of geriatric-women-targeted toys."

Outro Strategy Three: End with a Whisper

This approach is my all-time favorite "way out" of any essay.

Far too often, we tell students to restate the thesis and recap the essay's main points in the conclusion. This has never made common sense to me nor seemed a good use of space. I often say to my classes, it makes sense to recap at the end of a year-long trial, or in certain structured debate formats when competing, but not in a medium-length paper.

As English teachers, we so badly want students to be crystal clear in their final sentences, taking a definitive position on whatever they're arguing for or against.

I'm far more interested in teaching students a valuable lesson on symbiosis: Let the reader do some of the intellectual heavy lifting throughout your essay, but especially at the end. Don't solve the essay's problem; give them enough context and motivation to solve it themselves.

And when you "whisper" in real life, people have to lean in to hear you talk. It's almost a "law of power or attraction," to make others come to you – like a cat to a loose ball of yarn you're holding as you walk across a room trying to lure the cat outside.

What "whispering" in a conclusion means is: (A) refrain from over-explaining, and (B) say as little – directly – as possible: indicate, don't directly state.

A whisper should not be mistaken for a whimper: The former is a secret philosophy shared in hushed tones; the latter is a weak petering out – a kind of tacit forfeiting.

I worked with student Daniel Gray for two years in the English classroom. He – better than anyone – understood that an essay never needs a "hard stop." It's not a telegram. It's not a theme park ride. It's a matter of holding the reader softly in the palm of your hand and gently releasing them back into their world, to their life, thereafter. But they should still feel the sensation of your caress once finished.

Daniel's essay on "the crazy genius" – the notion that every brilliant mind is a bit off-kilter – concludes with an allusion to the O.J. trial, a key piece of evidence, and the Kanye West song Stronger (and how the three intersect). Importantly, Daniel trusts the reader to *get the reference*, and connect the dots between O.J. and Kanye as pop-culture figures who have been the centers of culture-wars serving as racial and religious flashpoints.

"Why any of us are flabbergasted by Kanye really eludes me. Still, if I had a time machine, one of the first destinations would be about two weeks ago, when I could stomach my favorite artist's music. His sentencing in the court of public opinion was due four years ago, when he said slavery was a choice, but the glove didn't fit then. The art isn't going anywhere, but it's now stained worse than OJ's Isotoners."

Outro Strategy Four: End with a Pun

The noted humor writer Dave Barry told me he is allergic to using puns in his own writing. His syndicated column has been read by 80 million people, but – from my understanding – it never contained a single pun.

Some of us live by Hemingway-level codes: Suffer in silence, have just one confidant in this world, save pain for nighttime ... never use puns.

I, thankfully, don't have such hard-and-fast rules. I grew up on the TV show Frasier, where puns were regularly traded by the two psychiatrist main characters who loved to *nerd out* whenever possible.

So much of what I'm talking about in this book is "being disruptive on paper." Teachers have grown complacent with their curriculum and their pedagogy. Students have grown bored of much of it. The world is changing – our classroom approach has not (at least not enough, and not in a way that shakes students out of their screen-comas).

What do we expect to see at the close of our students' papers? A quote? A return to the opening paragraph's hook? A recast thesis statement?

What about a pun?

Something I wrote for my parting shot in an essay about my year of fully remote teaching was, "The problem with distance learning is that it's not remotely interesting."

Wes – I see what you did there. You used the word remote to play on distance learning. I get it. I also get that puns can be corny or have the potential to be overlooked by your reader. They might not get the joke, and all of your *cleverness* will be for naught.

Instead, I see it as adding value to your reader's experience. Just like a chiasmus, puns are a form of wordplay that students (believe it or not) find pleasure in creating. Rap is still a dominant pop-music genre, and everyone from Lil' Wayne to J. Cole leans into their punnery.

Puns can be "dad-jokey," (as a father of two boys, I get that), but they don't have to be. They provide a quick and easy way to spice up an ending, make the reader smile, or underscore a sub-point your essay gently made.

Sophomore Lily Greenberg wrote a delicious rant about her battle with misophonia, ending the piece with a pun that I remembered without even having to search up in her Google Drive:

"The worst part of this pet peeve: there is no escape. Honestly, at this rate I would rather listen to James Charles' horrific new releases on repeat than have to hear someone nibbling at their lunch. But I guess beggars can't be chewers."

Outro Strategy Five: End Figuratively

Tenth grader Isabela Braga Figueiredo took two passes at recasting her What's Eating Gilbert Grape film review "figuratively."

Attempt One

"Long after the Grape house became unrecognizable, what were formerly window frames indistinguishable from burnt chairs, the residual ash did not spell "Grape," nor "family," nor "duty." Instead, it traced the names of the children, the kids too young to drink but not too young to care for each other when their parents couldn't, the siblings who were free to write their stories, to choose where they lived and who they were, their "responsibilities tab" closed without being saved."

Attempt Two

"When the Grape house – a large, not-at-all-grape-like, white (or white-adjacent) house that wouldn't look out of place in a colonial-era textbook or a rich Amish neighborhood – went up in flames like an overly-enthusiastic cigarette, only memories remained in the ashtray; the only indication of weakness, of shanked responsibility. The foundations were literally and figuratively incinerated; the remaining Grapes were able to breathe, free from their nicotine-burlesquing mother weighing their lungs down, staining their larynx, infecting their bronchi."

And let me tell you: Students love creating pieces that are rich in metaphor, simile, and analogy. Again, I credit the rap community. Some rappers – J. Cole, TuPac Shakur, The Notorious B.I.G., and many others – are gifted docents through poverty and fame, who dot their landscapes with figurative language. And it's funny: Isabela would often come to our class wearing graphic concert tees of deceased rappers. It's evident their verbiage, diction, syntax, and linguistic playfulness had seeped into her subconscious prose (as evidenced above).

And having students write conclusions (or introductions) that are *steeped in the figurative* is great training to read and write poetry, to unpack the subtext of Shakespeare's plays, and to return a childlike wonder about writing to something we claim to really care about – or used to.

I grade what I value, and what I value is (A) being clever, (B) moving to the abstract, and (C) generating *redolent voice* – in no particular order.

To me, a conclusion must make me think and feel. It must make me say "Damn, Son!" – or some complex equivalent of that physical response. Being figurative is yet another way to get your students across the finish line without being battered, bruised, or disappointed.

Outro Strategy Six: End with Strategic Ambiguity

As I write this chapter, it's early November of 2024 and a current radio hit is Chappell Roan's Good Luck, Babe! At minute 3:15, the track slows like the world might to a motion-sick toddler on a playground-spinner, as Roan's voice choppily croons the song's hook: "You'd have to stop the world just to stop the feeling" four times over, sounding like a child's interactive doll put in a blender at low speed. It's the end of the song. No need to worry if you've missed it – the same station will be playing it several times again within the hour.

Escapism by Raye (featuring the rapper 070 Shake) was released in 2023. At minute 3:27, the song slurs to a befuddled, drug-addled halt, then yields to a choral remix of the song's hook ("I don't want to feel, how I did last night") and resolves in an expletive-laced rap-break-finale that ends abruptly.

In many ways, the two songs end the same, or similarly, or as if one had directly influenced the other.

In those moments (nearly at the same exact timestamp, too), the songs feel strangely alien, even unrecognizable. Like different songs, alternate tracks, remixes, or reimaginings – perhaps even covers.

It's true that form follows function here: The narrators in both are arguing how to go about "stopping the feeling" – so – there's a literal "stoppage" to the song itself, even before it's over.

The track suspends, devolves, or distorts. It's confusing – on purpose. It's disorienting – by design. And that's an option for my students when writing their outros. There is the potential for real art and power in creating that level of disruption at the end of an essay.

Would you like an example?

Yasmina Levitsky (SHS Class of '24) ends her essay "The Art of Disaster" weighing in on the specter of actually being carried away by the sea, tsunami-style, vs. just being a voyeur watching disaster films (like Open Water, Dante's Peak, or The Poseidon Adventure).

"Most cannot visualize or comprehend the way that a person feels during such a disaster. Your life being held on a string by a force that you cannot control; the terrifying question of "will I live to see tomorrow?" is not something that your average person has to genuinely respond to, and when they do, it must be petrifying. I try to imagine the terror of facing something that not a single being in this world can restrain. I wonder, if I were there, what would my reflection in the water look like? How do you look when you stare into the eyes of death? And how do you act when death stares back? The fear as you watch the wave above you darken your vision must be thrilling, in a disturbing way. The survival instinct kicks in and you fight against suffocation and flee. But no matter what, the wave (usually) prevails. After all, blood is denser than water. Confined in the murky sea with my feet grazing the sand, maybe that is when the attraction of disaster wears off."

Outro Strategy Seven: End with a Tautology

Yes, it's true. If you Google "tautology," you'll find the A.I.-generated response informing you that tautologies are often seen as weak examples of rhetoric, "generally considered to be a fault of style."

What that means is – technically speaking – tautologies are a literary "no-no."

But what if your goal was to get your students to "overwrite" their conclusions? To create what I call the "journalistic flourish" at paper's end? Sometimes poetry is overwrought and overwritten. Sometimes The Great Gatsby could have benefitted from a heavier hand in the editing room (no offense Max Perkins).

I say that tautologies are *stylistic redundancies* that add a forced depth to a sentence. "Close proximity" just sounds more authorial than "close" or "proximity" do on their own.

Style – as I see it – is sometimes divorced from strict grammar and usage rules, but they're not mutually exclusive.

Even in my "outro strategy six" above, I found myself trotting out a tautology to flesh out my point, and to add some "ear candy" to my music (as producer Quincy Jones calls it). Quoting myself from a few paragraphs above: "In those moments (nearly at the same exact timestamp, too), the songs feel strangely alien, even unrecognizable."

Strangely alien? Alien isn't strange enough?

You can't be "very unique," but maybe that sounds more emphatic than just saying "unique." In the context of a conclusion, a tautology can have resonance – a kind of lexical tuning fork whose vibration frequencies go on to endure (another tautology).

Keep in mind that when I talk about conclusions in this chapter, I don't necessarily mean "one paragraph." Form should follow function. A conclusion can run a page-and-a-half, two paragraphs, one paragraph, or just a sentence.

The idea is that a tautology could be embedded in *just* the final sentence – to make it that vibration that continues to jostle or hum long after entering their inner ear as your reader goes about their day.

11
RANTING AND RAVING
Why Complaining Is Good for Your Students

An essay I read in 1997 – The Elevator Ride by Nathan McCall – taught me how to write with a sense of purpose and showed me how form could drive content. It's a masterclass in pacing, as well as in making razor-sharp distinctions on paper.

I met McCall in 1995 at a Boston area college. He was reading from his memoir Makes Me Wanna Holler. Director John Singleton had just purchased the rights to adapt the film to the big screen (it never materialized).

McCall is a walking paradox. He's got a history of violence against women and has spent time in federal prison for attempted murder and armed robbery. But he's a sensitive, thoughtful, and reflective soul and one hell of a writer. So there's a degree of cognitive dissonance you must exercise when reading his work or when having a conversation with him.

That aside, The Elevator Ride is a rant.

It's a breathless approximation of paranoia and claustrophobia. McCall is Black, grew up in the projects of Virginia, and has a chip on each shoulder. It's something he carries into the world with an odd sense of pride.

McCall writes the piece in second person (its very first word is "You"), allowing readers to – at least for a moment – see the world through Black eyes. To paraphrase the late tennis prodigy Arthur Ashe: to be Black is to be reminded you are so, each time you enter a room.

In the elevator, the narrator (a proxy for McCall) encounters a White woman who has "that look" – a face that telegraphs fear and loathing – a face that says, I have a concealed weapon and I'll use it against you.

Throughout the four-page essay, the author treats readers to a breakneck-speed history lesson on Whites who have scapegoated innocent Blacks (such as Charles Stuart and Susan Smith), by playing on existing societal fears and foregone conclusions about a minority group that comprises just 12% of the American population. "Criminal" – he offers – is synonymous with Black, while "law abiding" is "thinly-veiled vernacular for White."

Remarkably, nothing actually happens during the elevator ride from McCall's floor down to the lobby. There's not a single word of dialogue exchanged between the two passengers. They don't know each other. It's all happening in an anonymous office building. McCall is remarkably well-dressed in formal attire, carrying an elegant leather briefcase, with the bearing of a man who is gainfully employed, and moving with purpose.

But – he spends most of the essay ranting about the woman's objectionable physical appearance, her unspoken intentions (as if he's a precog in Minority Report), and about the broken state of race relations in late-1990s America (using recent history and age-old taboos as direct evidence of the here and now).

To write a rant requires one to tap into their rage, dissatisfaction, disgust, or (perhaps) disenfranchisement. It's a written attack, and one largely unconcerned with offense or alienation. The idea is to make your reader uncomfortable enough that they chafe or want to change (or you wear them down into tacit agreement), to make them feel overwhelmed with the quality and quantity of your information, and your emotional momentum. Pro-tip: Make them feel like they're trying to take a drink of water from a fully pressurized fire-hose. Don't let up. Ever. Overwhelm your reader with specific information at breakneck speed.

McCall's rant is layered because it has two parallel narratives running concomitantly: one is the descent itself – during which we see the tension between the professional Black man and the side-eyeing White woman in an enclosed space, standing still, but also in motion; the other is the author's rich interior monologue – the man vs. society that really becomes man vs. self. McCall is a self-educated and self-made man who is well-read and even became a Washington Post reporter before teaching Black media studies at Emory. For Elevator Ride (which is part of a larger collection of essays on race), he explores his own paranoia but calls the suspicions "justified." That's just one of many paradoxes or contradictions in the piece, but all of these messy hypocrisies help accelerate the rantiness.

When my classes unpack this essay, they're facile at pinpointing two dozen (or so) techniques that McCall uses to give his rant *velocity and voice*. Which is much easier to do – than say – when teaching James Baldwin's Stranger in the Village. Baldwin's piece is much longer and has the kind of nuance and deep thinking that are his calling cards. And – technically – Baldwin doesn't rant (not for very long, anyway). Perhaps he's too thoughtful and considered. McCall is still angry at the world, despite being a senior citizen and having been largely celebrated for his body of work and his contributions to Emory – the most prestigious university in the south.

Then there's the creator of the postmodern, dystopian TV series Black Mirror, Charlie Brooker.

Brooker is a seething, fire-breathing pterodactyl on the printed page, and in the case of Uninvent This: Ban Dancing, he turns the flamethrower directly on himself. Black Mirror is known for its anti-modernity, anti-tech, if-only-Orwell-weren't-such-a-Pollyanna (by comparison) tone and subject matter that it's hard to watch even one episode without feeling utterly hopeless about the future of the human race. Even the comparatively gentle Nosedive, starring the starry-eyed, red-headed Bryce Dallas Howard, has no redeemable characters, nor any compelling world-building.

But Brooker's short rant that calls for the end of dancing is a respite from the horrors of the short-term, from what will surely come next week or month, and is an exercise in self-deprecation and self-negation that's just as potent as anything David Sedaris has ever written (the king of verbal self-harm and self-sacrifice).

Just as McCall builds parallel narratives into Elevator Ride, Brooker is juggling too. Ban Dancing sets up a sustained attack on "dance culture" while simultaneously dismantling his own ego and identity as a bad dancer (and – at times – a negligent son). Much of the essay is a spoiled pot-luck supper of the things Brooker hates about the sensory world (methinks he's "sensory defensive"), haircuts being top of mind. When he's not attacking his own two left feet (while dancing he's a "distress signal made flesh"), he's railing against the public social spectacles (weddings, anniversaries, etc.) that demand we dance or die. There's a brilliant composite conversation between the author and any number of family members or event guests who've shamed, cajoled, or bullied him into getting down with his (very) bad self on the dance floor. Though more often than not, Brooker just refuses to take part in the festivities. He's formed a highly articulated rejection system that serves as both armor and lance.

So Ban Dancing has at least three layers baked-in to ensure its ranty goodness:

1 The narrative of self-deprecation and self-negation (I *can't* dance!)
2 Calling for the end of dance culture (None of us *should* dance!)
3 A hypothetical conversation between Brooker and pesky instigators (Get up *and* dance!)

The rationale behind having students write a rant is simple: we're an inherently negative species. Complaint and dissatisfaction are our natural state, our resting pulse. *On the gut-check level there is no nuance*; everything's binary: we love it, or we hate it, and – let's be honest with each other – a hoarder's trove fits into the latter category, while we're practically minimalists when it comes to the former.

When students enter my class in early fall, I quickly discover that many of them are too scared to take risks in their writing (the fear of being wrong), others have become too submissive to assert themselves (the fear of being offensive), and the balance can either do it (they're eager to let the inner child come out and play), *or they want to* – and will – given the right prompts and enough tarmac to get the DeLorean up to 88 MPH.

It's no different with my eight-year-old son, Brady. He loves to play games of chase with other kids on the playground at recess but was recently reprimanded for slapping when tagging someone *out*. Now, after school, he walks around our house saying he'll never play tag again.

That's what happens to our students. So many kids actually enjoy creative writing when they're young, when there are no rules (or reasonably few), and when the objective is "to play" and little else.

From a "common sense corner" perspective (that metaphorical place I stand and apply rudimentary logic), I started this process by asking myself: What essays have stayed with me over the years? What not "just resonated" with me but also got seared into my mind? Which ones do I return to and – more importantly – get excited about *performing* for my students?

Those kinds of question are so damn practical that it's liberating when you: (A) ask them to yourself and really spend time thinking about your supplemental dream curriculum, and (B) teach in an environment where you can actually execute it.

I was talking with a neighbor recently, Vernon, who taught in Texas for two years at a middle school that had a prescribed lock-step curriculum. Every English teacher in that Houston district had to be on page X by day Y or they'd be zig-zagging for a new job. The one time Vernon asked to deviate from the playbook (to incorporate the work of a Black author into a mostly Black school that exclusively taught dead, White men), he was told to put in a formal, written request before being denied without cause. In the aftermath, his principal told him he had a chip on shoulder.

That's an extreme case (if not an anathema). I've taught at four different public high schools, two colleges, and various summer programs, and I've only had one gig that had hints of Vernon's experience and bitter aftertaste (too much tannin).

But the rant-prompt lets your kids be actual kids again. Think of how many classic works are ranty: Catcher in the Rye, The Stranger, Moby Dick, Gulliver's Travels, A Room of One's Own, Othello, Macbeth, Brothers Karamazov, Bleak House, Atlas Shrugged, and large swaths of The Great Gatsby. This is a profoundly incomplete list that came off the top of my head. This prompt lines up with just about anything you might be teaching or aspire to teach. You could have your students read Swift's A Modest Proposal and write their own response to an injustice that is keeping them up at night. So much of what we do in English class is heavy, if not academically leaden. We teach books with redolent voice but fear the student personality that transcends the formal circumscriptions of our analytical prompts. We resent students who don't appreciate our essay assignments (oh, the moans and groans when we announce them), attentive feedback (often spending longer grading the paper than the student spent writing it), or *prompt* assessment return (one week service) – but how often do we check in with our students to ask,

> What would *you* like to write about? What's the thing you've been obsessing about or fixated on? What's something that you'd like to come to understand about yourself? What have you been trying to work out in your head that might be more fruitful to resolve on paper?

Students love to complain. There used to be "Rate My Teacher" – a website that was a clearinghouse for ad hominem attacks and a whetstone for battle-axes wielded by anonymous gripers. Many HS students cannot wait for college because "Rate My Professor" still exists and they'll get to return to old form.

Students winge about getting assigned too much homework, getting Google Classroom notifications after 4 PM, getting Teacher X on their schedule, getting kept out of an honors' level course, getting grade-locked, getting too little playing time, getting passed over for class officer, getting called to the vice principal's office for parking in the teacher's lot, getting ghosted from a group chat, getting a bad proposal, getting a B+, getting called-on last during class discussions, getting assigned to late lunch, getting called on when they didn't have their hand up, getting – well – you're getting the idea.

They are natural born ranters. So, let them rant.

My teacher's model for this assignment came about when I got on the elevator right outside my office on the third floor of Scarsdale High School Once cleared by the nurse (due to injury or ailment), students are allowed to use the elevator. There are only two functional ones in a school of 1,500 students and 162 staff.

It's an old building, put up in 1917. The stairs are worn down and relatively narrow. Able-bodied students are sometimes known to "hop on" to get from the first to fourth floor (expediently traveling from an English teacher's classroom to the foreign language wing, for example). Sometimes I chide them when the doors go "ting" and I see they're joyriding. Other times I'm too focused on how I'm going to start the class I'm heading to, to bother.

But mostly, the student passengers are on crutches, have casts, or can affect a convincing limp. And they bring friends with them. "Helpers" who can press buttons, hold doors, and carry obese JanSports on their behalf. (Oh the back problems these kids must have.)

This exchange below sufficiently rankled me to sit down and start writing that same day:

Teacher Model: The Rant Essay

Small Talk vs. Short Walk: My Not-So-Private Elevator Ride by Wes Phillipson

Of the two boys in the elevator, the one in the baggier-fleece pants, points to his ankle, or knee, or to some uncertain spot that is allegedly ruptured, giving him the right to ride the vertical commute to class with me. It's a box that reeks of robusta. It's a coffin-cable-car with the moldy melange of *sporific* hospitality. I'm descending just one short floor, or level, or stanza, to the landing that will take me to 207, to get my didactic dance on to the music of my own lesson-plans made flesh, and to my student's mellifluous musings about Camus or Frost.

The other boy off to my left is the hype man for the ad interim disabled dude.

"This side," he motions to the closed, steel doors with the puckered-lip running up-and-down the center where the doors eventually spring open after the ding. Vineyard Vines is telling me which side of the elevator to get off after I'd been a passenger for 21 years. I'd been a straphanger longer than he'd been blowin' snot through his kitten-nostrils.

I am Claudius in ancient Rome, feigning idiocy, feinting toward the wrong side.

North Face and Montauk laugh like Beavis and Butthead taken aback by the other door opening (they had Roulette-level-odds).

"We faked you out, dude," Bridgehampton Candy Kitchen quips.

"Maybe I was just playing along," I swagged slyly, "Been here 21 years."

"21 years!" REI's diaphragm sounds deflated.

I leave the liminality of the landing and the Dom-Perignon-bottle-filled-with-flat-sparkling-cider that was the exchange I'd just endured and considered like a constipated cobbler sitting on an unforgiving wooden bench making a really complicated pair of Berlutis:

With talk that's small, comes a mind that grows ever-smaller.

Lana Weiser once stopped me in front of the recycling containers and garbage bucket right outside 301-B, as I was smuggling my finest tomes (books of poems, after all – When in Rome, right?) into Zeliger's old office to put my stank on the space.

She'd email me:

"Thinking back to our encounter last week by the bins and your new office: we both SUCK at small talk, LOL (but at least our long talk proves to be better)."

1980s singer and Prince acolyte "Sheila E" cajoled listeners to live "The Glamorous Life," and that "boys with small talk, and small minds, really don't impress her," and I'm right there with Sheila in that Spotify mix: (some) boys, the decrepit elderly, the spry-aged, tweens, threenagers, or anyone "conversing condensely" is akin to getting your blood changed, and Keith Richards is the donor.

Say it small? I'd rather you not speak at all.

It's 100 degrees in the shadows? Your L-Train is so late that it must have derailed? The cost of petrol is percolating and depuffing your purchasing power? Your psoas muscle is locked up like Mubarak's cage in an Egyptian courtroom?

Care not I.

I want to be familiar with the inconsequential deets of your life as much as I want the Scarsdale Union Free School District to chip away at my summer vacay as if a half-blind Michelangelo finding the silhouette of David in that marble block, chisel in fist, eyes straining to eliminate the places that don't look human.

If the Beelzebub is in the bee-tails (vs. details), then I find the sting not worth the swollen hand. Time is the only resource that has no charging station – no takesy-backsies – no step-on-a-cracksy-break-your-mommas-backsies.

Meaning: My Amazon purchase was War and Peace, Moby Dick, maybe Wuthering Heights, but you want me to read a recap, blog-summary, or Wiki-entry of the books that have filled neural networks with more Cab Sav than a blood-bank-and-a-winery-crossover-pop-up-shop could decant.

And I can't.

The title of Debra Fine's "Fine Art of Small Talk" plays on her surname, and she's a sure dame, but it also suggests that it's "fine" (okay) to commit conscious chat, to chew the fat, to casually confab like you're rapping about Jack Sprat.

Drat.

* * *

I needed to conjure up the ghosts of satire past to bring something truly unique to this rant essay assignment, so I thought about that wonderful ranty scene from This is Spinal Tap when Nigel Tufnel goes off about his guitar amplifiers.

Nigel Tufnel: The numbers all go to eleven. Look, right across the board, eleven, eleven, eleven and…
Marty DiBergi: Oh, I see. And most amps go up to ten?
Nigel Tufnel: Exactly.
Marty DiBergi: Does that mean it's louder? Is it any louder?
Nigel Tufnel: Well, it's one louder, isn't it? It's not ten. You see, most blokes, you know, will be playing at ten. You're on ten here, all the way up, all the way up, all the way up, you're on ten on your guitar. Where can you go from there? Where?
Marty DiBergi: I don't know.
Nigel Tufnel: Nowhere. Exactly. What we do is, if we need that extra push over the cliff, you know what we do?

Marty DiBergi: Put it up to eleven.
Nigel Tufnel: Eleven. Exactly. One louder.
Marty DiBergi: Why don't you just make ten louder and make ten be the top number and make that a little louder?
Nigel Tufnel: [pause] These go to eleven.

The questions I asked myself were,

Why are so many students writing "level 1 sentences" that lack color saturation, personality, intensity, specificity, nuance, imagery, and – among other things – uniqueness?

What would a sophomore or junior "level 11 sentence" even look like?

Rants are really about sustained intensity and laser-like focus. People often think the opposite; rants are just rambling, sprawling, emotional fuel spilled on the highway – and BOOM! But not good ones.

1 They should be fun and cathartic for students to write.
2 They should push the boundaries of diction and syntax.

Sabrina Anders was a sophomore of mine when she ranted about misophonia. Her mother is Mimi Rocah, the District Attorney for Westchester County. Given the household she was raised in, she's no stranger to dinner-table arguments, overhearing rhetorical strategies, and the emphatic expression of one's viewpoint. Sabrina's mouth is faster than her brain; it's hard for one to keep pace with the other. And that's saying something – because her mind is perpetually swarming with ideas and plans. She's a fast talker, and a quick study. We'd often conference during class for just a few minutes: she'd listen to me think out loud about her essay, jot down some notes, have her AH-HA moment, racing back to her desk across the room.

With students like Sabrina, this kind of focused-yet-simultaneously-open-ended prompt really fuels creativity and sustains engagement.

World-building is also central to what I teach, and that's well represented in this piece on misophonia, as Sabrina naturally makes mythic Greek and Roman allusions throughout.

Here's Prompt Eleven

Assignment Write-Up: The RANT ESSAY

Pro-Tip: RANTS Are FOCUSED ATTACKS, NOT Tangents

If you don't know what a "rant" is – then look it up. I do not believe in defining things for people. And you should NEVER, ever, ever define something in an essay or a handout. It's bad writing.

This essay prompt is asking you to ACCOMPLISH 3 things in 650 words (the length of a college essay personal statement). There is a PLUS OR MINUS OF EXACTLY ZERO WORDS.

1. JOB 1 – Have a topic that really annoys you, pisses you off, makes you say – "that's a pet peeve of mine," or just outright makes you cringe, or gets you angry. It should be something that you "want to go OFF on." (Even if it's a small, harmless thing to most people; it should really bother – or worse – YOU). Perhaps it's something you wish you could uninvent (like iPhones, dancing, English class, grades, texting, etc.).
2. JOB 2 – Use highly detailed, specific, and "well-built" figurative language FOR THE ENTIRE ESSAY. EVERY SENTENCE. EVERY WORD MUST BE a metaphor, simile, pun, hyperbole, burlesque, caricature, onomatopoeia, chiasmus, tautology, enjambment, alliteration, allusion, consonance, assonance, oxymoron, imagery, OR (among others) a synecdoche. IF YOU DON'T KNOW what some of these are, and you want to, look them up.

    The WAY YOU USE figurative language must "MAKE SENSE" in relationship to the other cases in your essay. You can't really talk about sneaker metaphors in sentence one, and lobster metaphors in sentence two, UNLESS IT MAKES SENSE to do that.
3. JOB 3 – "Live sentence-to-sentence" (to quote classmate Katie Kendall). Each sentence must have SHARP details. Each sentence must BUILD UP your RANT, be essential to telling your RANT, and help us FEEL whatever emotion/s you want us to FEEL, and THINK what you want us to THINK. REMEMBER: you are manipulating your reader, or failing to.

This essay CANNOT tell us things we already know (unless it's part of the sarcasm, verbal irony, etc.). This essay CANNOT contain a SINGLE cliche or phrase that appears more than 100,000 times in a Google search. This essay CANNOT contain a single moment that RESTS, COASTS, or TAKES A BREAK. **That's the Spinal-Tap-Level-11 rule that we've discussed in class, so let's honor it.**

There can be NO "half-measures" in this essay. You can't be half-committed to it. You can't do it half-way. You can't make it half-good. You can't make it half-figurative and half-literal, either.

You must PUSH each sentence to its maximum occupancy, standing-room only crowd, words crowded up against the wall, gasping for air. Trach time ... making us say ... Damn, Son!

12
DAVE'S WAY

The Humor Essay a la Dave Barry

I live in Armonk, New York, an Ambien-tinged town with a lot of new-money finance people who get picked up early by their drivers in massive black SUVs, ferrying them to Greenwich or Wall Street. About 60 years ago, IBM opened its world headquarters here. There's an upscale ski and bike shop, two bagel places within spitting distance of each other, and boutique real estate agencies aplenty. Within its limits exist about 4,000 people. Two decades ago there was no grocery store. Today we have a small-batch ice cream shop (open till 10 PM on weekends), and a DeCicco's supermarket in the town's modest square that sells produce at New Canaan prices.

Dave Barry – at one point – lived here too.

He's likely the most successful humor columnist in syndication history and the surprised winner of a Pulitzer Prize for Social Commentary (a genre he claims he's never once engaged in). His best friend is the horror writer Stephen King, and, respectively, they form 1/19th of a rock-n-roll collective called The Rock Bottom Remainders. Amy Tan, Mitch Albom, and Matt Groening are also part of this deep bench of weekend-warrior musicians.

Barry wrote much of what Steve Martin presented at the 2001 Academy Awards, but he's known for being a hipper version of Garrison Keillor (of A Prairie Home Companion fame). His brand of humor vacillates between dry and absurdist, and he – in many ways – pioneered the dad-joke. For the uninitiated, I'd begin with reading "Tarts Afire" – the satirically delicious account of Dave and his neighbor (with his wife gone for the afternoon) testing out the flammability of Pop Tarts. "Lost in America" is a touching portrait of a shared road trip taken during the last days of Barry's mother. While there are some poignant essays in his body of work, nearly all are comedic.

My conversation with Barry (over email) began with two questions: "Any chance you'd Zoom with my literature students in the fall or winter (not that you have those in Florida)? I just want you to help students get at the idea of: How do I arrive at something worth writing about, and what are some approaches to executing my ideas?"

That message was sent on the last day of July 2022. I got Dave's response 24 hours later.

From a distance, Barry taught my junior classes a few priceless core beliefs that have helped change the way I operate or – at the very least – made me believe in my own practices:

- The writer's sole job is to entertain the reader. While Barry is an alleged "social commentator" (hence the Pulitzer), he never sets out to educate or inform. It's not even in the back of his mind. I don't know if Barry said it or I intuited it, but it seemed that his goal was to cut anything from a draft that creates wind-drag on the vehicle – to make essays as aerodynamic as possible. I had previously taught this idea as "winning the attention game." At his peak, Barry was syndicated in over 500 newspapers in America and abroad. Most of his 30 books were bestsellers. One reasonable conclusion to draw from these two facts is that he was (and is) an entertainer who keeps his audiences on the hook.
- The use of puns in your writing is the commission of a cardinal sin. Barry has never found puns to be a reasonable basis for comedy. He sees them as cheap and inelegant. He might have even used the word "hacky" when we discussed their absence in his columns. My argument to Dave was that the long-running TV show Frasier (which was revived in 2023) used puns as a staple of the repartee between psychotherapist brothers Niles and Frasier Crane. Barry either (A) didn't find the show particularly funny or (B) felt that there was a clear distinction between how puns played when recited by sitcom stars vs. how they'd be received by column readers.
- Writing never –under any circumstance or level of success – gets any easier. Barry's semi-promise to my students is that "writing is likely to get more fun the longer you do it." But he's never confident about whether he's finished with a piece – both in the sense of how to end it and when it's good enough to go to print. It was more like: I know it's done when my deadline comes and my editor takes it. The clear message was that even Dave Barry is never truly satisfied with any draft, and living with that uncertainty is just something professional writers must tolerate, if not endure.
- Exaggeration seems to be Barry's secret sauce. He doesn't write fiction or tell lies for fun and profit. Instead, he prides himself on distorting the details of an afternoon spent (for example) turning a toaster and a breakfast

pastry into something that could (A) solve the energy crisis, or (B) provide reliable missile defense, or (C) both. Tarts Afire is the account of Dave and his neighbor friend seeing how easily a toaster oven can be weaponized. His description of the flame height or its applications to society are the aspects of the story that get amplified or become absurdist, while the physical actions in the story are all faithfully recorded as they happened.

Prior to 2022 (and Barry's involvement with my classes), I'd used many models of comedic nonfiction writing to help students see "voice in action." I hadn't ever assigned a "humor essay" per se. My teaching of the college essay was definitely influenced by David Sedaris. I'd used selections from his well-known collection When You Are Engulfed in Flames with juniors and seniors working on their personal statements for the Common Application. "That's Amore," "In the Waiting Room," "Town and Country," and "The Smoking Section" are masterclasses in self-deprecation, radical honesty, profound vulnerability, and narrative structure. These stories are first-person accounts of Sedaris as a gay, Jewish New York intellectual bumping up against homophobia, bigotry, reverse-xenophobia, language barriers, class warfare, and public embarrassment. All of it is couched in a kind of self-loathing that is highly endearing and engaging. *And funny.*

Former junior Jessie Kwon had succeeded in writing an edgy showcase for her personality after modeling Sedaris' work. It had a direct-effect on the story of Jessie visiting her grandfather at the cemetery. In this piece, you can hear echoes of Sedaris' voice, the awkwardness Jessie builds through setting and characterization, and the humor that comes from it. If sitcom stands for "situation-comedy," then the comedy should derive from the context. That's not usually the case (it's often the laugh track that informs us "it's funny" when it's anything but). Jessie's college essay is organically so:

"Hey Jessie," my cousin Jonathan tapped me on the shoulder. "Have you ever played the Gameboy Advanced?" In seventh grade, he's at that obnoxious stage that we've all gone through – the one where he "playfully" (note: awkwardly) punches me in the shoulder and laughs, the way a cheesy TV show character would when saying, "how ya doin', sport?" My other cousins were chasing each other and laughing, two of them retreating to the minivan for a quick juicebox break. My mom was talking to my older cousin about driving in the city. My dad was asking a different cousin about summer internship opportunities for my brother. The perks of having a giant extended family, besides having enough relatives to start a small mafia (I can see the headlines now – Kwong family takedown: triad ravages Westchester County), is having connections.

All this would've seemed like a regular Asian gathering, and for me it was, except for the fact that we were in a cemetery. My grandfather passed away before I had a chance to get to know him, so visiting his grave every spring feels more like a tradition than an emotional trigger, as mundane as, say, getting a car wash; it's not something you'd do frequently, but when you do it's not a big deal: We go, bow, burn some incense and money (fake, of course; it's our way of funding them in the underworld – you know how cranky dead people get when you don't send them their annual Monopoly-style allowance by fire. Haunting you and giving you bad luck and shit. Yeah, I hate when that happens.) and when we're done, we pack up and continue about our day.

As we waited for some other cousins to arrive (I know, there are more?), my dad saw his sister at another tombstone a few rows down. "Oh right, that's where my cousin's buried," he mused.

"Oh please, Paul. I've never seen you visit them. We come here all the time, and I bet you don't even know where their graves are," my mom snorted derisively.

"Of course I do! Come on, Jessie, let's check it out." As we walked away from my mom, my dad leaned toward me conspiratorially. "Wanna know a secret? I've never actually been to their graves before." He chuckled as I rolled my eyes. Typical.

We passed a cousin and his immediate family stopped at his wife's niece's grave and walked down to my aunt, my dad calling out to her. They talked in Chinese for a bit, and then my dad explained that we were at his uncle's oldest daughter's grave. I asked my dad about some of the writing on the tombstone, and again he consulted my aunt. After translating, he turned to the grave and began to bow, the customary greeting to deceased family members.

"Wrong one," my aunt deadpanned.

My dad had essentially paid respects to a random corpse the same way he would his father.

Nice gesture, dad, but you really don't have to greet everyone in this place. Of course, I laughed, probably a little too hard given that we were in a cemetery where a couple was picnicking by a most lovely headstone a few feet away. And there was a funeral party just up the hill.

As we walked back to the main congregation around my grandfather's grave, I breathed in the refreshing scent of smoking incense. Everyone had arrived. I smirked, basking in the gentle sun and a slight breeze, on a hill (with a splendid view overlooking hundreds of tombstones), surrounded by family members (alive and dead), my younger cousins giggling and skipping through the graves (oblivious that they were running on skeletons) and feeling like the Mount Pleasant Cemetery was a perfectly suitable location for a family reunion.

As the remnants of the paper money crackled against the worn metal bin, we bowed one last time. On our way home, my dad stopped at a car wash.

* * *

What's most interesting about teaching humor writing to high school students is that they really don't believe an essay can be "laugh out loud" funny. While Sedaris may travel around the world to sell-out crowds that hear him live-read his essays (and the throngs most certainly do "LOL"), and Bill Maher decidedly does read out his scripted "New Rules" each Friday night on HBO's Real Time to the bird-song of audience hoots, hollers, guffaws, snickers, and audible groans all the way through … it's unlikely that Barry's **readers** (by way of one of the 500 newspapers that carried his column) rolled on the floor laughing.

When doing interviews for his memoir The Cobbler, Steve Madden said, "The truth is always more interesting." Honesty also has a better shot at making someone laugh.

Recently I used a Bill Maher "New Rules" essay (in print form) from his bestseller What This Comedian Said Will Shock You. It was an anti-screed: incredibly short, concise, efficient, and damn funny – not a wasted word to be found. **In it,** he attacked comic-book-loving Gen Zers and Millennials who fanboy out about The Marvel or DC Universe at the expense of their emotional development. The class' favorite line – that engendered a meaningful LOL – was: "That's not Iron Man, that's irony, man." And what Rohan, a prepossessed young man of about 16, said was, "It's impressive that a team of writers created that, but the voices are blended nearly invisibly into Maher's."

That's why models of writing are essential in an English classroom. I am profoundly mediocre at humor writing. To be fair (to myself), I haven't done much of it – four pieces come to mind: narratives about my wife's dream of heisting a panda from the San Diego Zoo, the difference between "mom face" and "dad face," an embarrassing moment from my senior year of high school that involved an inept sociology teacher and two class clowns, and my exaggerated experience at a Tony Robbins seminar in the 1990s. But it's not my forte. Comedy writing is not going to fund my 403(b), but it's going to help my students locate a brave voice inside of themselves – and tap into an irreverence and clarity that is sorely lacking in essays about Of Mice and Men or To Kill a Mockingbird.

The View's Joy Behar said (on Maher's Real Time) that "comedians are the modern day philosophers," and I like the utility of that statement. Lenny Bruce, Richard Pryor, and George Carlin were abstract thinkers and social critics who often got political and even more frequently attacked cherished, sacred institutions. And they were (objectively) funny more than they weren't.

Students need to have their own ideas and opinions before they can write anything that will mean something to themselves – let alone their readers. Think about what teaching humor writing can accomplish when done (even remotely) well. Walk into your English class armed with Sedaris (I'd start with The Waiting Room – it's a potent lesson in how shame makes for sparkling comedy; David is his own worst patient, relegated to the exterior waiting room in a paper gown while others sit among him, fully dressed, waiting to be called), Maher (use anything from What This Comedian Said Will Shock You; some pieces are shorter than others, some are less inflammatory, less acerbic, and even less political: Choose something that fits your school's culture, knowing that you still may need to edit for content), Chuck Klosterman (Perpetual Topeka is a study in contradictions about two cultural figures, focused on Klosterman's own parasocial relationship with Kanye West and LeBron James), and Barry (the aforementioned Tarts Afire is accessible and humanizing – and very funny).

But it's not enough to *just show models* of "funny" to our students.

You have to want to cultivate a room full of people who will take that leap of faith. Being funny – on purpose – is an act of stark vulnerability.

I began by borrowing from an XM Radio comedy talk show called Ron and Fez. It was a bit Ron and Fez dubbed "building a comedy pyramid." The premise was: The show's hosts would ask their audience to call in and (for example) create a nickname for a celebrity couple (known as a portmanteau). Each caller would attempt to outdo the previous example, until the "pyramid had been built" (someone had – metaphorically – placed the last brick in place at the structure's apex: **Peak funny** had been achieved). After listening to the show for years (and catching dozens of comedy pyramid segments), I realized that Ron and Fez had simply turned its listening audience into a writer's room where one caller would feed off another. Comedy doesn't exist in a vacuum. So much of it is reacting to stimuli.

So I tried it.

I called it Funny Fridays. My students had a blast – they fell over themselves presenting their own Google slideshows depicting how their group took a first-draft punchline and transformed it into one that would (ideally) get a big laugh. Most presenters were in unbreakable hysterics throughout. What I noticed was: The *presenters* found themselves irresistibly funny, but – in all honestly – they weren't. But it loosened everyone up. In spite of all the bad jokes told that day, and the decided lack of seriousness in the room, it was the quickest way to break my students of their worst habit: **writing for their teachers**.

That had forever been a problem I was trying to solve.

Through this, my mantra has become: Write for yourself first, and your teacher somewhere far down that line. Long-time SHS Physics teacher and Speech-and-Debate advisor Joe Vaughan (I've often referred to him as the smartest guy in the room) has the strong belief that students must learn to write for the teacher or professor they have *now*. We discussed it at a faculty meeting once and I said – at face value – sure, it's practical advice, Joe. I largely agreed. And I still do – for everyone else's English or History classes, but not mine. Why? It's because that's precisely what they've always done, and it's yielded (occasionally) a strong essay here or there, but rarely the chance to develop a persona over time that they can own, or to forge an identity on paper that has purpose and intention. That takes time. That takes commitment. That takes a course dedicated to that process, where everything else is secondary.

Avant-garde jazz trumpeter Miles Davis was right – "It's not the notes, it's the intention behind them." Delight in him or despise him, but Bill Maher knows who he is, what he wants to say, and how he wants to express it. **How many of your first semester students can you say that about? What about by the end of your course?**

Maher's voice is distinct: it's mellifluously ironic, dotted with a playful cattiness, marked by tongue-in-cheek wryness, and delivered with the authority of someone who wrote it (or co-authored it at least).

Maher's words have conviction and therefore potency. He embraces the contradictions in his thinking. His digressions pay dividends. And – oh yeah – he's funny. Yes, sometimes he walks right up to the line of good taste and smudges the wet ink so that it offends (or "shocks" as his book title suggests), but why don't we allow our students to locate and give life to their inner Bill Maher (or Sedaris, Barry, Pryor, Carlin, John Mulaney, Donald Glover, Amy Schumer, Ali Wong), or any stand-up comedy writer of the last 50 years?

The opposite of this practice is chilling. As a junior in high school, I was humiliated by my public-speaking teacher for using the term "brownnose" in a piece of original oratory I'd delivered. While it's true that my instructor was old (likely in her late 70s), and largely out-of-touch with the youths in the room, it was an adrenaline-filled moment that clearly forged something inside of me. I can't recall her name (I've entirely blocked it out), but I can recall the name of my favorite English teacher (Elizabeth Smith), and my beloved art teacher (Janet Armentano). *I think that means something that I can't articulate.* But whatever-her-name-was, she recorded my speech and played back the word "brown-nose" in front of the entire class like it was a viral remix video of an ill-fated politician's soundbite.

That moment made me believe that students should be given the permission to walk right up to the line of what's appropriate. Is our goal as teachers of writing to hold students back, penalize them for errant commas and occasional profanity? For using "I?" Did we get into this profession so we could sit and grade a stack of nearly identical, thesis-driven papers about the meaning of the green light in The Great Gatsby?

I didn't. And I won't live that way.

And that's why a humor writing unit early-on in your class (sometime in the first quarter) (A) helps students "buy in" to the notion they have something to say and (B) lets them explore, on their own terms, what's appropriate and what's inappropriate. Yes, the adult in the room has to be the arbiter or referee, but isn't building self-reliance more important than a few ruffled feathers?

Keep in mind that the students who enter your classroom in late summer or early fall are the same ones who – just last year – weren't allowed to use first person pronouns in their English or History essays. They're the same ones who were (likely) given a thesis-statement template for every essay or were dictated an outline of "what they had to write," and so much of what your job will be is helping them "unlearn" some of those prior practices.

Former student Axel Ahdritz, currently attending Claremont McKenna College, returned to Scarsdale HS in recent years to give my students a presentation on "How to unlearn everything high school taught you," after discovering that his path forward would be best cleared and swept of the (relative) detritus of the past four years.

And – to keep with the Miles Davis idea – comedy is a lot like jazz. It requires improvisation and expressing things that might be cacophonous. Jazz is about working within a structure but also breaking free of it. It's about irreverence as much as traditions. It's about "being cool" (hence: Davis' LP Birth of the Cool). It's performative. So, there are countless baked-in skills that come with this unit. It's like a child's toy that has no assembly required, and no parts sold separately. Nearly everything I eventually want to accomplish with my student-writers is contained herein.

Wild Wesley Wednesdays was phase two of my plan to warm up students. I slapped a ridiculous alliterative title on the event using my name and the day of the week (and the promise of alleged "wildness" to reel them in). My first volunteer was Lucas Heidbreder, a Latin scholar in the making who also loved to nerd out on sci-fi books. Lucas came to a Wednesday class meeting with a draft of his humor essay in hand, took a seat in the wooden high-backed stool at the front of the room, and proceeded to read a story of foreign hijinks and profound embarrassment: It was a farcical tale of mixed-up suitcases in Italy, involving an 80-plus-year-old playboy, his young mistress, and the imbroglio that unfolded once Lucas took home the wrong bag from the airport to his host family's home.

As we watched Lucas perform (and – at times – veer from the script: Remember the comedy and jazz connection I mentioned earlier?), it was clear that (A) students could be cerebral and funny, (B) Gen Zers could be funny without resorting to memes, viral videos, bathroom humor, or TikTok-level vapidness, and (C) students will take calculated risks when you give them the running room to do so.

Listen, Lucas' scripted comedy was raw and real. It had some adult content that resonated with the room and got the biggest laughs – and gasps – (because the truth is always more interesting). It shimmied right up to that line ….

But it was Lucas' bold turn that led classmates Amelia Fader to recite her essay about flatulence and sundry offensive odors, Eian Tsou to read his prepared "shower thoughts," and Isaac Tiomkin to give a rousing recount of a basement party in Scarsdale that bordered on criminal mischief.

Not to be outdone, Belen (Bee) Burgert stood and delivered (as if a Moth Radio Hour performer) the blow-by-blow of a car accident that was most decidedly not her fault (despite seeming entirely her fault – underscored by a questionable parking job in her mom's Fiat 500 during a Chipotle run).

That was my junior honor's English "Essay Two" assignment from early October of 2023, and it laid the groundwork for nearly every other good thing that happened that year that would likely have not happened otherwise.

Resources

Table of Contents:

- Humor Essay Assignment Write-Up
- Teacher Model: Mom Face by Wes Phillipson
- Student Model: Manifest Destiny – My Cracker Barrel Odyssey by Rishi Shadaksharappa

Here's Prompt Twelve

The Humor Essay Write-Up: Dave's Way

Dave Barry told my JR class last year something about the process that led him to win the Pulitzer Prize for – wait for it – **commentary**. And that process was:

> "**I didn't have anything to say**; I just wanted to entertain people." Super-duper ironic.

Dave Barry was just writing what HE found funny. He was a baby-boomer writing – at 25 – about baby-boomer issues, concerns, and topics. If you're a Gen-Zer, then perhaps it makes sense for you to do the same through that lens.

The Assignment

Dave Barry writes about America. He – also – writes about the places he knows really well (for the past several decades that's been Miami, Florida). But he was born in Armonk, NY, and he was a reporter in West Chester, PA (also ironic, right?). He's written about those places, too.

Dave writes about situations that are funny to him. On occasion, he writes **serious** pieces. Typically, those are prefaced with: "This is not a humor column today."

Most significantly, Dave said something that is 100% true for me, too: "I only write what actually happens to me. I don't make things up. I exaggerate, sure, but I tinker with my degrees of exaggeration."

And, when I asked him what was the most difficult part of writing an essay or article, he offered this:

"Every part of what you just described – the ending, the last line, the wordsmithing, the knowing when I'm done – all of it is hard." It's not easy for him, either. Quite the opposite.

So, if Dave lives in Miami, he writes about what happens to him in Miami. If Dave takes his mom on a road trip, he writes about what happens to him on a road trip. Then – what about you?

Write a column. What it has to be: something that happened to you and is entertaining to read.

What could I have assigned for this essay?

*I COULD say, write 1,500 words on what it means for you to be an American. (*for clarity's sake here I say "could" because since 2003 I assigned this EXACT essay every single year about "being an American," and I almost never got a good piece of thinking or writing out of it; maybe that's a "me problem," or maybe it's a design problem; I don't think **America** has figured out, yet, "what *it* is," so how could a 16 year old? And who's to say that any given student at SHS is "an American" or identifies as such? To any teacher who assigns this essay I can only say: If it works for you, that's great. I've taught at six schools over my career if you count teaching college, and I've never NOT seen this essay assigned by one of my colleagues OR by me, myself, and I; I wonder what that means? I just know that I'll never assign it again after meeting Dave Barry because these essays are NOT entertaining and they are RARELY enlightening for the teacher or the student.)

So, quite freakin' frankly, I don't care. I ONLY CARE THAT YOU ENTERTAIN ME.

Dave didn't have anything to say (according to Dave himself), but he sure as heck *said* something – and that something resonated with readers across the country.

He's the best teacher: the one who gets you to learn when you don't even know you're learning. And he's his own best student: What came out of him came NOT from a compulsion to "teach" us, but it taught, regardless. He (also) learned a great deal about himself while not having the **need** to teach it or say it.

What's NOT entertaining?

- Using cliches
- A lack of honesty

- Exaggeration that isn't calibrated (how MUCH do I exaggerate – what feels right?)
- Being "meta" in the worst possible way: let me write an essay that talks about how I have nothing to talk about, or I don't know what I want to write about, or how HS essays are just fluffy B.S.
- Trying to be something you're not
- Forcing a joke
- PUNS (according to Dave – they CAN be clever, but never funny)
- Repeating yourself
- Essays that don't "read well out loud" – or that are "not digestible" (using Helen's phrase)
- Taking yourself too seriously (Dave's superpower comes from being raised "not to")
- ANY ESSAY THAT FEELS LIKE AN ESSAY, OR – WORSE – AN H.S. ESSAY
- Writing what you DON'T know or aren't genuinely invested in

Specs:

- The length should be (approximately) the length of a Dave Barry column.
- The piece could be serious, humorous, or a mix of the two.
- Time frame/due date:
- Can be read aloud to the class (but it's not mandatory).

WHERE TO BEGIN: What's happening in your life? What's an entertaining story from your recent past? ***What will entertain YOU will (likely) also entertain ME.***

(maybe) HOW TO DRAFT THIS:

This assignment is VERY hard (I think). It DEMANDS that you be ruthlessly honest with yourself and CUT ANY + EVERYTHING that isn't entertaining.
For this article: There can't be ONE DEAD sentence, or bit of fluff, or cop-out, or repetition, or useless detail. There can't be a "thesis restatement" or summarizing a point you've already made. *There can be no wind-drag.*
So – the hard part isn't going to be writing it – it's going to be mowing down sentences with metaphorical machetes. Pulling up, by their roots, those useless things that are found in the rancid, rank recesses of your essay. The things you'd normally not see – because you want to make the word count, or you're tired.

But you've got a reader to please – or – if you're Dave – 80 million of them. And you owe them something. You owe them a laugh.

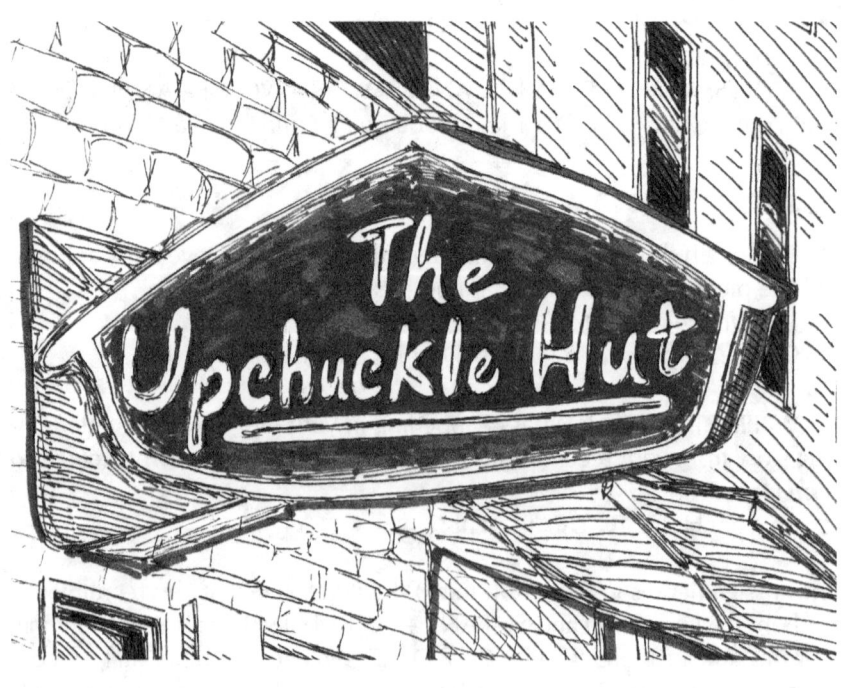

13
THE POETRY FORGERY UNIT
How Imitation Breeds Greatness

My father taught English at Newton North High School for decades (starting in the 1970s), and their Department eventually devised a unit called "Poems That Work." It was a massive three-ring binder of hundreds of poems that had some guiding questions and a few prompts for students to engage with. The idea was: here are classroom-tested poems that will break through the cynical armor of even the most jaded high school students (who believe poetry is for emo kids, middle school boys with crushes, or old professor types).

When I student-taught at NNHS in a classroom near my dad's in 1994, I only knew one thing about poetry: it was foreign and inaccessible to me (and by extension, my students). It was either too abstract or overly sentimental. But my father, Brainerd Phillipson, often recited Shakespeare's Sonnet 29 to anyone who'd listen:

> When, in disgrace with fortune and men's eyes,
> I all alone beweep my outcast state,
> And trouble deaf heaven with my bootless cries,
> And look upon myself and curse my fate,
> Wishing me like to one more rich in hope,
> Featured like him, like him with friends possessed,
> Desiring this man's art and that man's scope,
> With what I most enjoy contented least;
> Yet in these thoughts myself almost despising,
> Haply I think on thee, and then my state,

(Like to the lark at break of day arising
From sullen earth) sings hymns at heaven's gate;
For thy sweet love remembered such wealth brings

That then I scorn to change my state with kings.

He'd explain that the first seven lines presented the problem (in this case – isolation and desperation), and the second seven the solution (here – solace found in reflecting on one's true love and having an attitude of gratitude).

Even today, dad favors the Romantics – Shelley, Bryon, and especially Blake. He often quotes the first quatrain of William Blake's Auguries of Innocence as a reminder of his own personal credo and a call to action to anyone within the sound of his voice:

To see a World in a Grain of Sand
And a Heaven in a Wild Flower
Hold Infinity in the palm of your hand
And Eternity in an hour.

Growing up, I was surrounded by valuable volumes in my family's Holliston, Massachusetts home that was packed with books as if a microcosm of the U.K. bibliophilic town Hay-on-Wye: a first edition of Spenser's The Faerie Queene, the earliest Canadian publication of Shakespeare's 154 Sonnets, and an entire floor-to-ceiling bookcase of dust-jacketed originals by everyone from Robinson Jeffers, Robert Frost, and Edna St. Vincent Millay – to Soviet era poet Yevgeny Yevtushenko's collaboration with John Updike.

But none of that changed the fact that I didn't understand poetry, nor why it had taken hold of my father's imagination, leading him (as if in a Milton-esque trance) to walk around his backyard with leather-bound book in hand, passionately speaking couplets to the trees and flowers, or breaking into verse at family reunions when the mood struck. In those moments people were startled – if not impressed – by my dad's effusive performances, often left wondering: How did he do that? How does he know these poems by heart?

Years later, I'd discover a book in my father's library by American poet and academic John Ciardi (the only person in history to have his own talk show about poetry on network television). It was Ciardi's handbook on the subject: How Does a Poem Mean? An awkward, clunky title, where the word "How" feels like a misarticulation of "What?" It promised to (among other things) help the reader understand Robert Frost's Stopping by Woods on a Snowy Evening – that it wasn't a literal narrative of what the title implied, but a deeper meditation on how one's life work lies ahead, and death or completion is farther away than we realize or wish to admit.

While I tried using excerpts from the Ciardi book in my junior American literature class, it never really captured me or my students. The text was too dense, and I couldn't – for the life of me – explain why Ciardi used "How" vs. "Why" in the title.

For different reasons, the interactive and inventive book De/Compositions by confessional poet W.D. Snodgrass was recommended to me by friend and Literature and Composition professor David Solomon. It's 101 "good poems gone wrong" (as the subtitle reads). Snodgrass rewrites classics by masters from various eras, producing a side-by-side juxtaposition to show readers the brilliance and artistry of accomplished poets, pulling back the curtain on the heavy lifting that goes into producing an enduring poem.

But it wasn't Ciardi, Snodgrass, nor even the roving poet/English teacher/father Brainerd F. Phillipson who helped me engage with the medium, **it was a game I'd played as a kid**. My father (to this day) has a garage full of – not cars – but books. These are the lesser volumes that aren't worthy of being kept in the house. Some of them have gotten mildewed or infiltrated by termites. At age six (back in 1978), I came across a signed copy of John Updike's novel Of the Farm. On the front endpaper, Updkie's scrawl was loose and impressionistic, with some connected letters and others untouching. His casual double looped "J" gave way to what looked like a cursive "m" with three humps (that was supposed to be "ohn" in John). Shelving had been built into either side of my parent's garage from the floor up to the rafters. On one dusty, knotted plank next to Of the Farm was an unsigned copy of Problems (also by Updike). I walked the 20 feet back to the main house and got a pen. Two minutes later I'd "forged" Updike's signature on the front flyleaf of Problems. Sometime later, my father's friend found it randomly and was fooled by my childish attempt. At that moment my father and his friend learned they had a mini Tom Ripley on their hands.

It was about 20 years before I could use my copycat skills again – and productively this time. Newton North High School's "Poems That Work" *hadn't worked*. Ciardi had left me head-scratching. Snodgrass seemed like an anti-magician who violated the one rule they held dear: never reveal how the trick is done.

As a third year English teacher, I both needed and wanted to teach poetry, but I was decades away from deftly navigating the cerebral landscapes of Wallace Stevens, or willingly wading through the wastelands of Charles Bukowski.

But students are mimetic. Many of them have forged their parents' signatures at one time or another (for harmless reasons or just out of convenience – a school field trip permission slip, or a college application as their parent's proxy). Most teenagers are – to some degree – copycats. They love viral internet memes (the term coming from the Greek "mimema" – something that has been imitated). They are – according to Madison Avenue's VALS survey from the 1980s – overwhelmingly "emulators," attempting to pass themselves off as self-assured and successful.

So my thinking was, what if I took the idea of forgery and emulation – of being purposefully mimetic – and applied that to teaching poetry? It felt a bit like the Tom Sawyer fence-painting trick cross-bred with building a Trojan Horse – a backdoor to getting students into a literary form and medium they saw as foreign, mushy nonsense put to paper.

It had to begin with me, though. I had to sit down and figure out (A) how to codify it, and (B) how to convert that repeatable process into a poem that would fool a class of sharp-eyed 15 year olds. And it had to be a game: I truly believe in the gamification of teaching English whenever possible. Poetry is only fun once you understand it, once you become facile with its moving parts. So I started with Harlem Renaissance writer Langston Hughes, whose poems are either deceptively simple, or openly complex. I went with the former category, figuring it would be easier to forge (fake, approximate, convincingly recreate) a basic two-stanza poem by Hughes that appeared to have little depth or meaning beneath the surface. I quickly landed upon 1947's Snail.

How I Faked a Langston Hughes Poem in 30 minutes:

My model by Hughes is "Snail" –
Little snail,
Dreaming you go.
Weather and rose
Is all you know.

Weather and rose
Is all you see,
Drinking
The dewdrop's
Mystery.

Step One: **I "crack the code"** of the Hughes poem "Snail." It appears that he was using a simple nature observation (a snail in a garden) to "get at" a bigger idea: that – perhaps – little children (particularly Black children) don't yet know that life is more than just "weather and roses." Hughes is speaking of their innocence before the fall: when White society finds ways to exploit their labor, prevent them from equal access to facilities and institutions, and treat them as second-class citizens without designated rights. Again, this piece was written in 1947 and published two years later in his collection One-Way Ticket, so we're talking pre-Civil Right Act, in the thick of Jim Crow-era America.

Step Two: **I pinpoint the style techniques** (how the form drives the content). In "Snail," I see the repetition of one phrase ("weather and rose"), and the slight variation of another ("Is all you know" vs. "Is all you see"). There are two stanzas. The language is incredibly simple. There are two key verbs: "Dreaming" and "Drinking." The poem is addressed to someone (or thing) – in this case – a "Little snail." Stanza one is two complete sentences. Stanza two is one complete sentence. There is punctuation within (and at the end) of each stanza. All first letters of each line are capitalized. There's a clear and consistent rhyme scheme. The poem's message is deliberately understated. The first stanza has four lines; the second has five. Each line has four syllables (except for the second half of stanza two).

Step Three: **I think of an occasion that would inspire a Hughes poem** that never specifically became a Hughes poem. In service of this, I conduct ten minutes of Wiki research to find out something about the man himself, and I begin to form an idea. I find this quote on Hughes' Wikipedia page: "I was unhappy for a long time, and very lonesome, living with my grandmother. Then it was that books began to happen to me, and I began to believe in nothing but books and the wonderful world in books – where if people suffered, they suffered in beautiful language, not in monosyllables, as we did in Kansas." With his words in mind, I'm going to build my forgery around Hughes' grandma, books, monosyllables, and (indirectly) Kansas. I'm going to use (to a point) the structure and rhythm of "Snail" for formatting purposes, mimicking its thematics and structure (and resolution) as well.

I'll call it "Monosyllabic" – which is risky, because it's (at face value) more sophisticated from a diction standpoint than most Hughes' titles.
Here it goes:

"Monosyllabic"
By Langston Hughes (aka Wes Phillipson, the forger)

Grandmother's shelf
Lacks all the books,
For a Black boy
Whose mind's a brook.

> For a Black boy
> Whose mind's a stream,
> The words
> Evaporate
> Like so much steam.

There are many ways to approach – and implement – this assignment in your English classroom.

I use it in all of my classes each year as a group exercise to build esprit de corps and bolster self-belief about writing. My sophomores do a poetry forgery, my juniors (in American Lit) do an F. Scott Fitzgerald short story "embedded" forgery, and my seniors in Words and Images create passages in the style of Patricia Highsmith or Tim O'Brien (and weave them into an existing short story written by the real authors). All that means is: for my upperclassmen, I apply this "poetry forgery concept" I created to writing short fiction. It's the same assignment, just adjusted slightly.

Logistically, what does this look like for The Poetry Forgery specifically?

For my tenth graders it's making a packet of four poems. Three are real, one is their forgery. They are obligated to ensure that the three authentic poems are vetted and faithfully represented in the packet. That means (A) thoughtful proofreading, (B) careful formatting or reformatting, and (C) cross-checking it against published source material (which usually means a trip to the school or town library to get a physical copy of the book the poems came from).

I encourage students to work in groups of "up to three people." Four means that someone will sit and do nothing, and three is the tipping point. Students can work alone, but I find that there are (comfortably) three roles that students can delegate throughout the process of creating their forgery:

Role 1 – Researcher: What are the most celebrated poems by your chosen poet (avoid using those), what are some obscure titles of individual poems by your author (find and implement these), what form and style patterns (as well as thematic ones) get recycled, and what is some useful biographical information about your author that could aid you in the construction of your forgery, as well as help you unpack the deeper meaning of his work?

Role 2 – Curator and Vetter: Robert Frost, for instance, wrote 256 poems in ten published collections over his career. Of those, I probably know 20 or 30 of them well. Carl Sandburg penned roughly 1,600 poems, but I'm familiar with just a half-dozen. That means, if you've chosen a poet as prolific as Sandburg, or as famous as Frost, then you'll need to spend some time sifting through their collected works and whittling things down to the roads less traveled, by curating a handful of poems that are (A) not markedly better than what a high school student could conceivably write, and

(B) not too thematically or conceptually similar to each other, so that – in the end – your poem isn't just a "little bit of one, and some of another."

Role 3 – Writer and Editor: Writing a poem is deceptively hard. It's shorter than a short story, but much more challenging to lexically tune. When I write poetry, I riff off an existing poem (structurally speaking), or I write mine in response to an existing, published piece. If not that, then I've been inspired by an event or occasion that I want to reflect on. I'd recommend getting a few stanzas on paper before letting things like phrasing or rhyme scheme stifle or concern you. Creating a poetic forgery is (perhaps) like an act of Impressionistic painting: the goal is never to "copy," it's to approximate – to tap into the feeling, flow, trajectory, and velocity of another artist's work. As for editing the draft of a poem, I can say that English teachers have only four strategies to impart to their students: add, subtract, move around, or rewrite. In that sense, editing a poem is no different than editing an essay. In another sense, it's very different. I had a 50-minute conference today with a student working on three poems to submit to The Kenyon Review, but in the end we just focused on one partially fleshed-out piece that had failed to launch. After investing nearly an hour with my student Zirui Zhou, we'd mapped out several possible directions he could take the poem. His "brain was bursting" – as he'd put it – and much of our conference was spent unpacking Edna St. Vincent Millay's "Chorus" as a way to help him unlock (or at least unblock). In other words, spending an hour "talking out a poem" is not unusual. Zirui left energized, but he still must do the intellectual heavy lifting of writing, rewriting, and editing on his own.

It reminds me of Beat writer Allen Ginsberg's poem dedicated to his best friend Jack Kerouac upon his death. Ginsberg's eulogistic piece didn't come to him immediately (despite their long and intimate relationship). According to Michael Schumacher it "was composed over several sittings" from "recorded fragments of his thoughts and memories of Kerouac in his journals."

That means that to "forge a poem" is not so different from "writing a poem for oneself." It requires sitting with your discomfort and uncertainty, tapping into nostalgia, and contemplating in real time. In this case, it's just someone else's nostalgia, contemplations, and uncertainty.

The Steps

Step One – Make a group of up to three students.

Step Two – Select a major poet of the past 75 years (or so). It's first come, first served, so get your top choice approved ASAP. (Please make an informed decision before you commit to a name, though. Peruse a handful of their poems first.)

Step Three – Explore at least a dozen works by your poet. Make a Google Doc called "My Poet's Patterns" and dump as much insight and observation in the Doc as you can about how your author uses everything from stanzas, white space, figurative language, rhyme scheme, and repetition to understand how they construct "the poem's occasion," or the narrator's voice or perspective. You're really blueprinting the mechanics of their poetry.

Step Four – Narrow down your "dozen" to just three works by your poet. Verify (and double-check) that these three poems are faithful to how they were originally published.

Step Five – Write your poetic forgery in the voice and style of your chosen poet. If it seems fitting, base your faked poem on an occasion that would have likely inspired your author. Pay close attention to word choice (diction), rhythm, syntax, stanza breaks, as well as the mechanics of the poem (as explored in Step Three).

Step Six – Make a packet. Your cover sheet should include your poet's name, their photograph (please don't use "the first Google image result" that comes up – find something special, odd, or memorable), a brief biographical sketch (written by your group), and your group members' names. The body of the packet should contain four poems: one poem on each page – three authentic works and one forgery made by your group. The Brits on Savile Row have an expression about cutting yards of fabric for a bespoke suit – "Measure twice. Cut once." My application of that here is: read your poem (aloud) at least twice. Make each member of your group responsible for proofreading. When you hear your poem performed (in rehearsal) – listen carefully: does it have the same rhythm or meter as your other three? Does it have the fluidity of your other chosen poems? You can only "hear this" truth if you recite it (or at least sight read it).

Step Seven – Take your packet out into the world. Find some English teachers in the building, librarians, support staff, teachers from subjects you most respect, classmates (not in our section), and (outside of SHS) family/friends who will give their time and attention to trying to "spot the forgery." Listen to their feedback. Apply anything useful they say to your next draft.

Step Eight – Present your packet to the class. Your goal is to fool as many students as possible (and hoodwink your teacher).

* * *

And how do I assess this kind of student work? I assign two grades to the project: one is for the percentage of students who are fooled by the forgery – so it's a performance grade, and the other is for the poem itself: How well did the student use authentic voice and was faithful to the form and content choices of their chosen author?

By having both grades carry the same weight (100 points each), it keeps students honest in the sense that while they may fool a great many of their peers through gimmicks, trickery, or a secret pact, the other side of the assessment is more empirical (Is it a quality poem?).

Pro-Tips (to share with your students to set them up for success with this project):

- Put the titles of your three real poem titles (in quotes) in a Google search – see if the ones you intend to use in your packet are well-known or relatively obscure.
- Google search for – "Famous poems by_____" (your poet). Avoid using those titles altogether.
- Google search for – "Little known poems by_____" (your poet). Consider using one or two of those for good measure.
- Whenever possible, get a physical copy of your chosen author's collected poems. Cross reference your internet print-outs against the published "official edition" for inconsistencies (and resolve them).
- A "real poem" (by a legitimate poet) is typically rooted in logic, there's an event or occasion that inspired it and an argument at its center.
- Poets never "try hard" to be poetic – they (mostly) "live in the figurative world." Any line that is blunt, self-evident, or a crude example of "tell" is probably not written by a real poet.
- Read your forged poem "aloud." That is really the only way to catch the rough spots, inconsistent rhythms, and design flaws.
- Take your packet of poems (three real, one fake) to a handful of teachers or upperclassmen (or family members) to "stress test" your presentation. Listen to them. Get feedback. Make changes, accordingly.

14

THE FEATURE ARTICLE

Journalism Your Classroom Needs

My grandmother Elizabeth (Betty Grace Boyd) married Karl Nash of Ridgefield, Connecticut, long after my grandfather ended his life, and after Karl's wife left him for his tennis partner and good friend.

His home at 486 Main Street was the site of a blended, pre-Brady Bunch family that included my father and his innumerable siblings.

His stepdad Karl was a great deal like Atticus Finch. Beyond his principles and perpetual formal dress, his tenure as school board chairman for 17 years, and editor of a community newspaper he'd assumed ownership of with his brother in 1937 (civic-mindedness ran rampant through both men – one of those men being Atticus), Karl was a descendent of Ridgefield's founding fathers. As family-friend and journalist Jack Sanders laid out in tribute to my grandfather, "His Main Street homestead had been in his family since 1708." And that house was a 15 second walk to the town's public library. It's now an apartment building but is still within paper-cut-striking-distance of tens of thousands of books, magazines, and newspapers.

I don't – for one minute – believe that writing is "in the blood," or some "inherited trait" that's passed down through generations.

My great-grandfather (Thomas Boyd) was a novelist, historian, and biographer. His wife (Peggy) played a role in syndicating crossword puzzles. Karl Nash started a small-town newspaper empire called The Acorn Press that became the Hersom-Acorn Group (18 separate Connecticut papers eventually bought by Hearst Communications). He was its editor and publisher, until my uncle Thomas took over. His wife (Betty Grace) contributed bird-watching columns. Separately, my father (Brainerd) was an English

DOI: 10.4324/9781003600565-14

teacher who wrote several unpublished novels that dealt with recent-Boston-area history and family trauma.

And so on.

But none of that literacy was "passed down" through the gene-pool. It was earned. Thomas Nash didn't even have a college degree when he helmed The Press and still didn't have one when he assumed second-in-command at Hersom-Acorn. Uncle Thomas learned all that he knew on-the-job, wrote a running column, and thoughtfully reviewed automobiles, all while navigating the tensions caused by dried-up advertising dollars for print media, and the day-to-day running of a Connecticut institution that his father had put on the map. That's pressure – not nepotism or osmosis.

My father became an English teacher (in part) to have those precious summers off to write. His novels didn't write themselves (no ChatGPT yet). And they'd taken a toll on him long before the rejection slips came.

Karl Nash cobbled together a few thousand dollars in a (slightly) post-Depression-era-world to buy a struggling newspaper that couldn't afford to pay his $25-a-week salary (as reported by Sanders). Moreover, my original grandfather and reverse namesake (Wesley Brainerd Phillipson the 1st) died by his own hand after failing to write the great American novel. But when he passed, not a shred of its evidence revealed itself that he had even tried: no manuscript, no notes, no correspondence with publishers, no prewriting, and certainly no finished draft. His own father had written Through the Wheat – the moderately successful WWI story of an American Marine. It was also adapted to the big screen. But none of that helped the late Wesley Phillipson write his own war novel (he *was* a Navy pilot in WWII, after all, so that seemed like a natural choice of subject matter).

And while Journalism isn't "in the blood" either (nor for me, despite it being a long-held family business that was sold off for parts in 2018), it is what I ask my students to both: (A) formally write, and (B) aspire to.

Why?

In 2021, fewer than 3% of all North American-issued college degrees were for English majors. That means in a class of 20 students, there is a .56% likelihood that one of those kids will approximate your own academic journey.

In 2023, there were nearly 25,000 English Professors in North America. That means the odds of one of your students someday wearing tweed blazers with suede elbow patches and waxing poetic about Gertrude Stein is roughly 0.00735294118%.

But: there were 32,000,000 bloggers in the U.S. in 2020. Therefore if 35,000,000 people currently have a blog (adjusted by 11% every five years), but only 25,000 people are presently English Professors, maybe we should treat English class as a place to do some "sophisticated blogging," rather than a training camp for literary critics (which is something that – essentially – no one becomes). There are 72,350 museum curators in America. You're more likely to end up one of those, than the other.

I tell my students: *The biggest compliment I can give you as a writer is – Your essay has the look and feel of professional journalism. The thing you never want to hear from me is – Your essay sounds like it was written by a HS student.*

Students rarely share written work with their parents. Yes, they'll make one of their *friends* an editor of their English essay Google Docs to elicit feedback or simply commiserate, but our students are far more likely to share their music than their East of Eden paper.

But Journalism is different. It's alive. It has elegance: it whispers (especially at its end). Journalism is robust and often longform, especially in the case of The New Yorker magazine and The Atlantic Monthly. I savored Ian Parker's New Yorker profile (published in June 2024) of the Tadao Ando house that disgraced rapper Kanye West bought for 57 million dollars (and subsequently wrecked). It's nearly a 12,000 word piece, takes up countless pages in print, and took me several days to wade through.

As I wrote to Parker (who will soon be FaceTiming with my classes) back in July –

> I want to transform "the literary research paper" to the longform nonfiction essay, and I spent about 4 days reading your Ando piece in these slow cooked moments that have (basically) made me memorize the entire thing. It's just burned on my brain, and I remember thinking: I hope it just keeps going. I didn't want to see that dreaded "visual touchstone" that would signal its end.

And I really didn't. How many of your students' essays can you say that about?

It wasn't an English teacher who taught me how to write; it was Rolling Stone magazine (remember when that publication *meant* something?). Of all things, it was their album reviews that completely changed my understanding of what an essay writer's job was.

I was in my small-town public library (in Holliston, Massachusetts) reading the July '91 issue of Rolling Stone. My fingers raced to open the music critics' pages when I saw the write-up for N.W.A.'s sophomore effort. (A gangsta' rap collective helmed by Dr. Dre). (I had purchased their debut, Straight Outta' Compton, solely because it had a "Parental Advisory" sticker affixed to the front of the CD case. It disappointed not.)

Their second album got two stars out of five – by Rolling Stone's own metric, it wasn't classic, excellent, nor poor, exactly. But it wasn't a rave, either.

The review, by staff-writer Arion Berger, concluded on a meditative note about the alienating nature of N.W.A.'s lyrics and sound-design. In that moment, I understood there were meaningful alternatives to "restating my thesis" or "summarizing my paper's main points," or merely going "book to world" in my paper's outro. Additionally, in Journalism there are no rules about "where and when you're allowed to analyze." You can contemplate and dot-connect until the bitter end of your article.

Berger waxes:

"The Compton posse is well suited to this sort of foulmouthed sing-along. Meticulous about nothing, the group rides one beat until the song runs out, lets whoever is ready with a rhyme jump in and keeps the subjects simple. While the musical styles can be inspired – they vary from an ominous, Public Enemy-siren to quick-lipped Jamaican patter and R&B howling – the lyrics about life on the street feel like mere exhaust fumes from that big motor, Straight Outta Compton. The loosest stuff on the record, when the band members sloppily rant, is also the most difficult to follow; the rest is so hateful toward women, and in such a pathetic and sleazy manner, that it's simply tiresome. For N.W.A, making [this album] may have been something of a party – but not one at which everyone would feel welcome."

* * *

Over 30 years removed from high school, I find it challenging to remember much of the content I studied in Chemistry or History class, but I do remember (almost verbatim) the last line of an essay I wrote for my media studies teacher Don Iacovelli senior year:

"That's what made the Jazz Age trumpeters ring, and the Roaring Twenties' flappers sing."

The truth? I have no idea what I was arguing for or against, or what my actual topic was, but I *was* starting to play with voice, internal rhyme, meter, and viewpoint.

And it was reading magazines in my HS school library during free periods that made me want to manipulate language and sentence structure – *not* the lessons of my English, drama and media teachers Mr. Iacovelli, Mrs. Kadra, Mrs. Smith, or Mr. Park (whose big, steel classroom desk was covered with air fresheners that helped him not).

While 1990 was not exactly "peak magazine" time in American history (that distinction doesn't come along until 2012, when there were nearly

7,400 separate consumer titles), that year I regularly read (cover-to-cover) Sports Illustrated, The New Yorker, Rolling Stone, GQ, Esquire, Artforum, andNational Geographic.

But today in our English classrooms?

As Scarsdale HS friend and English Department colleague Stephen Mounkhall often says to his students:

"We teach fiction, but we ask you to write nonfiction."

Stephen is identifying one of the hypocrisies in our collective practice, but he's also mitigating it by moving toward teaching more nonfiction.

Salman Rushdie – not long before his stabbing – said that the world didn't need his magic-realism right now because it was so mired in fake news and tumult, and truth has become decidedly stranger than fiction (if not in short supply). His memoir Knife is an account of the attack that nearly ended his life and claimed an eye. As someone who lived under a fatwa for three decades (since writing The Satanic Verses), he understands better than anyone the importance of telling your story, controlling the narrative, and separating rumor and speculation from truth and scrupulous accounting.

With the tens of millions of bloggers in the U.S. alone, nonfiction writing is the current zeitgeist. Social media gives equal playing time to truth-telling and confession as it does hate speech, facade, and disinformation.

There are meaningful options for people who want to tell the stories of their community, their identity, and their experience interacting with media and popular culture.

Today, anyone could (realistically) write a guest essay for The New York Times and easily (for free) start a blog on Substack that can be monetized by its author within the hour.

When I was graduating HS in 1990, my parents bought me a thin yellow paperback called Jobs for English Teachers and Other Smart People that (A) I didn't read one word of and (B) wouldn't have bought into anyway. At the time, getting a public school teaching job was difficult (the Great Retirement wave of Boomers wouldn't happen for at least ten years), and there was no World Wide Web for another three.

For aspiring writers, that also meant: no submitting to Huff Post, and no way of launching a career in writing without getting past the gatekeepers at Random House, Knopf, Condé Nast, Kaplan, or McGraw Hill. In 1995, I secured a literary agent named David Andrew (a Brit working in Seattle), but he dropped me after my SAT Prep Book was "too funky" for Adams Publishing to greenlight. Adams had "too many titles that were underperforming to take the risk with an unknown quantity." I was barely 22 at the time and had already cold-called or written every single relevant agent found in the trade publication I'd photocopied at my local library. David Andrew had been my last hope.

That was – for many – a struggling writer's life in a pre-internet world.

And yes, I know that the lines of Journalism have been redrawn in the internet and 24-hour-a-day cable news age. And that anyone under 40 gets their news from social media or comedians posing as anchors. *But it's because of this* that much of my attention in the English classroom has shifted from "covering lots of novels" to having students *read and write* longform nonfiction.

It started happening very slowly.

In 2021, I read Yasmina Levitsky's essay on disaster media (a broad category that includes Lord of the Flies, Lost, Titanic, Twisters, etc.) and was left bereft by her conclusion.

She had titled it The Art of Disaster. Yasmina was my student for two consecutive years, but this was just the second essay she'd ever written for our class and was just 14 at the time.

She concluded with:

"Most cannot visualize or comprehend the way that a person feels during such a disaster. Your life being held on a string by a force you cannot control; the terrifying question of 'Will I live to see tomorrow?' is not something that your average person has to engage with, and when they do, it must be petrifying. I try to imagine the terror of facing something that not a single being in this world can restrain. I wonder, if I were there, what would my reflection in the water look like? How do you look when you stare into death's eyes? And how do you act when it stares back? The fear as you watch the wave above you darken your vision must be thrilling, in a disturbing way. The survival instincts kick in and you fight against suffocation and flee. But no matter what, the wave (usually) prevails. After all, blood is denser than water. Confined in the murky sea with my feet grazing the sand, maybe that is when the attraction of disaster wears off."

Yasmina accomplishes in that last line what I've come to call in my teaching – "Ending with a whisper."

No one had ever put words to that technique, or taught me how to execute it, but that "whisper" was ubiquitous in good (and great) Journalism. That's how so many New Yorker and Atlantic pieces were brought to a close: gently, and with thoughtful reflection and respect for the reader's intelligence. There was no need to over explain things in the 11th hour of your article. Instead, let the reader do some of the intellectual heavy lifting so that they're a part of the equation.

But the lessons of Journalism went far beyond what we could glean from just the conclusion.

It was Jon Caramanica's (NYT's The Critical Shopper) ability to take a would-be puff piece on consumer culture and the reimagining of the urban shopping mall (and just "buying too much stuff in general") and transform it into a meditation on death.

Caramanica had invented his own major while attending Harvard: rap music. He has gone on to write about music (as a critic), musicians (as an on-the-ground reporter, profiler, and feature writer), and shopping (for years he reviewed retail options in and around the five boroughs).

One "game-changing" moment for me was reading Jon's 2015 NYT piece (called "Shop the Pain Away") about Brookfield Place, a new mall located directly across from the footprint of the Twin Towers at 200 Vesey Street.

Yes, in it Jon covers the usual ground a fashion writer treads. He label-checks a number of brand-name-luxury-powerhouses that are sold within Brookfield Place (and their dizzying price-tags), but the piece – on point – features Jon reflecting on why we conspicuously consume, our "need" for yet another retail palace in Manhattan, and what it means that this new mall stands in stark contrast to a place of abject devastation (9/11's Ground Zero). Before this article – this review – this eulogy – I had never once seen a fashion writer use even one inch of their banal newspaper column to do something brave and daring. (As we live in the age of the advertorial). Right then, I decided to push student-writers in that direction: take a basic prompt, respond to it, but layer metacommentary on top of that. Jon proved that substance and style must coexist, even in the most unlikely places.

As I wrote to Jon in May of 2020:

"Your piece, Shop the Pain away, is everything I would want a college essay to be: it's a micro-focal point (a mall opening) that you use as a deep and textured meditation on how we deal with survivor's guilt, and use retail therapy to build on top of a gravesite, and – more importantly – how that's a metaphor for so much of what 'shopping' has become in our lives. Again, it's really a magic trick you pull off. Few, if anyone in history, have turned a shopping review into something so damn devastating and indicting, but also strangely uplifting and hopeful. It's an odd cocktail of emotions you experience, capture, and produce in the reader. And I think you do a lot of that with your journalism."

Jon was kind enough to give my students a few hours during the lows of the pandemic-lockdown and even stayed on the live feed (after the school day had ended) to field additional questions because – as he said at the time: "Why not? The world is burning. Might as well."

Here's that "journalistic ending" from "Shop the Pain Away" that I am forever helping my students move toward:

"Dazed, I smelled one candle after the next, barely able to make out the voice of the sales clerk preaching their charms. They all smelled the same until finally I landed on one – Sicilian tangerine – that was almost acidic. It had bite, the scent creeping up my nostrils and scraping away. Instinctively, I winced, but at the same time began to salivate. For a moment, death felt far away."

* * *

During academic year 2023–24, I resolved to make one of my essay prompts a "feature article." Some of my motivation came from a visit I'd made to a nationally-known English teacher at Townsend Harris High in Queens named Brian Sweeney. Beyond teaching, Sweeney runs the school paper which publishes daily and has over 150 contributors. That year he'd also won the $25,000 grand prize for the FLAG Award for Teaching Excellence.

When I got to Townsend HS, an imposing building that looks (from the outside) part Verizon-server-depot, part federal courthouse, and part hospital, I was scrutinized by security then escorted to Brian's pressroom/classroom. It's a 30 x 40 space with tall windows and banks of computers on the far end, and rows of desks on the other. Brian is mild-mannered and unassuming, with prominent glasses and slicked-back reddish-blonde hair. The job keeps him boyish.

His journalists, as young as 13, are unpaid for their reportage but have been responsible for breaking national news on several occasions. Their investigations have unseated their school's onetime interim principal (Rosemarie Jahoda) as well as uncovered inappropriate relationships between teachers and students, leading the DOE (Department of Education) to institute new teacher-training programs as a countermeasure.

Regarding his coverage of Jahoda, whose "combative management style" the school paper had held to account in a series of articles while she was acting principal, Sweeney said:

"It's incredibly nerve-wracking, but it's the best teaching that I'm doing. The idea that they're learning how to do this on the job, and it's my job to make sure that they get it right, is terrifying and rewarding," as WNYC reported in 2016 on Sweeney's ethos while advising The Classic.

When I taught at a West Nyack, NY high school, I'd also been the advisor to a student newspaper. That was over 20 years ago, and I can't find any evidence that it's still in production. There does exist a literary magazine called Arcadia, but no sign of journalistic endeavors at Clarkstown South.

The truth? I did next-to-nothing in my "advisory" role on the paper. The students made all the decisions. I can't remember a time when they even ran a story-idea by me, nor can I remember dealing with printers, purchase-orders, funding, or deadlines. I didn't attend any editorial meetings. It was entirely self-sufficient. And at that school it had to be: I taught five classes a day and had one full period of study hall duty and another of hallway patrol (leaving me not a single moment to meet with students, to grade, or advise).

But the world that Brian Sweeney has created for himself at Townsend Harris (which now sounds more like a Presidential ticket than a public HS) has a dedicated space and built-in curricular time to make The Classic a success. And by all metrics it is.

Right before the pandemic broke, I spent one day with Sweeney and his charges, auditing a freshmen class where he showed the opening scene of a Wonder Years episode featuring Daniel Sterns' voiceover narration of "adult" Kevin Arnold. It was in service of conjuring up what Sweeney calls "your voice from beyond," to make the hook of a personal essay more engaging and poignant. I hovered when he received story pitches from a small group of student-journalists, sending many of them off to write immediately and others to refine their projects' scope.

Keep in mind that The Classic has literally changed public policy, ousted bad administrators and teachers, and has functioned – essentially – as a "speaking truth to power" machine that is built on the same model as the 1970s incarnation of The Washington Post. Major efforts were taken to shut down Woodward and Bernstein's investigation into Nixon's Watergate imbroglio, and there have been (at times) administrative pressures on student-journalists at Townsend Harris as well.

Sweeney's model at The Classic reminded me of a scene from John McPhee's memoir Draft No. 4. McPhee – the brilliant essayist and longest running New Yorker magazine contributor who comes to mind – had a Princeton HS teacher who assigned three essays a week. Now, how much feedback his teacher gave on such a fast and furious output – who knows? – but The Classic publishes something daily.

Students don't get better at writing unless they're constantly writing.

So I took three specific inspirations from Brian:

1 Have students do some kind of writing each day.
2 Ask students to speak truth to power.
3 Students must have something at stake when they sit down to write.

A few years later I had back-to-back seasons with Harvard class of '28 student Natasha Pereira. She'd been in my sophomore regular and junior honors classes and worked on our school's literary and arts magazine Jabberwocky (for some unknown reason, two important publications at SHS are tied to a work by Lewis Carroll; Bandersnatch, our yearbook, is the other).

Natasha had been devastated by the ongoing renovations at the Scarsdale Public Library, a mixed-media building that was part mid-century modern and part Quaker meeting house. It was shut down for two years (2018–20), completely inaccessible to the community during that time. In the interim, there was no "pop-up" library so the town had lost its communal center. But that wasn't the worst part for Natasha: the new building lacked the charm, warmth, familiarity, and utility of the old one. Additionally, "physical books" seemed to be deemphasized. And that sense of "getting lost" in the nooks and crannies of an old building edged with concrete, steel, and walls of glass on one side was also absent.

At that point, I still hadn't assigned students to "write a feature article," but Natasha wrote one anyway. While reading it: Everything, everywhere, all at once – came together at that moment: times I'd spent at my family's Connecticut newspaper as a child, growing up with The New Yorker magazine, "advising" that student-run paper at Clarkstown South, visiting countless public high schools since 1994 that led me to meet innovative, serious-minded educators like Sweeney who were asking students to do one simple yet powerful thing: share their work with a community larger than one teacher, and beyond the walls of one classroom. That resonated with me like nothing else has in 30 years of teaching.

Natasha's piece, "Shelf Life: AD PER 102," is a 1,300 word feature article and nostalgic reflection on her long-term relationship with her local library, and how that dynamic has changed post-renovation.[1]

* * *

My first tenet of English class is: I never ask my students to write something that I haven't done myself. I also read my version of it aloud to them. Being vulnerable – myself – is the best way to get them to do the same.

My "feature" was on two young and exciting filmmakers who'd Zoomed with my classes about a Nicholas Cage and Elijah Wood film they'd made called The Trust. Watching that neo-noir, as well their next project with Cage (Arcardian), and the remarkable VFX team that Ben Brewer participated in for Everything Everywhere All At Once inspired me to write this.[2]

* * *

Since incorporating feature writing into my curriculum, I've reached out to noted journalists and cultural critics whose work has moved me (and my students). The response has been overwhelmingly positive and appreciative. A small sample includes the following: New Yorker contributor Dan

Piepenbring (he authored The Beautiful Ones for Prince), NYT writer Saul Austerlitz (who authored the definitive book on the TV show Friends), New Yorker and Guardian wunderkind Samanth Subramanian (who penned the only article you'll ever want or need to read about ancient board games), and the Pulitzer Prize winning Hua Hsu.

All of these journalists, and countless others, have worked with my classes entirely pro bono – and that includes multiple Pulitzer Prize winners.

All that says to me is: there's a community of professionals that anyone can tap into. As an English teacher who has thousands of files (both paper and digital), an infinite number of lessons, and helpful colleagues, I've found that the best resources exist outside of what I've done for 30 years, and far from the campus I've commuted to for 22.

Of the best journalists I've ever read and contacted, nearly all of them responded. The vast majority of them worked with my classes. Even John McPhee returned my snail mail, and that's saying something.

* * *

My personal favorite feature article thus far (from a student collaboration) was Gracie Liebman and Kate O'Connell's look at the alleged anonymity of graffiti at Scarsdale High School.[3]

Here's Prompt Fourteen

Essay Fourteen: THE FEATURE ARTICLE It's an Investigation – so Details Matter

Investigate something in Scarsdale (or NY) that actually matters to you. Next year most of you will be driving, but where will you park? You are all trying to get into Cornell: what actually makes the difference between rejection and acceptance at an ivy-league school? You don't like the smell of the Learning Commons? These topics should be timeless more than "breaking news" or "of the moment."

My former student Jimmy Vielkind is a top reporter for The Wall Street Journal. He grew up near Albany, NY, the state capital. He's a born newsman. He covers NJ, NY, and CT for one of the biggest and respected newspapers in America. His job – and his passion – is to "find the story worth exploring, sure, but really the one worth telling."

But you have to start with you. What interests you? What will matter to you, soon? What's of real consequence? Tip O'Neal said that "All politics is local," which really means: "What happens in your neighborhood is what actually matters; THAT is what impacts your life most powerfully."

First off: We have a school newspaper called The Maroon. It's a solid paper. It does some good work. You probably both have and haven't read it. My question would be: if you were going to write something for The Maroon, the article, story, feature or Op-Ed that YOU wanted to see in the paper, what would that be? What would it look like?

For me, it would have to be (HAVE TO BE) something that The Maroon hasn't already specifically addressed. It would have to be niche. Micro. It would have to be specific to me and my interests. A reporter or journalist is either: (A) Assigned a story by their editor, or (B) Following and developing a story that interests them.

What would make a good story because: (A) You want to "get after it," and (B) You think there is some heat, some energy, some life, some narrative, and some interest in that story?

And for me, I'd be truly interested in getting CLOSER to understanding ANY of the following hyper-local and hyper-specific areas of inquiry and investigation that have not been directly covered by the school paper in the past.

Why Gridlock at 3:00 PM?

Why is it so difficult to "get in and out" of SHS' campus at pick up time? Why such chaos? What happened to the security guard who used to direct traffic at 3:00 PM, and made things run so smoothly? He left two years ago, so why wasn't he replaced with someone else who could be the traffic cop helping parents, students, and teachers safely navigate the end of day? There are parents blocking the traffic circle out front. Double parked. Stopped in the middle of the road. Students driving through the track parking lot at 80 MPH. People going the wrong way "up" the traffic circle by the cafeteria entrance. Brewster Road itself is just a "parking lot" from 2:50 to 3:10. This is (mostly) avoidable, isn't it?

Why Is Wellness Getting in the Way of Rigor (If It Is)?

Since the Wellness Initiative began at SHS (perhaps prior to its official start), teachers at SHS have given up assigning schoolwork over ALL breaks and holidays, stopped assigning summer reading, are prevented from testing immediately after returning from vacation. Along with this, we've implemented (and encouraged students to use) "the mercy rule," and (as a school) we've LEANED HARD into the notion that students should be given extensions on work, make-up tests "when possible," giving out "compassion and empathy like never before" regarding missed work or late work, and now – even – we've moved to "rolling gradebook" (which is supposed to have a more favorable outcome for student's grades). What has been the impact of this on curriculum, academic rigor, and college preparedness?

Why Is There This Constant Game of Telephone at SHS (If There Is)?

Why are so many things at SHS like a game of telephone? Every year, my seniors going into Senior Options attend all kinds of informational meetings with their case managers, but over half of them have no idea what the rules are, what kind of journal entries they need to do (or that they have to do them at all). They have no idea about deadlines. Forms. Where to submit. When to submit. They don't seem to know anything about anything. RELATED: Why do Deans tell us teachers at faculty meetings that we only need to submit college recommendations on Scoir, yet I get many, many students each year sending me a request for a separate recommendation through a specific college's website portal, Naviance, or The Common Application site? Where is the breakdown in communication happening, and why?

The Constraints for Essay Fourteen:

- DETAILS MATTER, SO YOU MUST GET THE DETAILS RIGHT: The details that end up in your article must be fact-checked, they must be highly specific, and they must come from a place of rigorous research: you must either BE, or BECOME the expert, and the details MUST support or prove that YOU are the expert.
- YOU MUST PITCH: You are pitching me your story idea. It needs my approval. That's going to happen in-class OR you can do it one-on-one in my office. If you choose the latter, you must schedule an office appointment.

If we absolutely must, I will reserve seven spots (total from my two classes) for approval over email.

- Grading: If you don't grade this with me, during office hours, then you are self-grading Essay Fourteen. You've had 13 chances (with 13 separate essays) to get my feedback. For self-graders: I'll give you the self-grading rubric when the essay is due. I'll also "grade the self-grading" that you do to keep things honest.
- You are writing a FEATURE STORY: Not a straight news story, and certainly not a review. Explore on your own what that means.

"A feature article is a human interest story about a person, event, or place. Rather than simply summarizing the subject, a feature article highlights one aspect or significance of the story. This kind of content gives you the chance to go in-depth on a story or at least one angle of that story. It's less formal style may take an odd twist or heartwarming angle at the end."

The Resources:

- JOURNALISTS: We have a HS newspaper, a local newspaper, and countless magazines and papers in NYC and around the country (and globe). I have personally Zoomed with over 50 professional journalists because of something I read. I contacted them. Overall, 75% of the people I have written to responded, willing to talk with me and my students for free.
- PUBLICATIONS: Submit your work to any one (or several) of the following professional publications: The Cut, NYT Modern Love, The Atlantic, Huff Post, The Concord Review, Vulture, or any one of these places.
- ME: I would never sell myself short: I know my worth. My grandfather started The Ridgefield Press and came to create the Hersam-Acorn network of newspapers (owning over 17 newspapers in Connecticut). My great-grandfather (Thomas Boyd) was a successful novelist and best friends with F. Scott Fitzgerald and helped him edit The Great Gatsby. Several of my former students are professional journalists or editors. My great-grandmother basically invented the syndicated crossword puzzle that she sold to newspapers across America (Peggy "Woodward" Boyd). So – yeah – writing is in the blood.

> Important Dates: THERE ARE FIFTEEN FULL DAYS BETWEEN THE TIME I'M ASSIGNING THIS ESSAY AND THE DATE THAT IT'S DUE. AT LEAST HALF OF THE WORK YOU'LL NEED TO DO FOR ESSAY FOURTEEN WILL HAPPEN IN CLASS. SO – YOU CAN'T WAIT UNTIL THE WEEKEND BEFORE IT'S DUE TO GET STARTED. YOU'LL CRASH AND BURN. YOU'VE GOT TO START TODAY. YOU HAVE THE ILLUSION (BECAUSE IT'S 15 DAYS) THAT YOU HAVE A LOT OF TIME. YOU HAVE JUST THE RIGHT AMOUNT OF TIME. SO, CONSIDER THAT.
>
> Day One – Walk into class with a printed story pitch (complete attached PITCH DOC).[4]
>
> Day Three – During the time our class meets on Wednesday, schedule meetings with AT LEAST TWO people (separately or together) who you believe are "central to your story." PLEASE DO NOT schedule appointments with administrators (the Principal, or the Assistant Principals, or the Head of Deans, for example). Why? You will NOT

get time with them on such short notice, and YOU are VERY UNLIKELY to get anything "out of the ordinary" or "compelling" from them. Why? Because their job is to answer questions in a direct and straightforward manner, or to not answer your question at all (for various reasons). You must go to your interviews/meetings with your TOPIC/QUESTION DOC completed (see attached), and printed out. DO NOT have it on your iPhone.

These meetings could be virtual, through Zoom, Google Hangout, the telephone, or in person (on the SHS campus).

Day Ten – Come to class with a "working draft" of your 1,250 word story, in progress. There's every chance (by this time) you will have written 2,000 or 3,000 words (or more), but your goal is to get it down to (in the end) 1,250 "essential" words. Additionally – come to class with a list of specific things in bullet point form: What are the things you still don't know or understand about your topic/story, what are the questions you have yet to answer that will help you story, and who are the people you have yet to talk with (or to) that would assist you fleshing out your story? What are things that you haven't considered "enough" or haven't considered "at all?"

FLESHING OUT DOC (see attached)

Day Twelve – During the time our class meets on Friday, schedule meetings with the people you haven't yet talked with (can be in person, on Zoom, on the phone, etc.). Have your TOPIC/QUESTIONS DOC, and add the questions and concerns from your FLESHING OUT DOC.

*This might be the time to schedule an appointment with more in-demand people who are the "expert voices" on your topic.

Day Fifteen – Full period of writing and revising, in-class.

Article is due by end of class (VERY few exceptions will be granted to this due date). Use this period to do final fact-checking, quote-verification, writing a journalistic intro and conclusion, writing the essay itself, having me look something over for you as "your main editor" at The Wes Press, etc.

You are encouraged to post this to a Substack Blog that you create.

Notes

1 See https://www.routledge.com/9781032987842.
2 See https://www.routledge.com/9781032987842.
3 See https://www.routledge.com/9781032987842.
4 IF you are not "pitching in class" - you need to schedule an appointment to pitch me this week, before or after school, during lunch, or using my YouCanBookMe page. It must be this week. Otherwise, you can just pitch it in class. If you can't find a time on my sign-up page, email me.

15

THE AUTOPSY OF YOU

When Students Metacognate Good Things Happen

I don't know how valuable "student reflections" are in the English classroom.

It's a paradox, or some kind of catch-22: the students who are really good at reflecting tend to be strong writers; the weak ones tend not to reflect on themselves that well at all.

It becomes an engagingly reflexive process for some, and a chore or burden for others.

There's another snag: if you're not writing essays that you're initially invested in, it's difficult to return to those works and say something meaningful about them later. Sure, you could send your students back in time at year's end to rework a first semester paper, but that's like asking your children to eat last week's stale spinach. It may not be (technically) too late, but it's an exercise in bad digestion, and no child wanted the spinach when you served it hot and fresh.

I've been involved with four HS English Departments in my career, and most Department Chairs push teachers to do "portfolio work" with their students. It's a game of telling kids: reflect on this piece, and write comments on that paper – but what does it mean for a student to revisit an essay they've authored about Macbeth or Othello (for example)? Do they find something legitimately authorial about that artifact with their name on it (or often without their name on it), stashed in a manilla folder or hidden somewhere not easily found on their Google Drive? (Have you ever noticed how difficult it is for students to locate an old essay in digital form? They never know what they called it. Oftentimes, they've crafted so many versions or drafts that it's nearly impossible to produce "the one," or they never wrote it in the first place. Beyond that, they'd have to unsubmit it on Google Classroom to even have editing rights, let alone become the document's owner once again.)

Long before I have students complete "The Autopsy of You" in the 4th quarter (which I'll explain later), I ask them to do "My Former Self in Essay Form." It's simply an assignment that prompts them to look back on what they wrote last year, the year before that, and so on....

So – if you're a sophomore, I'll ask you to examine what your freshman pieces looked and sounded like. Do you cringe when you review that Ramayana Hinduism essay you wrote last minute? Do you feel good about your character study of Odysseus you labored over (or that standard "Hero's Journey" paper that is often just a checklist of Joseph Campbell's "steps")? Did you add something new to the conversation about the patriarchy in A Midsummer Night's Dream? And what – if any – personal essays did you write last year?

The idea behind "My Former Self" is to: (A) Have students make a clear separation between grade levels as they transition into my class and (B) Nudge students to be self-critical enough to break bad habits and rudimentary practices.

Every student needs that freshman English teacher to show them what a thesis statement looks like and how to construct one, which "pattern of argumentation" to use, but they also need that sophomore English teacher to say – last year you were practicing on a flight simulator, this year you're the co-pilot of a plane that could actually crash. And next year? You'll be flying solo.

So all of my students do this activity in September of Quarter One – from 10th through 12th grade. It's not a "gotcha" assignment. I am actually hoping that two things happen when students revisit their body of written work done for previous English classes:

1 They will see – glaringly – what isn't working about their prose.
2 They will see – subtly – what is working about their prose.

Senior Safiya Rahman found a paper she'd written in 10th grade on the novella Montana 1948. It's a book that many of us teach at SHS.
Safiya focused on this excerpt:
"There is nothing more magical than a wonderful father-son relationship; a satisfyingly indestructible bond where the father treats their boy to a football game while shouting at the top of their lungs, 'GO! GO! GO! RUN FASTER!' as they enjoy a bucket of popcorn, sitting centimeters away from their child as they guffaw at the sight of the opponent team collapsing once they read the tally."

Then she unpacks it:
"I created this for the opening to a thesis on Montana 1948, which was supposed to be relevant to the subject of close familial bonds. The process involved painting a picture of what a close bond with a dad feels like, which I tried to achieve by evoking the image of father and child intently watching a football game. This was supposed to paint a scene of familiarity, then the next sentence contrasts this warmth by expressing how not every family has such a close-knit bond. It felt awkward to read this again…? It feels weird to see my old writing, but strangely, I actually kind of like this opening – unlike my other 10th grade essay intros – and I could see myself writing something like this again this year."

Junior Grace Wu looked back on freshman year text Gilgamesh – the story of a demi-god and a man-beast who become human together – and one sentence from her 9th-grade essay gave her pause:
"Your love for him makes him immortal in your heart."

And she waxes:
"This line sounds cliché, but it reminded me why I loved Gilgamesh more than I'd like to admit. While the plot and metaphors were horribly executed, in my opinion, the underlying message resonated with me: even if my loved ones aren't here physically, they're always with me emotionally. Especially as most of my close family lives in China and I haven't gotten to see them since the pandemic, being apart from them has never held me back from taking any opportunities for my future because they weren't with me. I get sad thinking about how I'll never be able to play with my childhood friends in the park or get blueberry mooncakes from the best bakery outside my apartment, but the fact that I can never relive those moments doesn't mean those moments are relieved from me. The theme of Gilgamesh was probably what inspired this, but when it comes to writing, I tend to jot down anything that crosses my mind and pray some of it comes out coherent – and in this case, it did!"

And from sophomore English, Grace revisits an underwhelming result:
"Last year, I had to recreate a fairy tale from We Were Liars to encompass a moral lesson. Reading it again, it didn't feel like there wasn't much of my trademark language or phrasing in it, but I thought I twisted the narrative well to get across my point – that living in a household of perfectionists makes it impossible for you to feel truly loved. I always write better when I find meaning in what I'm writing, and I thought that essay briefly but powerfully conveyed its intended message. Also, rather than using tense, obscure language to try and sound 'fancy' in an analytical book essay, I found my writing more digestible and casual when I read it back."

Current sophomore Eli Zargari offered a brief history of his relationship with English when looking at his former self in essay form (more

holistically though – because he'd changed schools, and – despite emailing his old teachers to get access to Google Docs – no one responded):

"I have always excelled at composing pieces and essays. Since I was in 6th grade, I was one of the top students in my honors English classes, and, unlike math and science, the subject was one that I enjoyed working hard on. I live for words. As a speaker of 4 (and a half) languages (English, Italian, Hebrew, Spanish and some French), I have come to understand the meaning of wordsmithing even more. My skills in linguistics and word roots have given the English language a purpose for me. I spend hours a week rigorously studying my collection of languages, and I recognize that writing only allows me to better understand my mother tongue and its origins. As a younger kid, essays were a burden, which I only wanted to submit and never read again, but, overtime, I learned to love the feeling of forming words in my head, pouring out my spirit on to page in order to unravel my enigmatic beliefs. In 9th Grade, at the Leffell School, I opted into a creative writing class, in order to get the portfolio distinction on my report card. While most of the essays I wrote in English class were the standard 5 paragraph argumentative essays, I had the opportunity to explore other types of writing in my creative writing class. While I agree that five paragraph essays lack personality and 'soul,' I do believe that they have been some of the most helpful practices for language crafting, clarity work and wordsmithing in my career. Writing pages of analytical essays in 8th and 9th grade was not something I may have enjoyed, but it allowed me to become comfortable with the editing process and overcoming 'writer's block.' I learned how to put a little bit of myself into each of those essays, even though personal pronouns were prohibited."

* * *

As you can see, these students are critically engaged in a meaningful reflection of their writing process. And your students can be too. It really comes down to the questions you pose to them, and how seriously you (as the educator) *consistently* take the practice of writing in your classroom.

By the end of the first month of school, I've asked them to confront their former personas with some thoughtful, guided questions that simply don't let them off the hook.

My Former Self in Essay Form – Assignment Write-Up

Turn this PDF into a Google Docs and share it with me by the due date. Print a copy out for yourself to bring to class and have some specifics to share about how you wrote essays last year, and (when possible) beyond last year.

Directive: Go through your previous year's English class essays (and beyond) and find the following: Go back as far as 7th grade, but start with "last year's English teacher."

10 AREAS OF "LOOKING BACK" AT YOUR FORMER SELF THROUGH YOUR OWN WRITING

Your responses below must come from reviewing English class essays from PREVIOUS years: go back AT LEAST one year (last year's English teacher). Look at old DRIVES, Google Docs, and FOLDERS: Be as specific as possible; copy-and-paste from actual essays; you ARE NOT being asked to examine each and every essay ten different ways, NOT AT ALL: just reflect on your past history as an essay writer.

These are suggestions, not directives:

1. What are your best examples of phrase-making or wordsmithing? What sentences would ARREST me or make me say "Damn Son!" Where did you create beauty or poetry, or possibly even achieve "Google Zero" (or something close to it)? How did you create this language? What was your process like? What is it like to read it again?
2. What is a distinction that you made within (at least) one of your essays that you think is worth restating here? (Distinction = the distinguishing of a difference; pointing out a nuanced thing like – Travis Scott is a great performer, but not a great musical performer, as Jake Feuerstein once wrote). What was important to you, or meaningful to you, about making this distinction? What did you do with it?
3. What is the ONE essay from last year (or the year before if you're a junior or senior) that you would EAGERLY share with me and why? Share with friends and family? Post on-line? What did it mean to you to write it? Read it again: what is it like to read it again? Tell me about the experience:
4. What is the greatest SPECIFIC thing your English teacher from a previous year said about your writing? If there is more than one thing, or more than one teacher said it, please share that too. No names (of teachers) are necessary (unless it's purely positive, and then I'm happy to pass it on to them). I talk about this in terms of "your superpower in English class." I've already had 100 writing conferences this year, and I can say (confidently) that I've articulated – to at least 30 different students – what their "superpower" or great strength appears to be (in some cases, multiple strengths). What belief did it give you about your writing (what your teacher wrote or said to you last year or the year before), or what did it mean to you that they said it?
5. Give me the best opening line from any essay you wrote in the past. Unpack what made it "the best" (of your writing). How did you create it (the process)? The worst?
6. Give me the best conclusion you wrote, or the best "last line" from an essay that would leave me bereft, or thinking and feeling something. The worst? Unpack what made it good or bad.

7. What is a moment in one of your past essays when you meaningfully intersected with your topic (when you became a significant part of the essay)? Give me those sentences or passages (if you can). Tell me what it was like (for you) to get vulnerable (if that's what it was; an act of vulnerability). It was something else (emotionally or intellectually) for you to "intersect," (and not feeling exposed) then what was it?
8. Give me your best attempt at HUMOR and/or VOICE in a past essay, and unpack it.
9. Give me your most creative use of FORM and/or punctuation in a previous essay and unpack it.
10. What is an essay that your teacher graded and "got the grade exactly right." How did you know? What was the grade? What was the feedback?

Bonus Questions:

Your favorite rubric category from a previous teacher's rubric? Be specific.
Your favorite essay assignment from a previous teacher? Be specific.
Why did you choose the essay topics or prompts that you did? How did you feel about writing essays last year? To what extent was their choice? To what extent did you default into "the easiest thing to write" from what was on offer?

* * *

As I write this chapter, I'm reflecting on something my current sophomore Tom Degani wrote in response to this "Former Self" prompt. I think Tom represents the way many students feel about their relationship with writing and the English classroom. In spite of not seeing himself historically "as a writer," it's really impressive how engaged Tom is in reconciling the past with his present:

> None of my essays from the past have any **Wow** moments. I've been stressing, searching for a hot minute on ways I've wordsmithed in my past essays, but I never took the time because I wasn't taught or forced to, but I also never felt like it. I don't enjoy any essay I write. A prompt was always engraved in my mind by the teacher. Creativity was lit to flames before thoughts yet sparked. I've read paragraphs upon paragraphs stuck in a mindless dimension of boring cliches.

> One essay that I would like to share with you is on the novel Life of Pi. I didn't get a good grade. The work was mediocre at best. I was proud of it though. At the time, it felt as if I was Shakespeare carefully crafting each and every word into the places I saw fit. In reality, it was messy. I've even read it to my friends and we all laughed. I thought we laughed because they didn't expect me to write something so good, but I was feeding into my own delusional

thoughts of perfection. I tried re-reading it today for this assignment but it wasn't even worth finishing. I definitely had no interest in writing it either.

My latest compliment on an essay was probably in elementary school. Essays weren't even essays back then. Just small paragraphs that would be assigned with a lot of time to write them. My 4th grade teacher had a conference with me and my mom and she said that I was super creative and great at writing. Looking back at it, I realize it's hard to do badly on an essay in the 4th grade. I've genuinely looked back and thought of times my teachers could've said something positive at all and found nothing else. I feel like you as the teacher are assuming we are all good writers and have a spark in us that are waiting to be lit. Mine still is. I don't exactly like getting vulnerable in front of other people unless I can fully trust them.

In my past essays, every single essay was provided with a prompt. Therefore I have never tried to be humorous in my essays. I was never creative either. As stated, my teachers would make us form the most basic paragraphs possible. As long as my essays provided the information they needed, I would receive good grades.

In one of my essays on Heracles, I barely even read the text my essay was based on. I just wrote random stuff that didn't even make sense to me. I Googled what happened in the story and got a 74/100. I didn't even read the feedback. I knew the essay was terrible, so as soon as it was returned, I read the grade and threw it out.

My favorite rubric was in elementary school, where prompts weren't given to us. I enjoyed when a teacher would let us be free and wild and made writing fun for me. My spark was nearly killed in the following years.

In all honesty, my favorite essay assignment was the Wax Pack essay you assigned. I have never been able to write about the joys in my life and my actual interests to a teacher who cares. I'm glad I was able to talk about volleyball and football with my friends. I felt so bored last year. Writing was dreadful. It felt like a burden. Usually, we had two prompts to pick from. One side of a story or the other. For example you either thought something was good or bad. No opportunity to go your own way.

***

It's quite possible that Tom's experience in English class was your experience: some teacher came along and gave you a bit (or a ton) more freedom, and you took it and ran all the way to a liberal arts college, eventually earning your teaching degree. Touchdown.

Or, you're not a teacher and have no plans of becoming one, but you had a mentor or model of writing that flipped a switch on the library of content within, illuminating the words, sounds, rhythms, and vibrations that existed not-so-deeply inside of you – but near the surface, and you could coax them out with a little effort and some self-satisfaction.

So – here's how I roll out the first month of any academic year in terms of writing:

Step One: After I've assigned and graded Essay One (and introduced Essay Two), I ask them to reflect on previous years' essays by giving them the "My Former Self in Essay Form" prompt.

Step Two: Students bring their findings (the research they've conducted into their past writings) to a full class period discussion. There we unpack the good, bad, ugly, and beautiful as a class. Now – not everyone is going to participate – but many are eager to share just how cringeworthy some of their pieces were. In fact, students often want to read aloud a terrible last line, a cheesy or cliche opening sentence, tally up how many times they used the name Macbeth (the record was 43 times in a single essay), call themselves out for not having read the very book they were writing about, and – on occasion – catch themselves doing something right.

That "Former Self" activity is – from what many students have told me – the first time in their 15, 16, or 17 years of life that they've actually taken a hard and thoughtful look at their own writing. Most of them are embarrassed by what they discover – they can't believe they wrote so badly the previous year and are stunned by how differently they're writing already.

And – the funny thing is – I don't lead them to that conclusion. In fact, it's the opposite: I've constructed guiding questions for this assignment that asks them to locate the good, the special, the poetic, the arresting, the wordsmithed in those old essays – but what I usually hear is panic: I'll get emails the night before it's due that say, "Phillipson – I can't find anything 'well wordsmithed' in my previous essays. It's just a bunch of cliches and plot restatements. What do I write down for those categories? I don't have anything good."

Other students have no problem finding rich examples of voice and introspection. Many of them are proud of the way they crafted a hypothetical conversation with William Golding (Lord of the Flies), a character sketch of Odysseus and his Hero's Journey, a day in the life of Holden Caulfield at Scarsdale HS, and so on.

Some students keep remarkable records, able to access (even as juniors) their 7th grade papers as if they are Presidential Historians and Archivists.

Now, with everything digital, cloud-based and Google Docs facing, there's little content we create that "goes away." It's there to be data-mined in the best possible way.

And this first month of classes (September) is bookended by the last month (June). "Getting September right" makes a successful June possible.

In June, I assign "The Autopsy of You" – a review of one's personal body of work from the academic year with me. The idea comes from the basic practice of "Portfolio Work" that most English Departments in America do, say they do, used to do, or intend to do.

In modern times, asking students to "keep a separate Portfolio" is profoundly redundant – Google Drive makes it so. But teachers have a responsibility to create opportunities for their students to metacognate and make distinctions about their work.

I remember reading a Ted Sizer book from my student-teaching days that advocated for "mastery presentations" – students, by the end of their year or high school career, must be able deliver a series of presentations that show not just proficiency of the content matter they'd studied for four years, but a complete mastery of all subjects. Sizer was an ambitious man and a prolific author on the subject of authentic assessment.

I don't think Sizer's vision is remotely realistic today (given declining enrollments nationwide, an uptick in homeschooling, and America's dismal PISA ranking), but I've always appreciated his intent.

But it is surprising how rarely we have our own students return to the work we claim is so important to write in the first place. And when we do, it often feels like theater, or even worse, punishment.

"The Literary Autopsy of You" adds a layer of forced objectivity to the self-reflection process. It's asking students to take a step back and look at their work from the perspective of a literary critic. Here's the thing: We ask our English students to be literary critics all the time, examining and analyzing someone else's novel, play or short story, but they lack the expertise or wisdom of a graduate student, high school teacher, or even AP-level senior.

They're not the expert on Death of a Salesman, Waiting for Godot, Atonement, The Bluest Eye, As I Lay Dying, or Fahrenheit 451, but they are well versed in their own content creation: the author's intent behind it, the construction of things at the syntax level, the nuanced distinctions, and the personal rhythms of the writer.

Everything in my class is an artificial construct: I put frames around things, create forced restrictions, and add one skill while removing another (intentionally handicapping the writer).

My Essay 13 is no different: it's writing like someone you aren't, in hopes of discovering who you are, and who've you've been at different points throughout the course. It forces the student-writer to treat their work seriously, and with distance, as a professional critic might while making a study of an important author of historical and cultural significance.

***

Here's Prompt Fifteen

Essay 15: The Literary Autopsy of YOU Phillipson's English

BEFORE YOU GO ON TO NEXT YEAR'S ENGLISH TEACHER

INSTRUCTIONS: For this 15th paper, the idea is quite simple:

> You are a professional literary critic who has been tasked with looking into the body of literature that YOU produced during the past academic year in – and out – of Room 207.

You have completed 12 essays and 1 forgery. That's a lot to go back and thoughtfully examine, read, and consider AS IF YOU WERE SOMEONE ELSE.
The goal is to be objective in how you approach, well, YOU.
You should look at these 13 pieces as if for the first time, as if written by a stranger, as if you are the scholar or journalist whose job it is to research you (what can you find by Googling yourself?), taking a DEEP DIVE into the work you produced this academic year. Who are you OUTSIDE of what you write about, and how does that person (the real or private you) inform your writing (the guarded or public you)?
Standards and Expectations:

- You are not modeling or copying, but you should read some LITERARY CRITICS: To help you see how literary criticism is written, read a few essays by: Susan Sontag, John Updike, Harold Bloom, or Helen Vendler. Look at their essays' structure, pacing, tone, and voice. You can find reviews they've written of books other people wrote, through a 5 minute Google search.
- QUOTE LIBERALLY, BUT ALSO SPARINGLY: Drink deeply from many of your different 12 essays and one forgery project: selectively use quotes from various essays you've written this year; look for patterns in your writing; examine your growth – or plateau – or the extent to which an earlier piece was stronger than a later piece, etc. Look at stuff you wrote as a freshman, too, and compare and contrast. GO DEEP.
- ANALYZE + SYNTHESIZE: Essay 13 is all about putting your work from this year into a larger context. What are your superpowers, your weaknesses, your best paper, your worst paper, your most challenging "write," your writing process, your relationship to the written word? Scholars who write about an author tend to be the EXPERT on that author. YOU are the expert on YOU, so, you have a leg up. Pretend (for a moment) that you are a scholar who has been studying (YOU) for their entire tenure at Princeton, Harvard, or Yale. They've written your biography. They

know your literature like the verso of their typewriter keys. And this year you've produced writing that was a "departure from your past work." And isn't that true? Did you write like this last year? Did you think about your writing this way in previous English classes? Did you write these kinds of essays in 9th grade? Prior?

So – the premise is:

Write a comprehensive literary analysis essay that explores your 14 essays from this year, your forgery, at least 4 essays from last year's English teacher, and at least 4 essays from the English teacher before that (so, 10th, and 9th – or 9th and 8th grade).

For this essay, you may wish to argue something, reflect on something, determine something, or come to terms with something about YOU and YOUR writing. (And of course, you could do *all* of these things for this essay.)

Total word count should be approximately 3,000 words: Say 1,500 words of your commentary, and 1,500 words of quoted material.

* * *

One of my juniors, Chloe Liu, is a shining example of what a high school student can do with the "autopsy" assignment. What follows is a model of how to contemplate in real time, what metacognition in action looks like, and an approach to being vulnerable that is undeniably appealing and compelling.[1]

The Autopsy of You comes Down to Two Things

For the student:

Can you return to your essays and be real with yourself about who you were when you wrote them, and who you are now?

For the teacher:

Can you revisit whether you consistently grade what you truly value in student writing, and whether you are teaching the skills required to get them to the point where they can write as you want them to?

Note

1 See the link https://www.routledge.com/9781032987842.

16

EBERT'S WAY

Lessons from a Late-Great Film Critic

It's an up-down vote. Doesn't get any simpler than that.

But Roger Ebert and Gene Siskel's "thumbs up or thumbs down" delivered on-screen during their weekly film review show "At The Movies" (for ABC Television), belied the depth and intelligence that Ebert had displayed as a newspaper columnist at the Chicago Sun Times for decades.

Siskel and Ebert – two film critics who gave hot and measured takes on the cinema of the day (starting in the mid-1980s) — taught then-eighth-grade Wes Phillipson that it's not just acceptable to have an opinion about the movie you're watching, it's your responsibility. That was a big realization. Further, that critically engaging with a piece of media is an organic part of the process of consuming it – Who knew?

They helped me develop my taste in film, introduced me to the concept of weighing in on popular culture, and shared their own infectious joy in connecting dots: they were both gifted at that. As to the last one, movies didn't exist in a vacuum – an Arnold Schwarzenegger performance in Commando begged comparison to his turn in The Terminator and Total Recall.

Before age 13, I had probably never conducted any meaningful comparative analysis, nor understood why someone would endeavor to do so. What would have been the point?

Suddenly I understood.

Ebert's first movie review tackled La Dolce Vita in 1961 (predating his work at the Chicago Sun Times), with his final submission a meditation on To the Wonder in 2013 (published days after his death).

But it was Ebert's Chicago Sun Times' reviews that separated him from Gene Siskel. Ebert coined terms and phrase-made with such frequency, potency, and ease that he was the critical equivalent of Jerry Seinfeld.

Seinfeld gave us the ultimate shorthand for summing up humans and their behaviors – "close-talker," "low-talker," "sidler," and perfectly captured our tendency to gloss over the details that mattered: "yada yada yada." It was accused of being "a show about nothing," but it has endured as the best written sitcom in history, and that's certainly something.

"Bruised forearm movie" was a linguistic cultural innovation that described the effects of watching Indiana Jones and the Temple of Doom in theaters with your girlfriend. It came from Ebert's metaphorically fertile mind, and there were thousands more improvised phrases like that at the ready.

To Wit

In his takedown of M. Night Shyamalan's 2004 pseudo-historical thriller The Village, Ebert writes, "To call it an anticlimax would be an insult not only to climaxes but to prefixes." Of the taut neo-noir Tell No One he posits, "I've heard of airtight plots. This one is not merely airtight, but hermetically sealed." He skewers Chris Farley and David Spade's Tommy Boy as "one of those movies that plays like an explosion down at the screenplay factory." Writing about The Spirit, a comic strip-movie-turned-live-action, Ebert winds up to deliver a roundhouse punch: "To call these characters cardboard is to insult a useful packaging material."

And that's the kind of cleverness that made me a life-long reader and admirer. Anyone can watch a movie. And now, with blogging, anyone can write about them, too.

What Roger Ebert did was make the *review* as important and entertaining as the film itself, and that is not something most of us know how to do. Affirmatively, what Ebert says about Terrence Malick's To the Wonder (from 2012) is exactly how I feel about most five-paragraph essays written by students:

"Why must a film explain everything? Why must every motivation be spelled out? Aren't many films fundamentally the same film, with only the specifics changed? Aren't many of them telling the same story?"

Damn, Ebert. It's like you're inside my head in the classroom or during writing conferences ….

I'd argue that a handful of writers have taught me how to think: Nathan McCall, Chuck Klosterman, Stephen King, Dave Barry, Toni Morrison,

Don DeLillo, Zora Neale Hurston, Emily Nussbaum, James Baldwin, and Roger Ebert.

Ebert's last on that list, but he was the first of that rarefied bunch to get on my radar. And in my 30s and 40s, Ebert became my docent through the museum of great-and-terrible cinema. If I felt like watching something (which was a daily occurrence), I'd go through the archives at rogerebert.com to discover Ripley's Game, Redbelt, or The Pledge – or any other titles that made it into Ebert's Overlooked Film Festival held at the University of Illinois in 1999 – now simply called Ebertfest, held annually.

I suppose the modern-day equivalent to his 1980s network TV show "At The Movies" are podcasts like The Rewatchables, We Hate Movies, Blank Check, How Did This Get Made?, Films to Be Buried With, and Big Picture, or YouTube channels Deep Focus Lens, Chris Stuckmann, Red Letter Media, and James Rolfe (to name but a few of a few thousands public voices that are celebrated on Reddit, social media, and deconstructed in reaction videos across multiple platforms).

Back in 1986, there were only three major TV networks and FOX. Ebert's show aired on Saturday afternoons, with two million households tuning in to watch the gentlemanly joust (and to know which movie to see that night at the local theater).

When you're 13, you don't know that yesterday's movies are often far more compelling than the latest box-office releases. Since then, Ebert's recommendations have led me to gems like The Prince of the City, an early 1980s, slept-on Sidney Lumet neo-noir (starring Treat Williams), that sensationalized the ideas of police corruption first expressed in Serpico but also adopted the cinema verite of Scorsese 1974's Mean Streets while adding narrative coherence.

And Ebert's review made me watch Prince of the City *that night*. I finished reading it, then scrambled to find it on-line. That's the power of a good argument, like the Roman orators Demosthenes and Cicero – when the former would get off the podium the crowd would mutter, "Good speech," but Cicero's crowd, in the aftermath, would disperse, chanting one thing and one thing only: "Let us march!" (As I heard the motivational speaker Jim Rohn recount at the Lantana Conference Centre in Randolph, Massachusetts, in 1994; it should be noted that Rohn was *no* historian).

This is Ebert's "Cicero moment" in the Prince of the City review:

"This is a movie that literally hinges on the issue of perjury. And Sidney Lumet and his co-writer, Jay Presson Allen, have a great deal of respect for the legal questions involved. There is a sustained scene in this movie that is one of the most spellbinding I can imagine, and it consists entirely of government lawyers debating whether a given situation justifies a charge of perjury. Rarely are ethical issues discussed in such detail in a movie, and hardly ever so effectively."

And I'd found this movie after reading Ebert's The Parallax View endorsement months prior. And *that* film (more or less) begins and ends with a commission of judges conducting private tribunals regarding the assassinations of Presidential candidates.

And his Parallax View post showcases Ebert's ability to make delicate distinctions and hypothesize about how the evolution of society is reflected in the evolution of filmmaking:

"A couple of years earlier, the hero of 'The Parallax View' would probably have been a cop or a private eye. But what with Woodward and Bernstein and all, Warren Beatty plays a newspaper reporter instead. Like all good movie reporters, he never has to meet a deadline or write a story; his function is to show up at the office late at night so his kindly old editor can hand over the petty-cash fund to finance further investigations."

It's probably difficult for people not alive in the 1980s or 1990s to understand the strange attraction to Ebert – he wasn't telegenic and was a brusque public speaker. He dressed like a frowsy adjunct professor. And – in many ways – he was an elite who was actually a populist, a plain-spoken smart guy who chose (for whatever reason) to turn his attention to a medium that didn't get a lot of respect until guys like him (and there were *very* few critics on his level) made people see the art and the artifice of cinema.

And that's why I ask my students to:

a   Read and annotate a dozen Roger Ebert film reviews (looking for patterns that emerge). How does Ebert begin and end his paragraphs? What does he use his introductions to accomplish? His outros – same question? What "sentence-types" does he favor and in what combinations? Does he prefer metaphors, similes, analogies, allusions, or other kinds of figurative language? When he "phrase-makes," what kind of diction tends to show up: simple, plain-speak, or more SAT-level terminology? How does he introduce an idea, quote, or personal anecdote? To what extent does he "intersect" with the review or keep a semi-distance and the appearance of objectivity?

b   Choose one film from my list that Ebert (for whatever reason) did not review when he was at his most critically prolific: Capricorn One (1978), The Candidate (1972), or The Chase (1966).

c   Review that film "as if" you have called a seance and can channel the spirit of Roger Ebert. The goal isn't to copy Ebert but to "approximate

him," in that every single review he wrote was an intellectually honest indictment of a film or a specific and sincere acknowledgment of its brilliance.
d   The average length of an Ebert column is 700 words. You're encouraged to stick to a minimum of 750 and maximum of 850.

What Are the Lessons of Roger Ebert's Film Criticism?

Ebert was encouraging and balanced whenever he could be. He could be a filmmaker's greatest advocate, as when discussing Robert Townsend's pastiche biopic The Five Heartbeats:

"This is Townsend's first traditional feature film; his directorial debut, some four years ago, was Hollywood Shuffle, a series of comic sketches that parodied the cliched ways Hollywood has used black characters in the movies. Most of those sketches were under 10 minutes; this time, at feature length, Townsend shows a real talent, and, not surprisingly, an ability to avoid most cliches, to go for the human truth in his characters."

And when writing about the lesser Townsend film – Meteor Man – Ebert is still on the director's side, nudging him toward the future and simultaneously the past:

"Townsend is an engaging actor (see one of his best performances in the Denzel Washington sleeper The Mighty Quinn). As a director, he showed a gift for satire in Hollywood Shuffle, his put-down of Hollywood's attitudes toward Black movie characters, and his 'Six Heartbeats,' about the rise and fall of members of a singing group, overcame an uncertain start to build real power and emotion. But here he seems to be the victim of too many ideas, as if he wanted to make several films, and decided to shoot the best parts of all of them."

As a practitioner, Ebert didn't fawn. He wasn't obsequious. He was sometimes blunt and brutal if the screening moved the popcorn down the windpipe, as was the case with Vincent Gallo's Brown Bunny. Yet in the same review, he's able to change course, acknowledging the good that came from the bad. He never fears being wrong or perceived as a waffler. There are outright contradictions in some of his reviews that can be forgiven, because they fit inside a flexible and fungible framework:

"In May of 2003 I walked out of the press screening of Vincent Gallo's The Brown Bunny at the Cannes Film Festival and was asked by a camera crew what I thought of the film. I said I thought it was the worst film in the history of the festival. That was hyperbole – I hadn't seen every film in the history of the festival – but I was still vibrating from one of the most disastrous screenings I had ever attended...But then a funny thing happened. Gallo went back into the editing room and cut 26 minutes of his 118-minute film, or almost a fourth of the running time. And in the process he transformed it. The film's form and purpose now emerge from the miasma of the original cut, and are quietly, sadly, effective. It is said that editing is the soul of the cinema; in the case of 'The Brown Bunny,' it is its salvation."

Nuance is what makes Ebert worth reading – and returning to. In fact, I don't really watch a movie before I've read one of his reviews. That means there's very little cinema that postdates 2013 that I eagerly consume.

Ebert's Memento review – three out of four stars – has a line that walks right up to contradiction. He loved the Christopher Nolan film about a man with memory issues and a dead wife that he can't really account for. But there's a problem with a key detail that Ebert himself didn't even pick up on that gets featured in his column:

"I have here a message from Vasudha Gandhi of Queens Village, N.Y., about the movie Memento: Although I loved the film, I don't understand one key plot-point. If the last thing the main character remembers is his wife dying, then how does he remember that he has short-term memory loss? Michael Cusumano of Philadelphia writes with the same query. They may have identified a hole big enough to drive the entire plot through. Perhaps a neurologist can provide a medical answer, but I prefer to believe that Leonard, the hero of the film, has a condition similar to Tom Hanks' 'brain cloud' in 'Joe vs. the Volcano' – Leonard suffers from a condition brought on by a screenplay that finds it necessary, and it's unkind of us to inquire too deeply."

Again – the man was generous. He was willing to suspend his own disbelief, despite calling attention to it with his virtual megaphone one day, then reconciling his misgivings about it the next. He sees the problem (with Brown Bunny in this case) but is able to say what my mom often said to me when watching implausible or unresolved issues in the storyline of a film or TV show: "Wes, it's in the script."

Ebert wasn't highbrow or elitist, but someone just looking for a good time at the movies. His relationship with the early films of Jim Carrey is indicative of that. Ebert awarded (begrudgingly) one star to Ace Venture: Pet Detective (like a belligerent Yelper who wishes they could give zero stars) but found wonder and surprise in The Mask. The films were relased just months apart, yet Ebert had praise in July for someone he'd openly dismissed in February (of 1994):

"I was not one of the admirers of Ace Ventura: Pet Detective. Millions were, however. I thought the story surpassed stupidity, and not in interesting ways. But I could sense some of Carrey's unrestrained energy and gift for comic invention, and here – where the story and the decor and the idea of the mask provide an anchor for his energy – Carrey demonstrates that he does have a genuine gift. It is said that one of the indispensable qualities of an actor is an ability to communicate the joy he takes in his performance. You could say "The Mask" was founded on that."

And that's what I want students to embrace in their own writing: strong opinions that can be walked back, tempered, or reconsidered; the creation of sentences that sustain themselves, for years, under the weight of their playful lightness; and, among other things, criticism that isn't inherently critical or negative.

Ebert loved movies and spent more time celebrating filmmakers and actors than tearing them down, and I'd love for my students – and yours – to move a little further in that direction too.

* * *

Here's Prompt Sixteen

Ebert's Way: Significant Until Proven Meaningless

NOTE of warning: When you are a movie critic for a newspaper (like Ebert was at the Chicago Sun Times for 50 years), you don't typically get to choose what movies you review. You are sent out to "review the current cinema of the day." With this prompt, I'm trying to recreate that experience for you as authentically as possible by having you choose from three films that you've never seen, and ones that Ebert could have – but never did – review.

I have watched these films more than once (and really enjoyed them). For whatever reason Ebert never wrote about them, so you can't "seek out" his critiques, or be tainted by his bias. Your goal – for Essay Eleven – will be to "write an Ebert level and Ebert styled review" of one of these three works:

1 **Capricorn One**: Astronauts are forced to "fake" a Mars mission under the threat of death. Released in 1978.
2 **The Candidate**: An idealistic lawyer runs for Democratic senator of California but finds he's a frog in a pot of water, with the heat turned up very slowly on him. Released in 1972.
3 **The Chase:** A deep south sheriff both helps – and hinders – the investigation of a jailbreak murder. Released in 1966.

Your job is to:

First night:

- a Pick one movie from my list of three **to watch the first hour of tonight.** The full movies are linked for free or can be easily found on a combination of streaming platforms, including Tubi, YouTube, Hulu, Netflix, and Kanopy.
- b Take notes with the most active and open mind possible. As former student Jocelyn Weiss taught me: "Everything is significant until proven meaningless."
- c Make a Google Doc called "Movie Notes – First Hour" – and share it with me before our next class meeting.

Second night:

- Read four additional Ebert reviews (you've already read three prior to getting this handout).
- Annotate Them: look for patterns, things you can steal, how Ebert expresses ideas, emotions, and connects dots. BLUEPRINT how Ebert writes about movies. Does he "review" them, or get you to think about them? And how? What does he accomplish with his film study?
- Make a Google Doc called Ebert Reviews 2nd Batch and share it with me before that next class meeting.

Third night:

- Read four additional Ebert reviews (you've read seven up until this point),
- Annotate Them: see above (same categories).
- Make a Google Doc called Ebert Reviews 3rd Batch and share it with me before that class session.

Fourth night:

- i Finish your chosen film and figure out what you – ultimately – believe about your movie. A review shouldn't be focused on: it's good – or – it's bad. It should be focused on (at least) three things:

  1 **Metacommentary**: What is the film saying (to you) beyond the immediate plot? What larger issues does it (indirectly or directly) bring up or get at?
  2 **Intersectionality**: What other things in pop-culture (particularly in film and TV) does the movie make you think about and can you connect to? What can you reference and explain in an interesting

way that showcases your expertise and helps readers better understand the film's larger social context?
3 **Phrase-Making**: Ebert has his own WikiQuote page, which is a library of his richest phrase-making and delicate insight. Your job is to play with language, to phrase-make, to coin terms, etc.

ii Make a Google Doc called "2nd half of film" – with some notes reflecting what ideas are NOW starting to "take shape" for you (or are better fleshed out in your mind now that you've completed viewing your movie).

17
THE VIDEO ESSAY IS NOT JUST FOR YOUTUBERS

A moment of radical honesty here: *I can't make or edit video essays.*

Admitting to that makes me feel a bit like the old Van Halen and The Doobie Brothers producer Ted Templeman, who, at age 80, can't make music anymore because the technology had long ago outpaced him.

Templeman is no Luddite nor technophobe; he just never changed with the times. As soon as recording studios converted to digital equipment, he retired from the industry, leaving behind a body of work that includes everything from Nicolette Larson's "Lotta Love" to Van Halen's "Unchained" (in which he makes a legendary audio cameo).

I *did* take a video bootcamp once at Scarsdale High School (taught by budding filmmaker Matthew Beals), but I didn't have the patience or technical savvy to hunch over and edit a video essay when I could just sit straight in my chair and comfortably write one.

And as much as I admire Ted Templeman's contributions to modern popular music, I don't want to end up being the one who bristled and chafed against the shifting sands of time.

In this case, I'm talking about video essays.

It started with an English Department meeting many years ago. Stacey Dawes presented one of her student's Scarlet Letter/Easy A (book to film "adaptation") video essays. I don't think I'd ever considered doing them before that moment. Right after, George Olivier showed a short film on Macbeth (also made by students) that was part "art film" and part "text-based analysis." At the time, the consensus was that these projects took significantly longer to execute than traditional essays and had undefined benefits. Were students who made video essays more thoughtful

DOI: 10.4324/9781003600565-17

about quote selection? Did they probe for subtext in more engaging ways? Was it worth the multiple hours of pre-production, production, and post-production time to yield a finished product with a five-to-ten-minute runtime?

The Macbeth video (for George's class) was starkly emo and abstract, but did it have the same depth of thinking that a 1250-word essay could? The Scarlet Letter film (for Stacey's class) was slick and well-edited, but it felt more like a movie trailer with added plot summary than an intellectual endeavor.

At the same time, I had never even thought of asking students to do this kind of project. This was probably around 2014, long before YouTubers were (oftentimes) making meaningful content based on classic literature and film – dissecting one frame-by-frame and the other line-by-line.

Walking away from the meeting, I remember my friend and colleague Seth Evans had expressed skepticism about the process and the product. I was probably just intimidated by what George and Stacey had pulled off, knowing that I couldn't effectively advise anyone on how to make a video, nor articulate the vision that would sustain one. And I was envious they'd thought of it first.

But then Oliver Hong happened.

It was 2021, and countless video essay creators were (by that time) readily monetizing their content on YouTube and various social media platforms. Oliver's first essay of junior honors (American Literature) focused on his relationship to a single, tattered edition of the graphic novel Watchmen by Alan Moore. It was his father's copy, and what emerged from writing about that talisman kept in his bedroom was a deep love of nostalgia and the potency of objects in his life.

So – for whatever reason – seven years later I suggested, "If anyone wants to make a video essay this year, I'm all for it."

Oliver had never made one, and he didn't ask for my help. He instead (through watching YouTube video tutorials) served up the most exquisite approximation of what It's a Wonderful Life would be like if a thoughtful, brilliant, sentimental, serious, preposterous, Asian Scarsdalian recut the film and inter-spliced home movie footage of himself with Frank Capra's movie, while voiceover narrating the entire experience in a tone that can only be described as wistful, hopeful, and bereft (all at the same time). He ambitiously called his video essay "The Way to Live," and it lived up to its billing.

The first 10 minutes and 20 seconds of Oliver's film features a pastiche of various media that he's "collected" for its affirmative value, as well as a wistful exploration of 1946s It's a Wonderful Life. At 10:21, the video abruptly cuts to black and the viewer sees two-year-sold

Oliver treating his sister to ride on a toddler's push car, then gives way to a montage of parent-shot footage of Oliver fishing, swimming, and playing the violin, all scored by a sparse piano and his somber-but-substantive narration:

"I've thought a lot about what might happen if I were erased from reality after watching It's a Wonderful Life.

It starts with fun hypotheticals:

Would someone else be President?
Was there anyone I may have inadvertently saved from death?

It quickly turns sadder:

How much did that broken window cost?
How many trees did my life burn?
Are there people I've hurt who would have been happier?
The net value of a life is impossible to calculate, but that doesn't stop us from trying.
The Good Place tries.

According to the soul squad, the net value of a life doesn't matter. It is increasingly impossible in our interlinked society to take a moral action. The point system is flawed, with its unfair standards and vague explanations. The conclusion the show ultimately arrives at is that we are never past redemption and always have the capacity to be better. It's a Wonderful Life doesn't try to do that complex calculus. There are characters in this movie who are just clearly past redemption. Mr. Potter will never be a charitable soul, no matter how many times he goes through the system. While the simple morality here seems cliche, rich man bad, poor man good, I actually think it helps the film's message."

* * *

Oliver Hong's video essay covers a long list of narrative media that affirms the value of life and the power of community (The Office and World of Tomorrow in particular), dives deeply into the Capra film, and probes the ethos of The Good Place.

By its end, though, it's not a "collection of quotes" (like many essays are). It's not a cluttered paper that uses too many examples from too many works. It's not a half-hearted look at an assigned text.

No. It's a 14 minute and 8 second film that reminds me there are better ways to live and that watching It's a Wonderful Life might provide a roadmap for that journey. It's a video essay that makes me cry (sometimes), while also making me wonder why I assign anything *other* than video essays.

Reflexively, I often say to students that "an essay must make its audience think and feel, just as the finale of The Good Place accomplishes exceptionally well."

It's no small feat for a high school junior to make a finished product about a classic film, an Emmy Award winning TV show, and a myriad of rich, postmodern media that is – in many ways – as powerful as the source material itself.

After Oliver's debut video essay, I asked him – wait for it – to make a video essay guide to making video essays. Surprised by the request (as he'd only made one), Oliver was slow to create the tutorial, but (at eight minutes and six seconds), it arrived packed with useful advice, actionable strategies, and ethereal philosophy about the creation process.

Tip Number One:

"You need to care about what you're talking about. Is this one too hard to believe? This isn't a hard and fast rule, you might be extremely talented and dispassionate. But for the vast majority of us plebeians, we need the crutch of passion to create something meaningful. What's that movie you've been thinking about for three years? And just what have you been thinking about it? I want to know."

Tip Number Two:

"Watch video essays. Again, this isn't groundbreaking stuff, it's just stuff you may not have yet verbalized. There are video essays on forking everything, I've watched a three hour video essay on Lab Rats. That show on Disney. Three hours. Lab rats. Three hours. – Personally, Jacob Geller is my absolute favorite video maker on Tube. And to prove my point about just how much stuff there is on YouTube, he alone has talked about forests, Zelda, the WPA, and translating ancient Chinese poetry… all in the same video. There is no shortage of stuff. You just have to find what you want to learn about."

Tip Number Three:

"Steal shamelessly. You, we, us, me are high schoolers. We aren't going to create a perfect video essay in a vacuum. We need inspiration, and at times, just straight up thievery. To illustrate my point, I have stolen from 'How to Write' 'Jacob MinnMax,' 'Top Ten Games,' 'A Closer Look video essay.' And that's fine. As long as in the end you can honestly say you've played a bigger role in the work than your source material, you've done your job. Don't plagiarize though. But taking others' editing techniques and trying them on for size? Sure."

Tip Number Four:

"This one sucks, but it might be the most important. We have all been trained to watch moving pictures on a screen with audio. We've done it since Wonder Pets! That's probably more than a decade, and more importantly the audience are unconsciously primed to notice when something is off. Amateurish work is unacceptable. I want to be clear here, this does not mean the work needs to be perfect. It just means that it is incredibly distracting to have the music too loud, or a voiceover too monotonous, or a clip with one frame more than intended. It will be all the viewer thinks about for the next five seconds of your video. While this one is depressing, the good news is that all it requires is time to amend. If we all have that sense something is wrong, you have it too, so just put in the time and fix the problems.

- Make sure your audio levels are balanced correctly to the layman, make sure the music doesn't drown out your voice and vice versa.
- Make sure your editing doesn't leave any broken frames.
- Your voiceover should be appropriate for the tone of whatever section of the video you are making. If it's sad, if it's happy, get into that mindset. I find a good way to do this is to listen to the music of the section you are making while doing the voiceover. For God's sake don't be boring.
- Make sure your mic quality doesn't shart the duvet. Don't feel compelled to go out and buy expensive equipment, just find a quiet room and talk into a pillow to avoid echoes.
- Watch the entire finished product; you'll be confronted by anything that's wrong.
- I use Davinci Resolve 17, which is free.
- I am downloading videos and music off of YouTube, and you can too.
- I'm using a Shure MV5 mic which isn't cheap nor necessary.

This doesn't mean avoid the things you don't know how to do [there are plenty of videos on-line to assist you]. It does mean that you try your best to do them correctly and precisely."

Tip Number Five:

"This one is probably the most important. Words tell you what to think, music tells you what to feel. Go to YouTube right now and search up 'Ross Psychopath,' and you'll instantly understand the role of diegesis (sound or music) in a scene (courtesy of a twisted re-edit of a Friends episode). Once you find the right song, I promise you the video will become twice as good."

Tip Number Six:

"It sounds obvious – but this is not an essay. So when you're writing your script, don't write an 'essay' as you know it. Think about how you would say it. Think about it as looser and informal. I'll admit, there's the danger of going too far. You need to say something by the end of your video. You can't be so informal that you neglect all analysis and meaningful content. But don't be so rigid that you start counting the number of times you've used a subject word – like you. For me, in my own video essay on how to make a video essay, I've used it on 55 occasions, and that's perfectly fine: I'm talking directly to you, whoever you are."

Tip Number Seven:

"Last one. You are a person. Have a personality. It's hard to latch onto sentences, but it's easy to connect with people. Crack jokes, write as you would speak, make this video have a life of its own. The whole point of creating art at all is so we can see the world through a different lens, so show us your forking lens (to quote The Good Place)!"

Tip Number Eight:

"Have fun."

* * *

Around the same time, sophomore Toby Rosewater took a stab at creating his own video essay about liminal spaces.

Complete transparency: I had never heard the word liminal and had no idea what he meant by that. Apparently it just means: in-between spaces, hallways, abandoned malls, eerie "dead space" that has no clear purpose or current use. They might be temporarily empty (like an unused service elevator or school gymnasium in summertime), or they might feel like places of transition (such as capacious airport corridors that you wouldn't spend time in except to get from Point A to Point B).

Toby called his film "Grandma's Elevator: An Exploration Into Liminal Spaces."

Like Oliver's, it too ran about 15 minutes and was ambitious in its scope, making great use of everything from original footage of his grandmother's home elevator to clips from the 2008 documentary Man on Wire, Christopher Nolan's Inception, The Coen brother's version of Macbeth, as well as Justin Kurzel's adaptation of the Bard's tragedy.

YouTuber Jason Gastrow – better known as videogamedunkey – posted a 5 minute, 17 second video essay on Stanley Kubrick's adaptation of The Shining seven years ago that has garnered over 5.9 million views. I've watched a few dozen times at this point. It's haunting, crisp, and revelatory.

I sent the video link to Oliver at one point in 2022, and he was flabbergasted:

"WHAT IN THE WORLD. I would never have expected you to send me a Dunkey video essay. I've watched this video about a million times and I think about his style all the time. He was a big inspiration for my video. I think his video essays very much utilize the idea that short, supremely honed works are better (or more enjoyable) than longer ones. Even just a 7 minute video of his is better than most 3 hour videos I've seen.

It's just good filmmaking to be honest. I don't think there are too many "Damn son" lines, but the visuals and audio, paired with really smart juxtapositions make the video for me. I think his big trick is sharp shifts in sound and tone of music. I love the moment when he says "maybe we can hear it." It's just so good.

You should watch his "Playtime" video. It's wild how good it is. I haven't seen the movie, but I feel like I watched the whole thing through his video. https://youtu.be/iTBW6jbHgX0

I don't know how much the Shining video makes me think, but it makes me feel so damn much."

* * *

I return to a truth I've observed: **We don't share essays with each other**. But we do seem to be experiencing a Renaissance of sorts where we share video essays (because content creators have never been so varied, compelling, or prolific). My current student (of two years), Jay Hove, has frequently emailed me things to watch. Jay has stopped doing so only because I have stopped watching, and that's only because I've been working on this book.

Otherwise, I'd delight in anything Jay might send me, including films by Drew Gooden (How A.I. is Ruining the Internet comes to mind).

Back in 2014, George Oliver and Stacey Dawes were onto something. They saw that the landscape was changing, perhaps even fading to black. They recognized how vital filmmaking was to their students' creative process, and that adding many layers (video, audio, editing, storyboarding, clip curation, voiceover narration, etc.) may have come at certain costs. Yes, you might (possibly) lose depth and breadth when you create a five-minute film short – being unable to take the deep-subtextual-dive that 1,500 words affords. But they also knew that it wasn't an all-or-nothing proposition anyway.

All that means to me is: it's a nice break from a paper essay; it's a welcome respite from having to stare down yet another empty Google Doc before one can fill it up with diction, syntax, and form.

I've often thought of myself as a late bloomer, but I opened up to the idea when Oliver came along.

Don't wait for your Oliver.

(It's also not lost on me that George Olivier was the first to introduce me to the medium, and it's awfully close to Oliver. 'Twas probably a sign').

18

THE INTERROGATIVE MOOD

Questions Only, No Answers

In 2009 I was waiting for a date to show up at Barnes & Noble (a walking English teacher cliche, I'm aware), when I spotted a book with a strange title on the New Release table near the magazine stand: The Interrogative Mood: A Novel?, written by someone with an even odder name – Padgett Powell – one that sounded like Parker Posey's long-lost cousin, or the nom de plume of a rakish, war correspondent.

Regardless, it's where my inspiration comes from: I'm at a bookstore, watching a TV show, listening to NPR (in my case WNYC), test-driving a podcast – and something strikes, hits, nudges, or moves me to say – *I could use this in one of my English classes.*

In this case it was Powell's book, and I noticed that the word "novel" was followed by a question mark, so I became immediately intrigued.

My understanding is – as of 2024 – that Padgett Powell has written the only full-length fictional novel in the history of literature composed entirely of questions, and this is it. No statements. No direct exposition. Just questions. That's why it's called "The Interrogative Mood" because interrogatives are, well, questions.

To be honest, I'd lost interest after a page or three, and by the time my newish girlfriend had arrived, the discovery had escaped my mind altogether.

But Then It Quietly Haunted Me for a while.

As a concept, Powell had done the unthinkable. As an executed project, I couldn't muster the interest to engage with it.

DOI: 10.4324/9781003600565-18

This excerpt from his "novel" (?) is indicative of the genius of the book, but also its central problem:

"Are your emotions pure? Are your nerves adjustable? How do you stand in relation to the potato? Should it still be Constantinople? Does a nameless horse make you more nervous or less nervous than a named horse? In your view, do children smell good? If before you now, would you eat animal crackers? Could you lie down and take a rest on a sidewalk? Did you love your mother and father, and do Psalms do it for you? If you are relegated to last place in every category, are you bothered enough to struggle up? Does your doorbell ever ring? Is there sand in your craw? Could Mendeleyev place you correctly in a square on a chart of periodic identities, or would you resonate all over the board? How many push-ups can you do?"

The genius lies in Powell's ability to unleash thought-provoking or confrontational questions "on demand," like generative A.I. cross-bred with a beer-tap, its robotic disconnect and foamy goodness coalescing for 164 pages.

The problem, though, stems from the episodic nature of the questions themselves. They don't "stack" or build on each other nearly enough. They seem downright disconnected – non sequiturs masquerading as inquiry. Now, I didn't read the entire book so take that with a grain of salt? A corn of black pepper? A dollop of whip cream? A smattering of applause?

Anyway – you get the idea. If this passage is like the rest of the book (or anything like my silly reenactment just above), then it's just a tedious gimmick that flares out before it fully ignites.

But here's what I took away from Powell: he's really interested in form, and exceptionally good at the gamification of writing. And that's what our students need today: to view essays and creative assignments as *play*, not obligation or chore – not as something to send their sympathetic nervous systems into overdrive.

But there has to be a rhyme to the reason for what we do (and what Powell did).

Yes, I know. If you Google The Interrogative Mood: A Novel?, you'll discover that it's not really a novel at all, but a philosophical inquiry about where humanity presently sits, versus where it needs to be (and the gap that – perhaps – the right question can bridge *if* thoughtfully answered).

So then, technically, no one has ever written a question-based novel.

But Powell's questions don't build on each other. If I were going to assign some bastardized version of Powell's questions-only exercise to my students as a writing prompt, I would need to first think through, then answer, some questions of my own:

a   What's the point?
b   Is it possible there is no point?
c   To what extent could high school students do something meaningful with it?
d   What would Padgett Powell think about all this?

July 25, 2024, 1:11 PM on LinkedIn: "Any chance you can talk with my students about The Interrogative Mood?"
Padgett:
"Possibly can. Send details. I'll help someone inflicting Interrogative Mood on innocents. Powell."
What? No *questions as answers* in Powell's DM? I had hoped for something, well, decidedly more interrogative.
I haven't followed up with Padgett yet, which highlights the raw truth about me and my creative process as an English teacher:

It took me from 2009 until 2023 to operationalize this "questions only" idea for classroom use. That's why this book that you're currently reading may, against all odds, be incredibly useful to you: it will save you fourteen years (or more) of trial-and-error, or doddering procrastination.

And Powell was clearly onto something. I now give this prompt during the first quarter and see students' writing radically transform from "basic plot-driven sentences" to masterfully constructed prose jigsaw puzzles with the breathless quality of Nicholson Baker's postmodern masterpiece The Mezzanine, or passages from Don DeLillo's White Noise. Consecutive questions create, almost by default, a kind of gravitas that students can't otherwise muster for years and years on their own. What often results is a hypnotic rhythm and syntactical strong-arming that reeks of consideration and authority.
What I'm about to show you will probably shock you.
A sophomore I worked with during academic year 2023–24, Isabela Braga Figueiredo, wrote a meditation on a single episode of Criminal Minds – Strange Fruit – Season 09, Episode 09. It's a remarkable piece of writing on its own, but it's also composed of "just questions."
And Isabela is my proof of concept for this prompt: she did, in my opinion, what Padgett Powell could not do – make a compelling,

cohesive, and serial argument, using questions that masterfully built upon each other.

When you read Isabela's essay, you'll quickly forget there are no statements, nor a single direct claim. And it *should be* very difficult to write a powerful argument about a TV show, book, or historical figure with such "limitations," but it's actually liberating, or self-governing at the very least. Again, it's the notion that restrictions lead to creative solutions. And this is a wildly different assignment from my "No E" paper – but it's also the other side of the same coin. Ernest Vincent Wright has written the only novel in history without the use of E (in English), and Powell has written the only "all questions novel" in history. They're both lipogrammatic in their own way – which is another way of saying: each one is a parlor trick; each one is about omission; and each one is about preventing the author's boredom (and hopefully the reader's, too).

Isabela's hot take on the reverse-racism of this Criminal Minds episode is one of the best pieces of writing I've seen from a tenth grader in 30 years of teaching, but, as you'll see later in this chapter, *anyone can do this assignment well*. And that was the real violation of expectation for me: I had no idea what would come from this prompt, but it's likely the best thing I do in the classroom.[1]

***

What's useful to know about Isabela's experience in my tenth-grade English class is that she really chaffed against the "No E" paper prompt but found her greatest work in this one.

Now, if you remember my number one tenet of English teaching, it's to never ask my students to attempt something that I, myself, haven't done first.

At the time, my wife was attempting to make it through all six seasons of the sitcom Schitt's Creek. The show is beloved by millions, and at one point swept the Emmys. But we were "hate-watching" it for a few reasons. One was to see if it ever got good, over time. What was all the hype about, anyway? We couldn't understand what was funny about it, or why these stilted characters (paper-thin stereotypes and tired retreads) were resonating with Americans so profoundly. Two was to follow the characters to their bitter end to see for ourselves if they remained static caricatures throughout. The outcomes? It never got good, and it continued to devolve (or remain in a holding pattern) season to season.

If anything, Schitt's Creek gave me something to write about, and for my essay I combined "the rant" with "only questions" and wrote this during a rare free period.[2]

Notes

1 See https://www.routledge.com/9781032987842.
2 See https://www.routledge.com/9781032987842.

19

GRADING ESSAYS MEANS NEVER HAVING TO BE ALONE AGAIN

Marina Keegan died in a car crash shortly after graduating from Yale in 2012. She (famously) wrote an essay called "The Opposite of Loneliness," (for her school's daily paper) in which she describes the enduring yet ephemeral sense of community that she's experienced at New Haven. She recounts a late-night study session in the library (after a locked door is opened for her by campus security), but it's really just an ode to Yale: she'll never feel this "unalone" again in her entire life if she could just take Yale with her.

It was a theory she never got to test out.

Scarsdale's own Nicholas Kristof (a multiple Pulitzer Prize winning journalist) is responsible for rescuing Keegan's work from near obscurity by dedicating one of his NYT Op-Ed columns to her book of the same name. *The Opposite of Loneliness* is (largely) a collection of the articles and essays Keegan wrote for the Yale Daily News, but its title expresses my own experience with teaching after I began grading essays *with* students, instead of divorced *from* students.

And That's Been the Most Important Distinction of My Thirty Year Career

And you might ask,

Why in the world would a teacher want to grade an essay with the student who wrote it? And what student would want to endure that torture, as well?

DOI: 10.4324/9781003600565-19

Isn't it uncomfortable to give detailed feedback – sometimes critical feedback – in real time to a student in real life, sitting right next to you in an office ... an enclosed space, with nowhere to hide out?

And what about the act of putting a letter grade on a student's essay with them looking on?

To quote The Cars – "Oh well uh, you might think I'm crazy" – and that's okay if you do. For the past decade I've slowly-but-steadily migrated most of my essay grading to "optional, in- person" from "isolated, alone, and resentful in my villain's lair."

What in the actual fudge is "optional, in-person" you wonder? It's saying to students: I have an office, and I have office hours (Scarsdale HS is based on the tutorial model; each teacher has an office – many have roommates; if you stay here long enough, you have decent odds of getting a singleton), and – if you'd like – make an appointment on my You Can Book Me site and get *instant gradeification* (™ pending, LOL).

Almost no one at Scarsdale HS was grading essays with students when I began the practice in 2014. I believe that two teachers long ago – Tom McGwire and Stephen Mounkhall – required students to come and review the first assignment of the year in American Studies (a jointly taught English and History course). But that was it: one and done.

Within the past year or so, three English teachers in my Department have picked up the habit.

I didn't get the idea from anyone or anywhere. It just seemed the most productive use of my time, and the co-grader's time. Nearly every single teacher on the planet would agree that we do our best work one-on-one with students. Wouldn't it follow that we'd also do our best (and most meaningful) assessing one-on-one, too?

Anyway, it's just counterintuitive to grade an essay in isolation. Don't believe me?

Take Jay Hove as a Case Study

Jay's currently a junior of mine and was my sophomore last year as well. Jay doesn't have much free space in their academic schedule to meet with teachers. After canceling on me a few times due to conflicts, Jay said, "Would you mark my essay and put a grade on it?" I, of course, said yes. After leaving 30 or so comments on the paper, Jay read my remarks and immediately met with me to eloquently argue against everything I'd written. And it was a strange experience for me – because it affirmed why I was grading WITH students and not SEPARATE from them:

I had misinterpreted or misapprehended nearly everything Jay had written. I had failed to appreciate certain nuances, but also to get the gist of the argument.

Yes, it was an easy fix. It took twenty minutes with Jay to set things right, but it simply wouldn't have happened if we'd sat down and co-graded in the first place.

Warning: It's Not All Warm and Fuzzy – But You'll Never Be Lonely

Grades are the currency at nearly every high school and college in America. Bard President Leon Botstein gave a long lecture at SHS back in 2005. He claimed that students attending his preparatory BEC – Bard Early College – in Manhattan "only did things for intrinsic reasons," and that "all extrinsic motivators – like grades – had been stripped away from my program."

At the time, it sounded like a fantasy or utopic ideal to me, and it probably was. The number of my colleagues' heads shaking in the auditorium as Bostein delivered anecdote after anecdote about students operating solely from a place of sheer intellectual curiosity, spoke volumes.

While I admire President Bostein's vision for a reimagined educational system in America, it's also utterly impossible to achieve it as he articulated. Even SHS' Alternative (A) School doesn't have grades, but – well – also has grades. There, report cards and letter grades are replaced with "Evals" – longform reflections on student progress and their body of work over a given academic quarter, written-up by their teachers in all academic subjects.

Evaluations are grades. Grades are evaluative. Employees need to get paid. Students need to earn grades. Unless you were doing volunteer work, you wouldn't stay on a job pro bono. Unless you were taking a summer enrichment program, you wouldn't do the work unless it was being graded.

So when I begin each year with a (mostly) new crop of students, I spend a good deal of time establishing a culture of:

a   Sharing work
b   Grading work together

But (on both sides now) you take an emotional risk and make yourself vulnerable by co-grading. More than once, I've had students leave my office crying, and sometimes they stay and try to fight off the tears. Now, it's hard to know: Would they have cried when they'd gotten the essay returned to them a week later? Was it my tone that made them cry, or my specific words and comments? Or both?

Occasionally, students will even get defensive: that first grading session is going to be the most "charged" meeting you'll likely have with them all year. Remember, they've never graded an essay with the teacher that assigned it (nor anyone). They've never gotten criticism (or praise) on a piece of their writing delivered in a kind of surround sound "stereo" – **out loud AND on paper**.

Connor Meschewski is a really useful example of a student who both (A) took my feedback really personally and (B) used his hurt feelings to fuel his personal growth.

He wrote about the ritual of grading essays with me – something he had never once done with a teacher in his 14 years of life – in one essay from sophomore year called, Breakthrough to Category Two: An Anti-Validation Story.[1]

* * *

I'll warn you now that co-grading essays it not going to be easier than grading papers alone, at the desk of your home-office, marking them on your kitchen table overlooking a backyard of grass or snow, leaving comments on a Doc by way of a screen – perhaps even copying and pasting "ready made" comments like you're a ChatGPT in human form.

No – in many ways, it will take more out of you to *grade with said student*, and *sometimes* even feel thankless when you do so.

But the alternative sucks. Or, at least, the old way is for suckers.

Grading in isolation, by your lonesome, is *always thankless*. It's *forever* soul-sucking. It's the most denervating thing you can do as a teacher.

No one likes to grade essays. If you do – you're a wonderfully freakish creature who should immediately be dissected and studied by Strunk & White's next of kin. Slices of your tissues should be flash-frozen and squeezed onto slides and scrutinized like the rara avis they are.

I hate grading essays.

But that's not a complete sentence. It should read: I hate grading essays by myself.

You see, my *opposite of loneliness* is collaborating not with colleagues (although I've done that with a good degree of success in a dozen or so meaningful cases), but with my students. They begin writing their essay (in part) with me, in class, so it only makes sense that they end it with me too, in my office: dueling laptops at the ready, seated side-by-side, Flokati rug underneath foot, floor-to-ceiling bookcases surrounding us on all sides, the underlying static of my white noise machines under chairs, natural light streaming into the room from towering windows, and two people, in some ways just meeting each other for the first time in weeks, not strangers, only lacking the knowing of who we are today, in the moment, as we endeavor to make meaning of the written word (to paraphrase Richard Rudolph here toward the end).

And how does it work?

I start by giving them Connor Meschewski's essay on grading essays (with me). Then I give them my You Can Book Me conference sign-up link (I post it to Google Classroom and my SHS Teacher Page). I encourage them to sign-up during the two-week period after an essay is due.

I make it clear: *You don't have to grade with me.* And I make my core belief transparent to them: If you really want my feedback, then you'll come to my office and you'll get it, each and every time I assign an essay.

Years ago, I made peace with the fact that not everyone wants my input. And that's really okay. If you don't grade with me, the most I can offer you are three brief comments and a grade. For those individuals, I'll do the best I can to get to your essay eventually, but I have more pressing business: the students who are currently asking for my help. I can't think of a more egalitarian practice, or dynamic between teacher and student, than that.

By the way, "asking me for help" also includes emailing me and writing, "Mr. Phillipson, would you please give me some feedback on my essay?" By the end of the first quarter of this academic year (2024–25), I've gotten over 25 requests like that and I've gotten to about 20 of them within 48 hours. And that's an important detail for me to include, because you might be saying to yourself right now:

"So, he ignores the students who don't sign up with him? That doesn't sound very optional."

And you'd be right, if I didn't offer the supplemental "virtual service" that I do.

Next, students come to their office visit with one of two agenda items top of mind:

1 They want to grade their final essay draft with me.
2 They want feedback from me because they know their piece is not yet "fully baked."

Regardless of the choice, I tell students to reshare the Google Doc of their essay a few minutes before entering my office. I want to have it just "pop-up" immediately, ready to review without wasting time while they search for it, wait for their BYOD Wi-Fi to kick in, or even retrieve their laptop charger from their bottomless JanSports. If they're not ready for me, I want to be ready to (at least) engage with their essay from the first moments of our meeting. Yes, sometimes there's small talk, but oftentimes it's just me saying, "So, how do you think the essay turned out?"

To that question, they'll often give a generic, timid, or "hedged" answer, and I'll follow-up with: Tell me something specifically you liked about it? Take me to a place in your essay that you're proud of, or want me to appreciate. Or, if they seem hesitant or conflicted, I'll ask – what's something that didn't work as well as you'd hoped it would? Or – what was it like to respond to this particular prompt? Did you run into any challenges that were difficult to resolve?

That part of the "grading session" can take some time. Students book either 15 or 30 minutes with me (a class period runs 50 minutes, so I can get to three students max during a free). Someone might require 30 minutes to grade a research paper (something long and involved that's over ten pages). Other times they're doing "double duty" – grading one paper and brainstorming for the next, or they're making up for lost time: grading two papers at once (back-to-back) because it's been put off for one reason or another.

Why are they there to grade? That matters very little to me. The thing that counts, that I can't take lightly or for granted, is that they're in my office. It's my best shot at making a long-term creative partnership happen with them.

My metaphor for this whole process? I'm their music producer – the Mark Ronson to their Bruno Mars, Jack Antonoff to their Taylor Swift, Quincy Jones to their Michael Jackson, or Timbaland to their Timberlake.

Cast another way: I want to be the Elton John to their Bernie Taupin, providing a backing track that will pair well with their lyrical offerings.

If I can't bring out the best in my students, then what am I doing in this profession? If I can't be a partner in that room (my office is a kind of production booth, if you will), then am I their teacher or their tormenter? Their collaborator or their captor? My goal is to help them produce great art or something commercially viable. If I'm at odds with them, how can that happen?

During the meeting, I have their shared Google Doc open on my Surface tablet, and they have it accessed on their MacBook, Acer, or Dell.

I start by reading their essay out loud. Occasionally, the *student* wants to perform it. Rarely, a student will say: *Don't read it aloud!* It makes them embarrassed or self-conscious to hear their own words like they're Adam Driver.

Why do I read it aloud? It's a performative thing that former student and actor Peyton Lusk taught me years ago. Peyton had some small parts on TV shows (like the Unbreakable Kimmy Schmidt), and a role in a Broadway production. Every English teacher worth the salt left in an Auntie Anne's bag knows that the best way to proofread – or fine tune your essay – is to read it out loud and proud. Before Peyton, though, I didn't know the real test of an essay's cohesive and rhythmic power: Does it perform well? Does it have a natural momentum baked into it? Can you hear it?

Once a student gives me editing privileges on the Doc, I start making margin comments that have to do with the rubric's criteria, but I'm also responding (as I read it) to moments that feel light, move me with their poetic beauty, make me question my own philosophy or thinking, and make me proud to be their teacher (like – I taught them something they're *actually* using).

Sometimes I speak the comment as I type it in the Google Doc's margin. There are occasions when I don't write any comments at all. It's the end of the first quarter as I write this chapter in early November of 2024, and I can think of 20 or so essays from the past two months that "students came to grade" but it turned into nothing more than a celebration of their genius work.

During this 15-minute chunk of time, lots of things are happening, and they vary from student to student, season to season (I sometimes cough more than I talk in the winter months), and prompt to prompt.

In some cases I'm asking them questions about the use of a certain word, phraseology, or reference. That's for one of three reasons: I'm not sure if they wrote it themselves, so I'm (low-key) testing them, or I'm genuinely curious if they're using it correctly, or I want to understand the genesis of the idea, and how they came to know and use it. TikTok, for instance, has introduced a great deal of content to students who have never really experienced the context. Die Hard is a prime example: brief clips are frequently streamed or scrolled through, but a little knowledge is a dangerous thing. A student might reference Die Hard but know nothing of substance about it. When I'm not sure, I tend to probe until something gives either way.

In other instances, I'm asking them practical questions: I've noticed you don't have any quotes or examples from the text – was that a conscious choice? You've used an implied subject word a lot of times in the piece (the word *book, movie, or character's name*), would you like some strategies to address that? What's your approach to ending paragraphs? The statement in this sentence feels self-evident or "common knowledge" – what purpose does it serve? Some of your details feel "writerly" – but are they for show or tone-creation, or something else, because I don't see how they factor into the bigger picture? And so on.

That 15-minute conference is a chance for them to get a little bit closer to understanding me, the teacher, the keeper of the grades, the one who designs the prompts and other assessments.

I remember that Katie Kendall – a nationally ranked tennis player and dogged self-advocate in her writing journey – said to me last year during one of our 50 or so meetings: "No, don't tell me what you'd write here instead of the line I came up with," as we looked at her essay, "Tell me *how* you came up with that line." She wanted to learn how to "think like me," how my creation process works, the very inceptions of my ideas.

Listen – that can't happen if I go home to Armonk and sit in my library and co-grade with my HP laptop. No. That kind of magic can only happen with Katie sitting right next to me.

I don't collaborate with technology. I use technology. The Minimalists (three podcasters who believe that less is more) have a useful phrase for this moment: "Love people, use things, because the other way around doesn't work."

You have to love and respect your students enough to know that they're creative forces to be reckoned with who just need someone to believe in them as such.

By the end of 15 (or 30) minutes, I've covered a lot of ground with any given student, or – perhaps – I haven't accomplished nearly enough. Your mileage may vary. Your experience is not (necessarily) going to be the next patient or customer's experience. It depends on what you bring me to read, and what your attitude is when you do. It may also hinge on how much sleep I've gotten the previous night, or if my kids are sick at home. That's not to say that my mood will impact the grade – because it won't – but energy is synergy. All that means is: good and bad moods are infectious.

Regardless, we'll get to the end of the meeting and one of three things will happen:

1. I'll turn to the student and ask them: What grade would you put on this essay and why?
2. I'll literally type the word "Grade" at the bottom of the document (followed by a colon), I'll think for a moment, then write the letter grade that feels most appropriate.
3. I'll quietly ask them if they want to take a few days (or a week) to revise the essay, as it's not ready for prime-time (so to speak).

And I know what you're thinking: You would never ask a student of yours to assign a grade to their own assessment. It's akin to the jailor giving the prisoner a key to his own cell. But I bet you don't have a good reason not to. Reasons? Sure. But good ones? I doubt it.

Sure, there's the obvious problem: everyone is going to ask for the "A." But everyone doesn't. Full transparency: I am not against giving someone an A+ or telling them their paper is brilliant. I called a student a "prodigy" this year, as I really believe that he is one. I said the same to a student last year, and – again – believed it then as I believe it now.

Our job is not to be gatekeepers – shutting them out of the advanced class they want to gain access to, or proving to our Department that we're the standard-bearers when it comes to a truly rigorous curriculum (which often just means "I don't give anyone an A first quarter under any circumstances" – remember, I've taught at six high schools and I've run into someone like that everywhere I've set up shop).

So what if a student does suggest "the A" but it's far from "A worthy?" It happens. In fact, it's happened twice this first quarter with the same student. And that surprised even me, someone who grades (with some regularity) a dozen essays a day WITH the students who wrote them.

That young man who'd wanted "the A" wasn't (yet) a great judge of what constitutes a strong paper – despite providing dozens of "A level models" written by former students, expressed in myriad different styles, approaches, and voices.

Is it his fault? My fault? Probably both, but it's part of his ongoing education, and central to mine. I'm really into the notion that my job is dynamic and not static, even after 22 years of being in the same physical space (Scarsdale High School [SHS]). I constantly learn, on the job, the right and wrong way to communicate with students, and a more thoughtful way to talk about grades and what they represent. But I get to have so many "high stakes conversations" with students that they start to become "just conversations." I don't think most of my colleagues – at any place I've worked – get to experience this aspect of my practice. And I can only say they're missing out.

And it's true, I don't usually *hang* with my students and make lots of small talk, and I'm not the most cheerfully popular or bubbly teacher at SHS by a LONG shot, but I don't really like small talk with anyone, and I feel like – more than anything – I get up every morning to spend time in front of the client, face-to-face, talking about craftwork, thinking on paper, working out an internal problem by converting it to words on the page or screen, and making some beautiful music with my stable of metaphorical rock, pop, jazz, classical, R&B, and rap stars.

I really leave a lot of the warm and fuzzy stuff to the people in the building who are good at it.

That doesn't mean I don't care, or don't have deep connections with many of my students (because I do), it just means that – like a Michelin Star chef – I'm here to put out 40 kick-ass covers a day on tables with white linen, fine china, elegant flatware, and crystal goblets. I don't want some critic to come take away my Star. I want to earn it every single day I walk into the Brewster Road entrance as I have since 2003, suited up, pencils sharpened.

* * *

From Serena Wu, Cornell University '28/Industrial and Labor Relations

"I remember going to Mr. Phillipson's office hours for my first essay, getting feedback on areas to wordsmith but that I was generally "on the right track." After a bit more work to wrap up my final draft, I knew it could score an acceptable grade – but I was unsatisfied and I knew I could do better: so once I ensured my work was saved in my revision history, I drastically changed the structure of the essay, tailoring it and digging deep into self-reflection and my neglected creative wells to produce an essay that I felt reflected my true potential. He loved it, but more importantly, I did too: even the time spent on the fruitless first draft, paragraphs impulsively deleted, and late hours squeezing my creativity juices dry. There wasn't a single essay from that class I did not struggle with (creating several drafts and scrapping most at whim became a habit), but Mr. Phillipson's encouragement for engaging in the tumultuous process of meaningful writing helped me produce what I proudly consider to be some of my best work thus far."

* * *

From Stephen Mounkhall, Veteran AP English Teacher

"I teach honors seniors, about a third of whom I inherit each year from Wes Phillipson's junior honors class. They are immediately recognizable in their writing as having been opened to the potential of their own voices. They write with verve. They also expect me to meet with them in person to grade and provide feedback for their work, which I have resisted, choosing to keep to my cloistered marking rituals, until this year. I offered in-person grading for a poetry close reading assignment collected in October (for which we had two rough drafts), and half of the class (including several students Wes Phillipson had not taught) volunteered. The results were encouraging. Marking an essay face to face gave an immediacy to the process that is mostly missing when I am home alone eating popcorn and trying to get through a set of papers before sleep. The students next to me read my comments in real time and agree with them (often with vocalizations rather than words) or respectfully disagree with them in ways that help me see their work (and the ways that their brains perceive their work) differently. I have met with students to provide formative feedback on drafts for decades, but the experience of meeting with students to provide summative feedback gave a task that can feel burdensome a welcome lift. I offered the same opportunity for the November assignment, which was an 'inspired-by' creative assignment (in that students choose a literary work we had discussed and refashioned it toward their own ends).

I already have eleven students signed up, and I have met with two of them for their grading/feedback sessions. I can feel their belief in their writing as they sit there next to me. I can feel how invested they are in what they have done. And when I laugh at a part that they meant to be funny, we both get a kick out of the mutual charge that passes back and forth between us. Real communicative writing, the kind done far away from the assigned and the graded, often feels out of reach in a school context, but this new method (new for me, inspired by Wes Phillipson, who has been doing it for years), has helped to bring student writing one step closer to the meaningful exchange of emotions and ideas that I always hope my students' work will embody."

Note

1 https://www.routledge.com/9781032987842.

For Product Safety Concerns and Information please contact our EU
representative GPSR@taylorandfrancis.com
Taylor & Francis Verlag GmbH, Kaufingerstraße 24, 80331 München, Germany

www.ingramcontent.com/pod-product-compliance
Lightning Source LLC
Chambersburg PA
CBHW070246230426
43664CB00014B/2418